Contemporary States and Societies

This series provides lively and accessible introductions to key countries
and regions of the world, conceived and designed to meet the needs of
today's students. The authors are all experts with specialist knowledge
of the country or region concerned and have been chosen also for their
ability to communicate clearly to a non-specialist readership. Each text
has been specially commissioned for the series and is structured according to a common format.

Published

Contemporary Russia
Edwin Bacon with
Matthew Wyman

Contemporary South Africa
Anthony Butler

Contemporary America
(2nd edn)
Russell Duncan
and Joseph Goddard

Contemporary China
Alan Hunter and John Sexton

Contemporary Japan (2nd edn)
Duncan McCargo

Contemporary Britain (2nd edn)
John McCormick

**Contemporary Latin
America** (2nd edn)
Ronaldo Munck

Forthcoming

Contemporary India
Katharine Adeney
and Andrew Wyatt

Contemporary France
Helen Drake

Contemporary Spain
Paul Kennedy

Contemporary Ireland
Eoin O'Malley

Contemporary Europe
B. Guy Peters

Also planned

Contemporary Asia
Contemporary Germany
Contemporary Italy

Contemporary States and Societies
Series Standing Order
ISBN 978–0–333–75402–3 hardback
ISBN 978–0–333–80319–6 paperback
(*outside North America only*)

You can receive future titles in this series as they are published by placing a
standing order. Please contact your bookseller or, in the case of difficulty, write to
us at the address below with your name and address, the title of the series and the
ISBN quoted above.

Customer Services Department, Palgrave Macmillan Ltd
Houndmills, Basingstoke, Hampshire RG21 6XS, England

Contemporary Latin America

Second Edition

Ronaldo Munck

First edition 2003
Second edition 2008

Published by
PALGRAVE MACMILLAN
Houndmills, Basingstoke, Hampshire RG21 6XS and
175 Fifth Avenue, New York, N.Y. 10010
Companies and representatives throughout the world.

PALGRAVE MACMILLAN is the global academic imprint of the Palgrave Macmillan division of St. Martin's Press, LLC and of Palgrave Macmillan Ltd. Macmillan® is a registered trademark in the United States, United Kingdom and other countries. Palgrave is a registered trademark in the European Union and other countries.

ISBN-13: 978-0-230-51494-2 hardback
ISBN-10: 0-230-51494-4 hardback
ISBN-13: 978-0-230-51495-9 paperback
ISBN-10: 0-230-51495-2 paperback

This book is printed on paper suitable for recycling and made from fully managed and sustained forest sources. Logging, pulping and manufacturing processes are expected to conform to the environmental regulations of the country of origin.

A catalogue record for this book is available from the British Library.

A catalog record for this book is available from the Library of Congress.

10 9 8 7 6 5 4 3 2 1
17 16 15 14 13 12 11 10 09 08

Printed and bound in China

Contents

List of Figures, Tables, Boxes and Maps

Figures

Tables

Boxes

Maps

Preface and Acknowledgements

To write a book on 'contemporary' Latin America is to invite almost instant obsolescence. The continent is changing so fast that texts which seemed to be at the cutting edge a decade or so ago are now decidedly stale at first glance. It is also courting the danger of writing in relation to what is newsworthy or academically fashionable. It almost certainly runs the risk of being superficial in that it is impossible to do justice to such a complex continent in one small book. So, it is with considerable reluctance that I undertook to write this book. That I did so was due to a number of reasons.

I believe, firstly, that Latin America is too important to be left to the specialist 'Latinamericanists', and that the main issues, developments and debates about the continent deserve a wider readership. What is happening in terms of economic collapse in Argentina, or the new president in Brazil, or indigenous political movements in Mexico or Ecuador has ramifications across our globalized world. Secondly, I think it is important that Latin America should be presented by Latin Americans, not exclusively of course, but 'positionality' (where I stand in the world, socially and spatially) is surely an issue. For Latinamericans, it is not an exotic land where they dance the samba and drink rum while talking revolution or carnival. For many outside observers there is still this fascination with the exotic 'Other', however well-intentioned they may be. Thirdly, I think it is a stimulating challenge to synthesize such a vast body of knowledge as encompassed by 'contemporary Latin America' and present it in a rigorous but approachable manner. So, while this book is self-conscious, it is not naïve and will, hopefully, lead to a better understanding of the complexity of its subject matter. It will work, to my mind, if the reader is encouraged to delve into the Recommended Reading section and pursue some of the excellent material contained therein.

I should perhaps clarify what I take 'Latin America' to be. Do we include the Caribbean? Is the term the same as South America? If we include Mexico which is in North America geographically, do we include Mexicans living in the USA (Chicanos)? Could we not include French-speaking Québec? There is more than geography and language at stake in these debates. There is, for example, the problem with citizens of the USA (and others) using the term 'America' to refer to those United States when in fact many republics share the American continent. There is also the Latin American aspiration, going back to colonial times, to constitute a large unified American nation: *la patria grande* in Spanish. So, to be clear, I am taking Latin America to be the South American republics, those of Central America and, of course, Mexico. Cuba and Puerto Rico are part of this definition though this text does not deal with them in any detail given their particularities. The text does not deal at all with the Caribbean islands even though the United Nations body dealing with the region is called the Economic Commission for Latin America and the Caribbean. It is just I think this part of the world is distinctive and complex enough to be dealt with separately and not lumped in with the part of the world I know best where Spanish and Portuguese is spoken.

Finally I would like to thank Steven Kennedy at Palgrave Macmillan for suggesting I should write this book, and following through with meticulous suggestions to improve it. Also, the anonymous readers who generously praised the proposal and avoided easy criticisms. To my brother Gerardo Munck for not trying too hard to dissuade me from writing the book and then making helpful suggestions to manage the difficult task of writing an introduction which was not too simplistic. Ian Sharpes took a messy handwritten script and turned it into a product acceptable to the publishers, and Clare Horton did the last-minute tidy-up. Thanks to all of them.

RONALDO MUNCK

Preface to the Second Edition

In the five years or so since this book was drafted, Latin America has gone through dramatic political upheavals. It is thus appropriate that this edition includes a substantial new chapter on Politics. Latin America is a world region where there are not only radical social movements but also radical governments in terms of international affairs. Where possible socio-economic data have been updated as have all the original chapters, especially those on the international context and on the alternative futures the region faces. There are a lot more boxes illustrating the main text with little vignettes. Thanks again to Ian Sharpes for typing and even more so to readers of the first edition for buying it.

RONALDO MUNCK

List of Abbreviations

AFL-CIO	American Federation of Labor-Congress of Industrial Organizations
AFSC	American Friends Service Committee
ANRA	National Action Plan for Agrarian Reform (Brazil)
BA	bureaucratic-authoritarian state
CARICOM	The Caribbean Community
CEB	Comunidades Eclesiais de Base (Ecclesiastical Base Communities)
CIA	Central Intelligence Agency (United States)
CLAD	Latin American Centre for Development Administration
COMAL	Alternative Community Trade Network (Honduras)
CONAIE	Confederation of Indigenous Nationalities of Ecuador
CONTAG	National Confederation of Agricultural Workers (Brazil)
ECLAC	Economic Commission for Latin America and the Caribbean
EU	European Union
EZLN	Zapatista National Liberation Army (Chiapas)
FARC	Colombian Revolutionary Armed Forces
FMLN	Farabundo Martí Front for National Liberation
FTAA	Free Trade Association of the Americas
GDP	gross domestic product
HDI	human development index
IDB	Inter-American Development Bank
IMF	International Monetary Fund
LAFTA	Latin American Free Trade Association
LANIC	Latin America Network Information Centre
MERCOSUR	Mercado Común del Sur (Common Market of the South)
MST	Movimento dos Sem Terra/Landless Movement (Brazil)
NACLA	North American Congress on Latin America
NAFTA	North American Free Trade Association
NATO	North Atlantic Treaty Organization

NEM	new economic model
NICs	newly industrializing countries
NGO	non-governmental organization
OAS/OEA	Organization of American States/Organización de Estados Americanos
OECD	Organisation for Economic Co-operation and Development
OPEC	Organization of Petroleum Exporting Countries
PB	participatory budget
PRI	Institutional Revolutionary Party (Mexico)
PRONASOL	National Solidarity Programme (Mexico)
PT	Partido dos Trabalhadores/Workers Party (Brazil)
RAMAS	Mutual Support Network for Social Action
SATO	South Atlantic Treaty Organization
SEDESOL	Social Development Secretariat (Mexico)
TINA	'there is no alternative'
UN	United Nations
UNDP	United Nations Development Programme
URNG	Guatemala National Revolutionary Union
USA	United States of America
WTO	World Trade Organization

Map 1   Latin America: countries and capitals

1

Introduction: Setting and Issues

Latin America is one of the largest of the world's cultural regions, covering an area of nearly 8 million square miles. From the border with the United States to the tip of Tierra del Fuego in the south it is 7000 miles long, and from west to east it is 3200 miles across at its widest point. It is twice as large as the European Union and nearly as large as the USA and Canada combined. The backbone of the Latin American landmass is formed by the 4000-mile-long Andes mountain range and the Sierra Madre ranges in Mexico. Three massive river systems – the Amazon, the Orinoco and the River Plate – cover almost the entire continent east of the Andes. At the turn of this century the overall population of Latin America (and the Caribbean) was 516 million. This text deals only with Latin America and not the Caribbean, which means it includes the 12 republics of South America, the 7 in Central America plus Mexico, Cuba and the Dominican Republic.

Latin America has a considerable and possibly growing economic, political and cultural significance in the world today. This introductory chapter sets the scene for subsequent chapters on specific topics with a broad-brush description of the region and its republics. It also outlines some of the major themes that will be tackled in detail subsequently, with particular emphasis on political economy and social issues.

Physical Setting

Latin America's physical landscape is characterized above all by diversity: Map 2 provides an overview of the various regions, their geographical location and their natural characteristics. Starting from the north we have what is called Middle America, embracing Mexico, Central America and the Caribbean. Mexico contains a vast diversity of physical landscapes from the humid tropical lowlands in the south to the dry highlands of the north (for some basic facts on Mexico see Box 1.1).

1

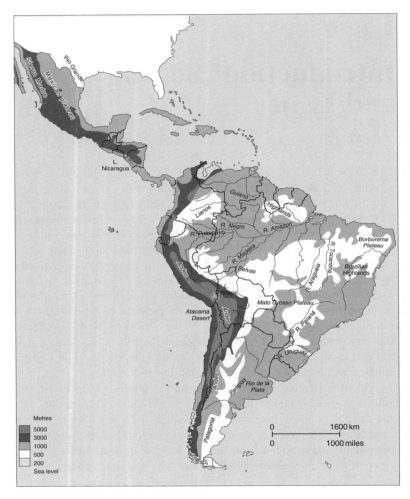

Map 2   Latin America: a continent of contrasts

A range of volcanoes crosses the country from east to west, and the Sierra Madre range encloses vast plateaux. Turning to Central America, Clifford Smith describes how 'Wet, forested lowlands and a confusion of dissected highlands with volcanic peaks and small-scale basins at varying altitudes define a region from Panama to Guatemala' (Smith 1992: 45). This picture of fragmentation is also typical of the Caribbean in a different way; all countries are islands, but some are low-lying

Box 1.1   Country profile: Mexico

Mexico in 2006 had a population of 107 million and it is growing rapidly, having a major impact demographically on the United States given the continuous flow of migrants across its borders. Mexico's GDP is now US$693 billion and per capita GDP works out at US$10 000. Like Brazil it has a substantial industrial sector that accounts for 26 per cent of GDP. Nearly 90 per cent of Mexico's trade is with the United States from which it imports motor vehicle parts (to assemble in the border region plants) and electronic equipment, while it mainly exports petroleum and motor vehicles. Economic growth since Mexico joined NAFTA (the North American Free Trade Association) in 1994 has been dynamic. Mexico has also joined the 'rich nations club', the OECD (Organisation for Economic Co-operation and Development), and was a founding member of the WTO (World Trade Organization) in 1996. This does not mean that Mexico has become an advanced industrial society nor that it has entered a period of accelerated and sustainable economic development. Social contradictions and political instability are still major issues, perhaps only postponed by a close relationship with the USA.

Nearly three-quarters of Mexico's population now lives in urban areas, and the capital Mexico City, defined broadly, has a population of 24 million people, which makes it the largest conurbation in the world. Mexico City was already an important centre during the colonial period, but it grew dramatically with the industrialization that characterized the twentieth century. Migrants poured into the city and its environs from the poorer rural areas in search of work, but much of this was precarious and since the 1980s industry has largely moved to the Mexico–USA border. Mexico City is known most notoriously for its transport gridlock and legendary levels of air pollution. In the 1990s concerted efforts were made to deal with air pollution based on higher taxes, even at the cost of job losses. Environmental reconstruction, if we can call it that, has had a measure of success, although it is still estimated that 2 million people suffer from illnesses directly linked to air pollution. As with other capital cities in Latin America, Mexico City displays a huge dynamism mixed with massive social (as well as environmental) problems.

coral islands, others are volcanic peaks and some are characterized by substantial highland massifs.

Making our way down to South America we find the Andes mountain range dominating the whole of the north-west and west coasts of the continent. From Venezuela and Colombia in the north down through Ecuador and Peru there is a common general pattern. There are coastal regions, then the Andean range, and then the interior lowlands. Chile is different in so far as the coastal regions predominate in this narrow country, with the Andes representing its backbone and its border with Argentina. In southern Peru and Bolivia the branches of the Andes diverge to create a huge plateau known as the Altiplano. Here the climate and the vegetation show considerable variation in accordance with altitude and temperature changes. The contrasting ecologies of the Andes have dictated where human settlements have occurred and these, in turn, have created productive basins with high rural densities. Pressure of population has led to an increasing level of agricultural colonization in the more sparsely populated lowlands of the interior, a region rich in mineral deposits.

Moving across to the east coast we have the extensive territory of Argentina, which in the north-west shares the broadly Andean features of its neighbours but in the south is characterized by 'the desert and steppe area of Patagonia [which] is unique in that it is the only mid-latitude arid climate in the Southern Hemisphere' (Gonzalez 1998: 37) From the frozen, underpopulated Patagonia we move north to the lush pampas and the River Plate basin. The temperate climate in these natural grasslands and the fertile soil makes them a rich agricultural zone. The rest of the interior lowlands are sparsely populated. Smith refers to this area as 'the empty heart of South America' (Smith 1992: 41). By contrast, the interior lowlands of the Paraná basin (feeding into the River Plate) are densely populated and constitute the main agricultural zones for Paraguay and Uruguay as well as Argentina (Box 1.2). The Buenos Aires–São Paulo axis provides a major pole of attraction for population across this whole area and dominates the physical landscape too.

The east of South America is dominated by two massifs, the Brazilian Shield and the Guiana Highlands. As Smith describes it, 'the geological structure is complex, the major physiographic features are those of an eroded plateau tilted towards the north west ... sinking imperceptibly towards the lowlands of the Amazon and the basin of the River Uruguay' (Smith 1992: 43). The Guiana Highlands are not very populated in contrast to the narrow coastlands. The Brazilian Shield (or Plateau) is the second-largest natural region in Latin America after Amazonia, and approximately a third of Latin America's population lives in this natural area. The southern section in the Paraná plateau is humid and subtropical, providing fertile ground for coffee cultivation. The north-east region suffers periodic droughts which lead to periodic waves of out-migration. The interior plateau is fairly underpopulated but is now undergoing rapid development and growth.

The physical environment provides the vital backdrop against which people build their lives, or try to, and natural resources and climate are

Box 1.2 Country profile: Argentina

Argentina at the start of the twentieth century was among the five richest countries in the world, but at the start of the twenty-first century it was facing economic meltdown, a situation only partially reversed by 2006. In 2006 it had a population of around 40 million and a GDP of US$182 billion. While per capita GDP in 2006 had risen again to a respectable US$13,700, still between 35 and 45 per cent of the population are living in poverty. Argentina was an early industrializer and until recently 36 per cent of GDP was accounted for by industry. The country's exports still reflect its agricultural past and include mainly grains and meats with some manufactured products. The country imports machinery, vehicles and chemicals. Interestingly, only 10 per cent of trade is with the USA, with Brazil accounting for 25 per cent and the EU some 20 per cent of the total trade volume. Argentina has left behind its days in the non-aligned movement to become a firm supporter of free-trade economics. It also strongly supports non-proliferation efforts worldwide and is a strong advocate of regional stability in Latin America.

While Argentina may have declined economically in recent decades, the capital city Buenos Aires with 13 million inhabitants is still a significant global city. However, it is far from the 'Paris of the South', as it was described in the 1920s. The city began to flourish on the basis of overseas migration, and in the postwar period it industrialized rapidly as it became a pole of attraction for urban migrants. At its height Buenos Aires was the epitome of the modern city with fine boulevards, the biggest opera house in the world and a city life to rival any in the world. Today the urban middle classes have moved out to the suburbs and once fashionable areas are becoming slums. Motorways remain half-finished and the housing stock is crumbling. As Beatriz Sarlo puts it, 'These processes are occurring in a city which is changing with a speed previously experienced only at the close of the nineteenth century, when the ideal of expansion and the extension of services to all prevailed' (2000: 122). Buenos Aires, once the shiny future for the rest of Latin America, is perhaps today a sign of the crises to come.

key factors in determining the prospects for social and economic development. According to the Inter-American Development Bank (IDB), if we take the approximately US$10,000 difference in per capita incomes between Latin America and the Western nations, US$2000 of that difference would be accounted for by geographical factors (IDB 2000: 56). The presence of vast tropical areas, the problems with transportation over vast inhospitable areas and the distance from the centres of world trade all go into this geographic factoring. Interestingly, while demographic factors account for another US$2000 difference, the IDB calculates that US$6000 of the differential is due to the effectiveness and predictability of public institutions. Although these calculations are to some extent subjective and even arbitrary, it is important to note that the physical environment matters in terms of the development prospects of Latin America.

There is a general consensus that Latin America has suffered an unusually high proportion of natural disasters in recent years. According to the IDB (2000: 132) there were 638 natural disasters in Latin America (and the Caribbean) in the course of the twentieth century, which amounts to nearly a quarter of all disasters worldwide! Hurricanes and earthquakes, floods and landslides happen with monotonous regularity. Clearly it is not only geographical causes which place a region at risk from natural disasters; it is also the structural socio-economic factors which place populations at greater or lesser risk. Certainly earthquakes and volcanic eruptions have as their main causes the four active tectonic plates the continent sits atop. But it is the pattern of human settlements, the adequacy of dwellings and the presence or absence of risk-mitigation strategies that determine the level of human casualties when natural disasters occur.

The internationally shared phenomenon of El Niño is one of the most dramatic permanent or at least recurring disasters in Latin America. Basically every 2 to 7 years a vast tract of the Pacific Ocean warms up by a few degrees and this sets off a chain reaction with the trade winds leading to great storms and frontal systems springing up haphazardly and changing temperatures across the globe. What it means, immediately off the coasts of Peru and Ecuador, is a disappearance of the vast catching shoals the fishing industry depends on as the fish flee the warmer waters. In addition, the volatility of the climate causes severe droughts, prolonged flooding and storm-strength winds across Latin America, and the trail of death and destruction makes it extremely difficult to achieve sustainable growth in the region. El Niño may or may not be caused by 'global warming', although there are some indications that the phenomenon is becoming more pronounced, but it is emblematic of the type of natural disasters that occur in Latin America.

Finally, it must be noted that Latin America is at the epicentre of international concerns over the degradation of the environment. Throughout the 1990s the international environmental movement focused on the exploitation of the Amazon, considered to be the 'lungs of the Earth' owing to its oxygen-producing role. There was widespread concern over the commercial development of the region through cattle-ranching, large agricultural projects and, above all, deforestation projects. The

Box 1.3   Country profile: Brazil

Brazil is almost a continent in its own right with a population in 2006 of 188 million and the tenth largest economy in the world. In 2000 it had a gross domestic product (GDP) of US$620 billion, and a per capita GDP of US$8500. A substantial industrial sector which includes steel, petrochemicals, machinery and vehicles now accounts for 40 per cent of GDP. Brazil is also the world's largest producer of sugar-cane and coffee. The country has vast mineral and agricultural resources in reserve, not least in the Amazon Basin which is the largest rainforest in the world. Brazil's foreign trade almost doubled during the 1990, but this picture of a dynamic economy masks a huge level of inequality between regions, namely the prosperous south-east and the poor north-east, and between those who are part of the growth process and those suffering from social exclusion. What happens in Brazil from now on will have a major impact on the rest of Latin America and the world as a whole.

Over 80 per cent of Brazil's population live in cities and the largest of these, São Paulo with 23 million inhabitants, is one of the biggest cities in the world. São Paulo grew out of the nineteenth-century coffee boom, the profits of which helped create a diversified industrial base. It is part of an industrial triangle with Rio de Janeiro and Belo Horizonte which constitutes the industrial powerhouse of Brazil and, indeed, the whole of Latin America. This triangle accounts for 75 per cent of Brazil's industrial employment. Industrial concentration drives urbanization and the creation of a sizeable industrial working class. It was the strikes by the São Paulo auto-workers and keenness of the industrial entrepreneurs to build up the internal market which led to the collapse of a long-lasting military dictatorship in the 1980s. São Paulo, while a dynamic economic, political and cultural centre, is a city plagued with massive social dislocations – from transport and housing to crime and pollution. It can be said to show the full complexity and contradictions of urban development in Latin America.

Transamazonian Highway and a massive hydroelectric project were a particular focus of these campaigns. Now, while Latin America is far from being the worst region in the world in terms of environmental degradation, there are serious grounds for concern. Deforestation in the Amazon in particular could have incalculable effects in terms of species diversity due to removal of vegetation and in terms of its impact on atmospheric chemistry. The use of burning to clear the forest releases huge amounts of carbon dioxide into the atmosphere and has created climate change of such magnitude that regeneration of the Amazon forest may no longer be possible. While Brazil (Box 1.3) is not the only Amazonian nation, its massive economic role in the region places it in a most responsible role.

Box 1.4   Country profile: Venezuela

Venezuela, with a population in 2006 of nearly 26 million, is best known, of course, for its petroleum industry that has dominated postwar economic development. GDP in 2006 was US$106 billion, and per capita GDP stood at US$6400. The petroleum industry accounts for 28 per cent of GDP and is by far the main export, earning nearly US$29 billion out of a total US$34 billion. Other exports include aluminium, steel and chemical products. Venezuela imports machinery, manufactured goods and construction materials, and its main task has been to construct an industrial base for when oil reserves run out. Manufacturing at 20 per cent of GDP may fulfil that role, but the overall economic future must be in doubt. Until recent years the Venezuelan political system was characterized by a legendary stability which was even able to defuse an incipient guerrilla movement in the 1970s. That has all changed now with instability the only certain factor. Although maintaining a higher standard of living than the other Andean countries, Venezuela has growing levels of social inequality and absolute poverty.

The other type of area very susceptible to environmental degradation is that characterized by steeply sloping lands, as for example in most of Central America. The ecologically sound terraces and irrigation systems of pre-Columbian times have long since fallen into disrepair, leaving these lands extremely susceptible to rapid loss of soil. Traditional systems of land use are making a gradual comeback, particularly in the Andean countries, but the imperatives of market production conspire against conservation measures. There have been some 'debt-for-nature swaps' in Costa Rica and Bolivia in particular, where foreign debts are cut in return for the creation of protected national environmental parks. There are also other problem areas such as the coastal pollution caused by petroleum drilling, for example in Venezuela (Box 1.4), but perhaps the main environmental problem lies not in the rainforest or sloping lands but in the mega-cities where urban growth has been such as to outstrip any attempts to control urban pollution in all its myriad forms.

Population Setting

As everyone knows, when Christopher Columbus sailed into the Caribbean in 1492 he did not actually 'discover' America in so far as people already lived there. America was first settled by people crossing from Asia some 30 000 years ago. The Andean region and what is now Mexico were the first regions to be settled in Middle and South America, which led to two major ethnic and political entities, namely the Aztec confederacy and the Inca empire, although there were many less-organized tribes and bands settled across the rest of the continent. The Aztec, Mayan and Inca civilizations were complex social and political structures possessing a class system, a division of labour and a developed philosophical/religious body of knowledge. The Amerindian peoples possessed vast armies, built sophisticated road systems, and practised astronomy, mathematics and, of course, sports. The impact of the Iberian conquest on these cultures was to be devastating, and is still felt today.

There is very little agreement even on the numbers of indigenous people inhabiting what is today Latin America at the time of the Iberian conquest. Estimates vary from 8 to 80 million people, although we can safely estimate some 25 million people for the Mexican region and maybe 6 million for the Andean region. Population decline consequent on the Spanish invasions is also contested, ranging from a 50 per cent to a 95 per cent decline between around 1520 and 1600 (Newson 1992). What is quite clear is that the indigenous peoples were systematically subjected to mass killings, deadly disease, overwork and a move to totally destroy their cultures. However, even at the start of the twentieth century around 80 per cent of Mexico's and Guatemala's populations were indigenous, as were also a high proportion in Bolivia, Ecuador, Paraguay and Peru. While some countries like Argentina pursued the North American model of simple extermination of the indigenous peoples, elsewhere the indigenous American influence remains strong to this day, and is indeed strengthening. Everywhere, the Spanish and Portuguese invaders sought to subjugate the native population and force them into various forms of bonded labour to work the land and the mines. However, this labour force was sometimes recalcitrant and sometimes became integrated through the *mestizo* (indigenous–Hispanic) intermarriage route.

Thus, in part owing to labour shortages, African slaves were sought out and between the mid fifteenth century and the mid nineteenth century some 30 million people from Africa were forcibly brought to America. The slave trade in the Atlantic was developed in the first instance by Portuguese traders, with around a third of all slaves crossing the Atlantic being destined for Brazil. Over half of all slaves brought to America ended up in the Caribbean with only a small proportion going to North America. Throughout the rest of Latin America there was a sprinkling of African slaves working in various trades during the colonial period. Apart from Brazil, Colombia (see Box 1.5) was the country with the highest proportion of African 'forced immigration'.

Box 1.5   Country profile: Colombia

Colombia is the third-largest country in Latin America in size of population, which stood at 43.5 million in 2006. Colombia now has a GDP of US$98 billion, which is substantial, but the preponderance of Brazil and Mexico with their US$600-plus billion figures is all too clear. Per capita GDP stood at US$7900 in 2006. Industry accounts for 34 per cent of GDP and includes textiles, chemicals, metal products and cements. Colombia exports mainly petroleum and coffee with some textiles and garments along with other light manufacturing products. The country predictably imports machinery and equipment, transportation equipment and consumer products. The USA accounts for around half Colombia's trade, with the EU (European Union) having a considerable presence. Until the mid 1990s, Colombia's was probably the most stable economy in Latin America. Since then a long-running civil war has erupted, endangering the stability of the whole country. Colombia, of course, as is widely known, is also the world's leading coca cultivator and major supplier of refined cocaine to the world market and particularly the USA, and is fast becoming a major financial money-laundering centre for the global drugs trade.

African slaves came from a broad swathe of West Africa stretching from Sierra Leone down to Angola, and they came from diverse economic and cultural backgrounds. They were regarded as private property and thus not really part of the social hierarchy at all. Unlike the situation in the West Indies and North America, 'In the Catholic cultures of Latin America, slaves were offered rights to marriage, to protection from cruelty, and, under special circumstances, to manumission [freedom] by self-purchase' (McFarlane 1992: 141). While in practice this did not make a huge difference in terms of their treatment, it did represent a significant cultural difference from the US slavery–discrimination–racism system. The emergence of a *mulatto* (mixed African–European blood) population was a major feature of Brazil but also Cuba, the Dominican Republic, Panama and the Caribbean as a whole. We turn next to the Iberian invaders who decimated the indigenous population and stole people from Africa to work for them.

The Spanish and Portuguese conquerors of the sixteenth century brought with them Catholicism, a mercantilist economics and notions of an absolutist state. It is estimated that between 1500 and 1600 some 300 000 people at most migrated from Spain to America, with the numbers from Portugal being maybe a tenth of that figure. Spain declined in the seventeenth century, the number of migrants increased and previous strict controls on 'Jews and heretics' and other 'undesirables' were relaxed. It is significant that at the very moment when Columbus was arriving in America the last of the Moors were being driven out of Spain. The Moorish invasion of Spain in the eighth century was coming to an end through a military campaign of reconquest, which goes a long way to explain the militarism and the *machismo* of the Spanish *conquistadores* when they arrived in America. Likewise it helps explain the absolutely central role of the Catholic church in what was also seen as a religious crusade against 'infidels' to match that just coming to an end against Islam.

The small Iberian population rapidly became wealthy, or at least some of them did. The merchants, landowners and mine owners would return to Spain and Portugal to display their wealth or to retire. However, as John Fisher writes: 'When they began to cease to do so in the first decade of the nineteenth century ... the shift was symbolic of the fact that the American empires of Spain and Portugal had outgrown the mother countries' (1992: 138). The shift was practically imperceptible at first and could simply be a social preference to retire in Rio rather than Lisbon, Mexico City rather than Madrid. There was, of course, an economic motivation in so far as the colonial connection became simply an economic drain on resources. Politically and culturally there was, finally, the emergence of an American or criollo identity which impelled the one-time settlers to struggle for political independence duly achieved in the early to mid nineteenth century, except in Brazil where it occurred towards the end of that century.

By the mid nineteenth century, Latin America was seen as a land of opportunity in Europe, surpassed only by North America. From the mid nineteenth century to 1930 some 8 million Europeans migrated to Latin America compared with the approximately 33 million who went to the United States. This wave of immigration was particularly significant in Argentina and Uruguay where they populated the country and pushed back the agricultural frontier. In other countries European migrants were significant, including Chile, Brazil and Costa Rica, but for the first two in particular this was concentrated in very specific regions (like the Brazilian south-east). Elsewhere the European element in the population was predominantly derived from the earlier period of migration during the colonial period. Where indigenous or African slave labour was readily available there was no overwhelming reason to attract land-hungry impoverished peasants from Italy or Spain. In the post-Second-World-War period, Venezuela attracted many immigrants from Europe drawn by the oil boom.

It is really only Argentina (apart from the much smaller Uruguay and Costa Rica) which is a truly immigrant country. If one walked along the streets of Buenos Aires in the early 1900s every other person one would meet would have been born overseas. A degree of economic growth from the mid nineteenth century onwards attracted thousands of Italian farm labourers in particular, sometimes even on a seasonal basis. Agriculture, cattle-rearing and sheep-farming were the main occupations for the migrants but they also began to occupy the urban trades. Italian migrants also led in the industrialization boom, with names like Di Tella in Argentina and Matarazzo in Brazil standing out. The Hochschilds in Bolivia are another immigrant family that did extremely well for itself in the new world. There is a strong concentration of Japanese migrants in the south-east of Brazil and in Peru, and there are a number of German colonies in the south of Chile. Many thousands of Europeans went to Cuba in the early 1900s to make up 15 per cent of the population in 1930, and out of every 10 of these, 5 would be from Italy, 3 from Spain, 1 from Northern and Western Europe and 1 from the Balkans or Eastern Europe.

After the great influx of overseas immigrants between 1850 and 1930 the population of Latin America began to grow rapidly without substantial levels of immigration, and between 1930 and the end of the century it increased nearly fivefold. This population growth exceeded that of all other regions in the world except for Africa, and even then the difference was not great. In 1930 this population was mainly rural with only around 15 per cent living in cities of 20 000 inhabitants or more. By the end of the century, Latin America was predominantly urban with around 76 per cent of people living in cities of 20 000 or above. By any comparative standards this constitutes a massive process of social transformation that has had an impact on the economic structures (see Chapter 3) and the cultural expressions of the region (see Chapter 8). At this stage we have provided only a bare introduction to the social transformations that are dealt with in detail in Chapter 6 (Social Patterns).

In Table 1.1 we can see the broad sweep of the population increase between 1950 and 1975 and from that date to 2004 how the total population increased dramatically. Annual growth rates, however, are set to slow down slightly from 1.9 per cent for 1975–2004 to 1.2 per cent for 2004–15. Uruguay is the only country that did not dramatically increase its population, while Brazil, Mexico, Colombia and Peru (Box 1.6) stand out as countries where the population increased more than fourfold. In terms of population density, only El Salvador, Guatemala and the Dominican Republic are significantly above the

Box 1.6   Country profile: Peru

Peru had a population in 2006 of 28 million people and a GDP of US$74 billion, with GDP per capita standing at around US$6400. While manufacturing accounts for 26 per cent of GDP, exports are still mainly the traditional products of minerals, fishmeal and coffee. Imports include machinery, chemicals and pharmaceuticals as well as household appliances and automobiles. The USA accounts for nearly a third of foreign trade, with the EU and Japan also playing important roles. Slightly over 70 per cent of the population live in urban areas. Peru has suffered considerably since the 1980s from the impact of the rural insurgency of Sendero Luminoso (Shining Path), and the authoritarian government of President Fujimori who fled the country in 2000 after a political scandal. The country has also suffered from natural conditions including the weather phenomenon known as El Niño which has led to a collapse of fishmeal exports, decimated agriculture and caused damage to the infrastructure on a regular basis. In 2006 Alan García, who was the last president before Fujimori, was elected once again as president promising social reform and fiscal responsibility at the same time.

world's average, although Mexico and Honduras are catching up quickly. The reality is that in terms of overall settlement patterns most countries of Latin America have vast areas that are still sparsely populated: on the whole in most countries over half the population lives in between one-fifth and one-quarter of the national territory. How these people live is the subject of the next section.

Social Issues

What are the prospects for social development for the 516 million people of Latin America? Since the population density is half the global average, there is no overwhelming overpopulation problem as some economists and demographers argue, for other developing regions. But demography does matter because age and gender profiles, for example, have a strong bearing on economic development. What is called the 'dependency ratio' – the consumption needs of children and the elderly that surpasses their contribution to production – is a key issue in this type of discussion. It is estimated that in Latin America the average age of the population will rise from 26 in 2000 to 32 in 2020, and there will be a marked rise in the proportion of the population who are of

Table 1.1   Latin America: demographic trends

Country/Region	Population (millions)				Population density (people per sq km)
	1950	*1975*	*2004*	*2015 (projected)*	
Argentina	12	26	38.4	42.7	14
Bolivia	2	4.8	9.0	10.9	8
Brazil	34	108.1	183.9	209.4	20
Chile	4	10.4	16.1	17.9	20
Colombia	7	25.4	44.9	52.1	41
Costa Rica	0.5	2.1	4.3	5.0	71
Cuba	–	9.3	11.2	11.4	–
Dominican Republic	1.4	5.1	8.8	10.1	177
Ecuador	2	6.9	13.0	15.1	46
El Salvador	1.4	4.1	6.8	8.0	303
Guatemala	2	6.2	12.3	15.9	105
Honduras	1	3.0	7.0	8.8	58
Mexico	17	59.3	105.7	119.1	51
Nicaragua	1	2.6	5.4	6.6	42
Panama	0.9	1.7	3.2	3.8	38
Paraguay	1	2.7	6.0	7.6	14
Peru	8	15.2	27.6	32.2	20
Uruguay	2	2.8	3.4	3.7	19
Venezuela	5	12.7	26.3	31.3	27
Latin America	166	318.4	548.3	628.3	26
World	–	4073.7	6389.2	7219.4	–

Source: *Human Development Report* (2006: 297–300).

working age. For the IDB this represents a 'window of demographic opportunity' (2000: 58). In absolute terms we can also note that by 2030 the demographic gap between Latin America and the developed countries will close, with the population in both groups becoming more or less equal.

The optimistic view of the IDB is based mainly on the 'youth' of Latin America's population. It is estimated that the 15–26-year-old cohort will rise from 102 million in 2000 to 122 million in 2025, while at the same time the population of the developed countries is 'greying' and thus absorbing more savings. But the IDB scenario is dependent on capital flow from the developed countries to Latin America that will create jobs and generate a yield to cope with their own ageing populations. In practice these capital flows depend on profitability opportunities and political stability, both of which are necessarily uncertain. The pattern is for the number of workers coming into the labour market to outstrip the number of jobs on offer. It is estimated that in every country in Latin America the secondary city, like Guadalajara or Belo Horizonte, will very soon outstrip in size the current primate or dominant city – usually the capital. The labour-saving bias of industrialization has become more pronounced in the information economy and thus this growth will probably not be reflected in social development.

Table 1.2 presents a quick overview of social development indicators, that is to say quantifiable measures of underlying social processes (which are examined in more detail in Chapter 6). Life expectancy at birth is a crude but effective measure of the 'quality of life' in a given country, and on this basis we do note a considerable level of social development over time. In 1950 the average life expectancy stands at 72.2 years, almost five years above the global life expectancy

Table 1.2   Latin America: Human Development Index, 2004

Country/ Region	Infant mortality rates	Life expectancy at birth (years)	Adult literacy rate	Carbon dioxide emissions per capita (tonnes)	Human Development Index
Argentina	16	74.6	97.2	3.5	0.863
Bolivia	54	64.4	87.0	1.2	0.692
Brazil	32	70.8	88.6	4.7	0.792
Chile	8	78.1	95.7	3.6	0.859
Colombia	18	72.6	92.8	1.3	0.790
Costa Rica	11	78.3	94.9	1.4	0.841
Cuba	6	77.6	99.8	–	0.826
Dominican Republic	27	67.5	82.0	2.5	0.751
Ecuador	23	74.5	91.0	2.0	0.765
El Salvador	24	71.1	91.0	1.0	0.729
Guatemala	33	67.6	69.1	0.9	0.673
Honduras	31	68.1	80.0	0.9	0.683
Mexico	23	75.3	92.0	3.8	0.821
Nicaragua	26	70.0	76.7	0.7	0.698
Panama	19	75.0	92.0	2.0	0.809
Paraguay	21	71.2	93.0	0.7	0.757
Peru	24	70.2	87.7	1.0	0.767
Uruguay	15	75.6	98.0	1.2	0.851
Venezuela	16	73.0	93.0	4.3	0.784
Latin America	26	72.2	90.2	2.4	0.795
World	51	67.3	–	3.9	0.741

Source: *Human Development Report* (2006: 283–6).

(see Table 1.2), so Latin America can be said to have advanced considerably in overall terms. Still, to be born today in Bolivia, Guatemala or Brazil is not as good for your longevity as to be born in Chile or Costa Rica. Of course, these overall figures mask huge differentials within each country. For example, in Brazil a white-collar employee in the urban south-east will have a much better life expectancy than a landless labourer in the deprived north-east of the country.

Infant mortality rates are usually taken to give a rough indication of the quality of a country's healthcare and social development levels generally, and infant mortality rates in Latin America have declined dramatically in the second half of the twentieth century. In 1950 it was estimated that for every 1000 live births there were 126 deaths in the first year of life in Latin America, which was brought down to 61 in 1980 and stood at 38 in the year 2000, compared with a global average of 78. Latin America's nations are mainly semi-industrialized urban societies with healthcare systems in some cases matching those of the developed countries. Nevertheless, this advance, as that of life expectancy, is uneven. Again it is best not to be born in Bolivia, Guatemala or Peru compared say with Chile, Costa Rica or Uruguay.

Literacy is universally taken to be an indication of social development. The Southern Cone countries already had quite high literacy rates in the early twentieth century given the commitment to universal and free education. Today the only countries with persistently high levels of illiteracy are those of Central America with the exception of Costa Rica. This reflects the poor state of welfare regimes in those countries and the general neglect of social development through the many decades of corrupt and authoritarian regimes. One could also add that the historical successes in terms of eradicating diseases such as malaria, typhus and smallpox have been reversed since the 'lost decade' (in social terms) of the 1980s. Even the casual visitor to Latin America now knows that many illnesses that were once assumed to be vanquished are back with a vengeance.

The fourth item of Table 1.2 refers to carbon monoxide emissions, low levels of which could be taken to indicate a commitment to sustainable social development. Yet if we take the 'high scorers' – Mexico, Brazil and Argentina – these are also the countries with the highest levels of industrialization and urbanization. Industry may be 'dirty', but it is also a precondition for social development. Conversely, 'clean' countries can be so because of a degree of social regulation over the economy such as in Costa Rica or Uruguay, or on the other hand because there is hardly any industrialization as in Paraguay and Nicaragua. In international terms, Latin America can be seen to account for a very small proportion of carbon dioxide emissions, the Amazon rainforest depredation notwithstanding.

The final figure is the Human Development Index (HDI) published annually by the United Nations, which is a comparative measure of life expectancy, literacy/education and standards of living for countries worldwide. It is essentially a composite index for what we might call the 'quality of life'. Latin America's overall index of 0.795 in 2006 is quite similar to the global 'middle income' category of country, compared with 0.556 in low-income countries and 0.942 in high-income countries.

If we turn from the broad national figures to household income distribution we obtain the social picture portrayed in Table 1.3. We immediately detect a highly uneven distribution of income across households. Brazil tops the inequality league with the richest 10 per cent of households obtaining very nearly half the total income generated in the

Table 1.3   Latin America: household income distribution, 2002–4 (date varies per country)

Country	Year	Share of total income of:			
		Poorest 40%	*Next poorest 30%*	*20% below the richest 10%*	*Richest 10%*
Argentina	2004	16.0	22.3	24.5	37.3
Bolivia	2002	9.5	21.3	28.3	41.0
Brazil	2003	11.2	18.3	25.7	44.9
Chile	2003	13.7	20.7	25.5	40.0
Colombia	2002	11.9	22.2	26.8	39.1
Costa Rica	2002	14.5	25.6	29.7	30.2
Dominican Republic	2002	12.0	22.6	27.0	38.3
Ecuador	2002	15.4	24.3	26.0	34.3
El Salvador	2001	13.4	24.6	28.7	33.3
Guatemala	2002	14.2	22.2	26.8	36.8
Honduras	2002	11.3	21.7	27.6	39.4
Mexico	2004	15.8	23.3	26.3	34.6
Nicaragua	2001	12.2	21.5	25.7	40.7
Panama	2002	14.2	25.0	28.2	32.7
Paraguay	2000	12.9	23.5	26.4	37.3
Peru	2003	14.9	23.7	27.9	33.6
Uruguay	2002	21.6	25.4	25.6	27.3
Venezuela	2002	14.3	24.9	29.5	31.3

Source: ECLAC (2006 : 332–3).

country, while the poorest 40 per cent obtain only slightly over 10 per cent of the total. The Andean countries and those of Central America are only relatively more equal. Again, it is only Costa Rica and Uruguay that stand out as having anything approximating a concept of social development based on wider access to economic and social citizenship prerequisites. The brutal fact is that Latin America as a whole spends only 20 per cent of its GDP on central government spending compared with an average of 41 per cent in the developed countries. The IDB resists the temptation to conclude 'that the small size of Latin American government *causes* poor income distribution' (2000: 65, my emphasis) but that correlation could easily be argued.

In the era of globalization and the new information economy, an index of social development could be the level of electronic 'connectivity' of a population. If a country's citizens are part of the new global networks created by the internet they can be seen to be part of the flows of information essential to the flourishing of the 'new' economy. On the other hand, if people are cut off from the 'information superhighways' they will not have access to the levers of economic and social development. If we go back to the communications technology of the 1950s – the radio – we see in Table 1.4 that Latin America still has a high level of ownership. Likewise with television becoming the prime communications technology from the 1960s onwards, although here the global average figure is slightly higher. When we turn to personal computers the picture is much more uneven. First, the global average of 58 PCs per 1000 people masks absolutely enormous differentials between a Manhattan and a Mogadishu, and even in between those extremes. In 2006 the latest data on internet users showed that 15 per cent of Latin America's population was connected up, compared with 70 per cent in North America. In terms of PC ownership and the number of internet hosts we can say that Argentina, Brazil, Chile, Mexico and Uruguay are 'semi-connected' with other countries lagging far behind the global averages. This very uneven connectivity of Latin America in terms of the new network-based global economy will have an increasingly serious impact; as Manuel Castells writes, 'Exclusion from these networks is one of the most damaging forms of exclusion in our economy and in our culture' (2001: 3).

Political Economy Issues

It is most common to find a global region such as Latin America defined in terms of the 'struggle for development' or 'overcoming

Table 1.4   Latin America: communications and connectivity, 2000

Country/Region	Radios per 1000 people	TV sets per 1000 people	Personal computers per 1000 people	Internet hosts per 10 000 people
Argentina	677	289	39	18
Bolivia	672	115	–	0.5
Brazil	435	316	26	13
Chile	354	233	54	20
Colombia	565	217	33	4
Costa Rica	271	403	–	9
Dominican Republic	177	84	–	6
Ecuador	342	294	13	1.5
El Salvador	461	250	–	1.5
Guatemala	73	126	3	0.8
Honduras	409	90	–	0.2
Mexico	324	251	37	12
Nicaragua	283	190	–	1.5
Panama	299	187	–	2.6
Paraguay	182	101	–	2.0
Peru	271	143	12	2.0
Uruguay	610	242	22	47
Venezuela	471	172	37	4
Latin America and the Caribbean	414	263	32	10
World	380	280	58	75

Source: *World Bank* (2002: 266–7).

underdevelopment'. I would argue, however, that to view Latin America simply as an underdeveloped or developing region is not particularly helpful, and certainly should not serve as the overarching perspective. Basically, if we measure development in terms of industrialization we find Latin America sitting squarely on the global average (see Table 1.5).

While agriculture contributes slightly more than the global average – 8 per cent as against 5 per cent – to the gross domestic product, these are hardly agrarian societies any longer. In terms of the services sector – also taken as an indicator of modernization – Latin America is only slightly below the global average. This is not to say that development is not a pressing issue in Latin America as the Social Issues section above amply testifies. The point is that there is a huge difference within Latin America in terms of the structure of production. Thus we see from

Table 1.5   Latin America: structure of production, 2005 (value added as percentage of GDP)

Country/Region	Agriculture	Industry	Services
Argentina	10	36	54
Bolivia	16	31	53
Brazil	10	38	52
Chile	6	47	48
Colombia	13	34	53
Costa Rica	8	29	63
Dominican Republic	13	27	60
Ecuador	6	28	66
El Salvador	11	30	60
Guatemala	23	19	58
Honduras	13	31	56
Mexico	4	26	70
Nicaragua	19	30	52
Panama	8	18	75
Paraguay	27	24	49
Peru	9	33	58
Uruguay	11	29	60
Venezuela	5	52	44
Latin America and the Caribbean	8	32	60
World	4	28	68

Note: 'Industry' covers manufacturing and mining/petroleum, hence high figures for Venezuela, Bolivia or Peru.

Source: *World Bank* (2006): 294–6.

Table 1.5 that agriculture still matters in Guatemala, Nicaragua and Paraguay in a way that is not even remotely approached in Argentina, Mexico or Venezuela. Conversely, industry makes a major contribution to economic development in Chile, Brazil or Argentina in a way that cannot be said about Ecuador, Guatemala or Panama. This differentiation can also be extended to the national level where there are vast disparities in terms of regional development. In most countries the urban areas are clearly more modernized than the rural areas. Also, in Andean countries such as Ecuador and Peru there is a virtual and socio-economic structure with a developed *costa* (coastal) region and underdeveloped *sierra* (highlands).

Modernization is thus clearly uneven and society is characterized by a structural heterogeneity. Development has occurred in Latin America, but not only has it been uneven, it has also been marked by a dependency on the world economy that has set limits even while creating opportunities. In the current era of globalization with increased economic integration of nations in the global economy, this characteristic of dependent development has become even more pronounced.

Structure of the Book

Following on from this introductory chapter, in Chapter 2, I outline the historical context shaping the current economic, political and social dilemmas in Latin America. From the postcolonial period through the formation of independent republics to the present era Latin America has been characterized by conflict, but in recent decades democratic regimes have prevailed. In Chapter 3 the main phases of dependent development are examined. Suffice it to say at this stage that we are currently at a crossroads in Latin America in terms of development strategies. The neo-liberal market-oriented strategy promoted since the 1980s has simply not delivered sustained economic development, still less sustained social development. What occurs next will depend fundamentally on the governance processes we turn to in Chapter 4, which addresses the issue of why governance is problematic in Latin America. The chapter also explores how a democratic political process can be sustained under conditions of huge socio-economic disparities and growing poverty. We might also add the question of violence, no longer linked solely to guerrilla movements (with the important exception of Colombia) but becoming an endemic or integral element in most Latin American societies. Political corruption is also an issue, and political reform is clearly as necessary as the economic reforms of the 1980s designed to overcome the inefficiencies of state-dominated, inward-looking economic systems. The reform of the state in particular is now a vital issue, not only to make it more 'lean' and economically efficient, but rather to make it more accessible to the citizens of the Latin American republics.

What is a crucial issue is how the economic reforms have coincided with a period of intense political democratization in Latin America, as we see in Chapter 5. Indeed the most significant fact in the recent history of Latin America has been the wave of political democratization since the 1980s. Not only compared with previous periods in the continent's history but in global comparative terms, Latin America is living in a democratic era. This democracy may be limited in its extension and it may be devalued in many areas but it is nevertheless being consolidated. There is, however, the danger that market economics may overwhelm political reform. Unless the state is democratized and strengthened, as the guarantor of democratization, then market-oriented economic strategies will tend to dissolve social and political bonds. The danger then is that an 'anti-politics' will emerge as the population become disenchanted with actually existing democracy. The electorate may then turn to charismatic 'apolitical' candidates at election time, the myth of the providential saviour becoming stronger at times of economic despair.

Chapter 6 turns again to the social patterns of development in Latin America and how different social categories live the economic and political processes outlined in the previous chapters. The particular social relations of the region are critically examined, and the massive impact of urbanization on people's lives is described and evaluated. Poverty, the constant backdrop to the lives of the majority, is closely examined as are the various attempts to introduce some form of welfare provision.

Another notable characteristic of Latin America today is the reactivation of civil society. For long it was argued that the continent's societies were dominated by the state that promoted all areas of politics and society. Now, as we see in Chapter 7, various social movements are emerging from within civil society seeking a transformation of the *status quo* and the dominant political economy model. Traditional social patterns still play an important role, as do patrimonialist politics, but the activation of civil society which began under the military dictatorships of the 1970s is changing the face of politics. Some social movements, such as the Zapatistas, may be better known internationally than others, but across Latin America the forces of social transformation are becoming very active.

It is often said that in Latin America politics are cultural in the same way that culture (think of Latin American literature) is political. In Chapter 8 we address various aspects of Latin American culture in the belief that, in terms of political transformation, culture is a vital terrain. For example, the indigenous peoples were largely suppressed from the Conquest onwards by cultural repression. Likewise their reawakening in recent decades has been, to a considerable degree, a cultural process. Globalization has also had a massive cultural effect in Latin America in various ways. On the one hand, as was the case in Eastern Europe prior to the late-1980s collapse of the state socialist regimes, the US consumer society image is all-pervasive and is a dangerous comparator as inequality, poverty and violence increasingly impact on the population. On the other hand, the cultural domain is where new, more independent, autonomous and diverse terms of politics are being expressed across the continent.

The main issue facing Latin America today is democratization and the constraints placed on its development by the dominant global economic model as examined in Chapter 9. Unlike the state-led industrialization period of the 1950s and 1960s, there is not even the pretence of social redistribution today as 'competitiveness' becomes the sole watchword. Periodic economic crises such as those in Argentina, Brazil and Mexico have placed the international economic agencies such as the IMF and the World Bank on the alert. For the new global order – based on economic integration of the world's economies – to be sustainable it will need to be more responsive to society's needs. Latin America may well be a test-case region for globalization in the decade to come. With considerable economic and human resources, and a thriving democratic political culture, the region is well placed to develop a more democratic and sustainable development model if the current crisis can be overcome.

As Chapter 10 shows, the future, albeit imperfect, is open. The global context is turbulent. The economic and political challenges are considerable. But we can be sure that the inexhaustible creativity of this world region will continue to offer alternatives to the global order as we know it. In many ways it is a barometer of where world affairs are heading, not least because it is, or it is perceived to be, the backyard of the world's only present superpower, the United States of America. And even the frequent use of 'America' to stand simply for the USA is contested by most of those people living in South and Central America, who also consider themselves truly Americans.

2
Historical Context

To understand the situation in Latin America at the start of the twenty-first century – in economic, political, social and cultural terms – we need to set the basic historical context and the parameters it established for subsequent developments. Latin America, more than elsewhere perhaps, is living a present which is very much shaped by its history. After a quick review of the colonial and postcolonial periods, this chapter focuses on the period since the 1930s when most countries began to move 'beyond oligarchy', the subject of the first section below. After the Second World War most countries moved into a phase where democracy was consolidated but in a variant that can be called national-statism, given the importance of the state as a matrix for social change. Democracy collapsed under the contradictions of dependent development in the 1970s (if not earlier) which led to the era of military authoritarianism in many countries. Finally, the current period can be said to be one of democratic openings across the continent, in spite of the constraining effects of the economic programmes of neo-liberalism set by the international economic bodies such as the IMF (International Monetary Fund). Whether that democracy will be consolidated is the great unanswered question for the period to come.

Beyond Oligarchy

When the European invaders arrived in America towards the very end of the fifteenth century, they first met the Mayan people who had been building their civilization since 500 BC in what is now Mexico and Central America. Further south in the Andes, the Inca empire stretched for over 3000 miles from what is now northern Ecuador to southern Chile. Along with the Aztec empire which occupied contemporary Mexico's central valley, these indigenous American peoples were gradually subdued by the Spanish *conquistadores* (conquerors). Technology, divide-and-rule tactics, but above all plagues all played a part in this massive reversal of fortunes. Spanish (and Portuguese) America sought to recreate a society in its own image. Iberian-style cities and complex social structures were soon springing up under the political jurisdiction of colonial *virreinatos* (viceroys) appointed by the crown. The Catholic church also played a key role in legitimizing monarchical rule in the Americas.

Through the 1494 Treaty of Tordesillas, Portugal acquired from Spain the eastern part of South America. This territory, which was to become Brazil, lacked anything comparable to the Aztec or Inca civilizations but it also showed no trace of silver or gold, the great lure for the Spanish settlers. Social differentiation proceeded more slowly than in the Spanish-dominated areas, which would undergo profound changes from 1600 to the mid eighteenth century. Spain was losing its pre-eminent position in Europe, and with its decline the New World became a vital arena for inter-European rivalry. British and other European interests began to take an active interest in this part of the world. The criollo (creole, or simply local-born) population began to exert its independent interests, and with the relaxation of imperial control began to take over the political processes as well as the levers of economic power.

Towards the end of the eighteenth century, the Spanish crown sought to tighten control over its American territories. The *intendentes* (local governors) were directly responsible to the crown and the Jesuit order was expelled in 1767 as a potential alternative power source. But resistance to colonial rule was mounting. In 1780 Tupac Amarú II, a direct descendant of the Incas, led an 80,000-strong indigenous army in revolt. In other areas protests against tax increases by the crown spread rapidly across the Spanish-controlled territories. Back in Europe, the Spanish fleet was defeated at Trafalgar (1805) and Napoleon Bonaparte occupied Madrid (1808). This was the signal for the criollos under their local authorities (the *cabildos*) to rebel. A citizens' army quickly dispatched an attempted English invasion of Buenos Aires in 1806. It was evident that the Spanish crown was a spent force and that the citizens of the American territories were becoming an autonomous social and political force.

From 1810 onwards, the municipal *cabildos* assumed political power in most areas, albeit at first nominally on behalf of the crown. While it was the wealthy criollos who supported the home-rule movement, some of its more enlightened military leaders were unambiguous proponents of independence for America. One such was the Venezuelan-born Simón Bolívar who justly earned the title of 'The Liberator'. His dream of one Latin American nation has endured and has even been revived in recent times as a counter to the effects of globalization. Further south, José de

Box 2.1   Simón Bolívar, The Liberator

Simón Bolívar (1783–1830) – 'The Liberator' of South America – is a key military and political intellectual figure of the anti-colonial struggle. He was part of the group that took Caracas from the Spanish and declared the First Republic of Cartagena in 1811. After a period in what is now Colombia, where he began to articulate the larger South American liberation project, he returned to Venezuela but his forces were defeated. In exile in Jamaica he issued his 'Jamaica Letter' through which he sought to rally his supporters behind a programme for government. He eventually returned successfully to Venezuela in 1816 and by 1822 his armies had also liberated the whole of Gran Colombia. In 1824 the Battle of Ayacucho sealed the victory of *El Liberador* and Upper Peru was named Bolivia in his honour. From his 'Jamaica Letter' we can get some insight into the political thought of this early politico-military leader with continent-wide aspirations for freedom:

> Success will crown our efforts, because the destiny of America has been irrevocably decided; the tie that bound her to Spain has been severed. Only a concept maintained that tie and kept the parts of that immense monarchy together. That which formerly bound them now divides them ... The veil has been torn asunder. We have already seen the light, and it is not our desire to be thrust back into darkness. The chains have been broken; we have been freed, and now our enemies seek to enslave us anew. For this reason America fights desperately, and seldom has desperation failed to achieve victory ... It is ... more difficult to foresee the future fate of the New World, to set down its political principles, or to prophesy what manner of government it will adopt. Every conjecture relative to America's future is, I feel, pure speculation ... Notwithstanding that it is a type of divination to predict the result of the political course which America is pursuing, I shall venture some conjectures which, of course, are coloured by my enthusiasm and dictated by rational desires rather than by reasoned calculations.

Reading the 'Jamaica Letter' in full <www.hyperhistory.net/apwh/bios/ b4bolivarsimon.htm> is recommended in so far as Bolívar's legacy is now increasing in importance, not least through Hugo Chávez in Venezuela proclaiming a new Bolivarian revolution with continent-wide aspirations.

San Martín, born in today's Argentina, was waging an extraordinarily successful military campaign against the Spanish forces. His victory in Chile and Peru led him to Ecuador where he met up with Bolívar in 1821. The Brazilian elite preferred a monarchy to a republic, but elsewhere Iberian America began its independent republican era, a process that had been well consolidated by the mid nineteenth century.

Spanish world power had been in decline from the turn of the century and Britain was emerging as the new dominant power at the global level. Trade with Britain was needed without intermediaries, and the colonies were beginning to assert their own needs. For Brazil the republic came late, with slavery being abolished only in 1888 and the empire collapsing in 1889. Elsewhere there was a conflictual process struggling for independence, but also between centralism and federalism as a way of governing the new emerging states. By mid-century, however, the nation-state system was well-established in most regions and it was also firmly enmeshed within the new global system of British economic hegemony. The second half of the century saw a great increase in the volume of international trade, with the Latin American republics witnessing considerable prosperity, albeit punctured by the various world economic crises.

Independence did not provide the Latin American republics with a much more independent economic policy than they had in the colonial era. Indeed, the structural dependence on foreign trade, foreign investment and the vagaries of the world market probably increased. Britain, in particular, invested heavily in Latin America's railways, docks, banks, public utilities and trading companies, thus securing a controlling interest in the export-oriented economies. The export of primary goods – beef, grain, minerals, for example – fed into Europe's industrial revolution. In some republics, such as those of Central America, the degree of structural dependence was even more extreme. Veritable company-nations were created where, for example, in Guatemala the United Fruit banana company practically controlled the whole economy (and hence the political process). The 'enclave' economy, where the imperial power actually held a piece of the Latin American country (as with the Panama Canal), was an extreme version of structural dependence but indicative nevertheless of the new (or neo-) colonialism which was emerging.

The criollo (local-born) elites were totally committed to the European notions of progress and civilization. Progress was essentially defined as following in the footsteps of the European nations inspired by the achievements of the Enlightenment. Civilization was thus inextricably linked with the European model and the recalcitrant American reality (and its indigenous peoples) was deemed the 'barbarism' that needed to be defeated. At best the local level would be seen as 'folklore' which could be later incorporated into the making of the national mythology as quaint 'ethnic' backdrop. Progress, civilization and culture, however, were the prerogative of the white European and hence the big drive to secure immigrants from Europe, preferably from the northern countries that were deemed more 'civilized'. The world created by economic and political liberalism was not, clearly, a harmonious one. As one historian from Argentina put it, 'Liberalism promised a theoretical garden of happiness which historically became a jungle of poverty' (cited in Burns 1977: 90).

What could make a few rich – for example Brazilian sugar and Bolivian tin – could also make the majority poor and actively 'underdevelop' a country. Thus in the north-east of Brazil, because conditions suited sugar, that is what was produced to the exclusion of fruit or vegetables, for example. The consequences are still felt today in north-east Brazil where hunger is endemic owing to a genuine 'underdevelopment' of the regional economy when the world market for sugar collapsed. Roads and railways had been tied to sugar, as were the credit and marketing systems. The notions of sustainable development were totally alien in this context and development 'after sugar' was never thought about. The same could be said about tin in Bolivia, which produced the legendary wealth of the Patiño family and a few prestige projects, but otherwise nothing but corruption and the dispossession of the communal indigenous lands to feed the tin machine. These are the types of cases which led to the famous phrase 'development of underdevelopment', which implied that modernization (or economic growth) could cause social underdevelopment.

The nation-states in Latin America did, however, become consolidated by the end of the nineteenth century and a certain degree of optimism prevailed. There was a considerable degree of political stability and the civil wars were put to rest and compromises found; great cities were built and a national infrastructure constructed. For the elite, and a growing middle class, this was an era of economic prosperity. A degree of industrialization was even occurring in the larger countries, based on the agricultural sector, such as wine production, tanning, meat-packing, sugar-refining, flour-milling and so on. The concept of 'progress' held by the elites seemed well-founded. European sociology, in the shape of Auguste Comte's concept of 'positivism', had considerable influence, promoting order, stability and growth. When the Brazilian republic was formed in 1889 its flag bore the positivist motto '*Ordem e Progresso*' (Order and Progress). In Mexico at the turn of the century the official state ideology was positivism and ministers were aptly dubbed the *científicos* (scientists) as keepers of the rational faith in progress.

The end of colonialism led to the emergence of a local oligarchy that controlled economic and political affairs in the new nation-states. This was quite a small grouping based largely on the huge estates and also control of mining. They did not feel the need to incorporate the incipient middle class and professional layers, let alone the working classes who were seen to be truly beyond the pale. Where the enclave economy prevailed, this oligarchy had limited power because as Cardoso and Faletto explain:

> [T]hey had little defense against the external sectors and were often transformed into groups patrimonially tied to the enclave economy in so far as national administration came to depend on the income generated by the externally controlled sector. (Cardoso and Faletto 1979: 72)

Where there was, on the other hand, national control over the key economic sectors such as in Argentina and Chile then the local oligarchy was better placed to consolidate a national state and achieve a more hegemonic and legitimate role in society. In these cases success would actually lead to the end of pure oligarchic rule.

It was the incorporation of the middle classes which would bring about both the success of the economic model and the start of politics 'beyond oligarchy'. In Argentina the revolt of the middle classes through the Radical Party had already begun at the turn of the century. They sought to gain access to the oligarchic political system through reform or revolt if necessary, and were in fact successfully incorporated and in a way which did not threaten the integrity of the agro-export model which all social sectors could be seen to benefit from. In Mexico the incorporation of the middle sectors occurred in more dramatic fashion through the 1910 revolution and subsequent moves towards political incorporation. In Brazil the urban middle sectors engaged in an alliance with the non-coffee-producing regional oligarchies that provided the basis for the development of an industrialist class, especially in the southern state of São Paulo. Elsewhere, the incorporation of the middle sectors was uneven, with at one end of the spectrum Uruguay and Costa Rica which became 'middle-class countries' early on, and at the other end true oligarchic regimes such as those of Nicaragua and Paraguay.

In the early twentieth century the larger Latin American countries such as Argentina, Brazil and Mexico were looking like stable semi-democratic republics. As Burns writes: 'Their governmental apparatus followed the most progressive models of the day. Political stability replaced chaos ... New industries existed' (Burns 1977: 145). Yet this apparent modernization masked the fact that the agrarian oligarchy (or aristocracy) still largely held the levers of power. Dependency had actually increased since independence and the crisis of the world economy from 1914 onwards was to have a major effect. The collapse of the international capitalist market caused by the First World War produced a crisis in the Latin American primary-goods export sectors, which coincided with many countries placing wartime limits on imports. Given the great disruption of 1914–18, followed by the depression of the 1930s and then the 1939–45 disruption caused by the Second World War, the stability of the old agro-export model never truly recovered.

The effects of the global context could be seen most clearly in Chile, which relied heavily on the production of nitrates. While the First World War boosted international demand, this was followed by a sharp drop and by the 1920s the whole power scheme had come into question. As Cardoso and Faletto show, 'The slump following World War I affected the enclave economy and – through the connecting mechanisms of banks, domestic trade, and import–export trade – the economy as whole' (1979: 113). A new political balance had to be found and while dramatic massacres of insurgent workers occurred, on the other hand the middle sectors were brought into politics. These sectors began to use the levers of the state to generate an industrial economy in which they were to be the key players. The other major dimension of the world system that was to have a major impact in Chile, as elsewhere throughout Latin America at around this time, was the shift in dominance from Britain to the United States. By the end of the 1930s and particularly after the Second World War, the newly dominant world power would be a key player in the region.

While politically oligarchic rule had already begun to crumble before the international economic crisis of 1929, it was this event and the subsequent depression of the 1930s which finally sealed the fate of the *ancien régime*. Quite simply the old economic/political model could not be sustained and an adaptation to the new conditions of the world economy had to be found. The 1930s had demonstrated the radicalism lying just beneath the surface in Latin America: Cardenismo in Mexico, the Popular Front in Chile, Aprismo in Peru and various peasant revolts in Central America during the 1930s severely jolted the complacency of the ruling classes. The response could be more repression as seen in Central America where oligarchic rule was simply intensified, but the dominant trend was towards a new political economy of development based on industrialization and the internal market. The national-statist order that began to emerge after the Second World War was to create a virtually new society, more urban, more educated, more commercialized and more integrated.

National-Statism

Outward-oriented growth and the unshakeable positivist belief in orderly progress were both brought into question during the long disruption of the world economy, stretching essentially from 1914 to 1945. The slump in external demand for agrarian produce due to the depression and the disruption of international trade for industrial goods both promoted the cause of industrialization in Latin America. This certainly took place unevenly across the continent and did not always respond to a conscious policy initiative. Nor was it particularly progressive in social or political terms in many cases. Thus the Vargas regime that dominated Brazil from 1930 to 1949 saw a considerable industrialization effort, particularly in relation to the iron and steel industries. However, as Cardoso and Faletto note, the 'strengthening of the industrial sector oriented towards the domestic market was more an *ad hoc* response to market conditions than an attempt to change the economic bases of the system of power' (1979: 92). Furthermore, there was no attempt to incorporate the popular sectors into this *de facto* national-statist model of development, which we shall now examine in its various facets.

Nationalism was to become the dominant ideological force across most of Latin America after the Second World War. From the Argentina of Perón in the early 1950s, to the Cuba of Castro in the early 1960s, nationalism was the main motivation behind movements for social change. This was more often than not a form of economic nationalism that offered a critique of the growing foreign (especially US) influence over the Latin American economies. Dependence on foreign investment and its exploitative relation to the nation was blamed for underdevelopment and the general poverty of the population. This nationalism was an echo of that articulated by the nineteenth-century Cuban nationalist José Martí, for whom 'a people economically enslaved but politically free will end by losing all freedom.' This nationalism would develop mainly in a vague 'populist' direction but could also take on a more decidedly socialist direction as in the case of Cuba. Nationalism was, from 1945 onwards, perhaps the major political force in Latin America but it was also a powerful agent of economic transformation and also a key component of Latin American cultural processes (see Chapter 8).

If nationalism was the main ideology, it was the nation-state that was the main motor of development in the postwar period. The intervention of the state and its capacity to generate a dynamic capitalist development process was a hallmark of this era. It was largely state investment that laid the basis for economic expansion from the mid 1950s onwards and

Box 2.2 José Martí: the 'Apostle' of revolutionary freedom in Cuba (1853–1895)

Before he died in a self-immolating dash against Spanish troops in the Cuban rebellion of 1895 Martí had begun to articulate the notion of Latin Americanism in the context of anti-imperialist struggle. José Martí spent considerable time in the United States and he had great admiration for the mythologies of freedom in that country. His most famous essay *Nuestra América* (Our America) extracted below is notable for the fluid, not to say fluctuating, view of what 'America' is. While this 1891 essay is widely seen as marking the beginning of a new epoch of resistance to empire in the Americas, the United States is often viewed quite positively by Martí. The importance of Martí as an iconic revolutionary figure owes much to Fidel Castro's naming of him as the 'Apostle' of revolutionary freedom in 1959. In *Nuestra América/Our America* Martí writes:

> To know one's country and govern it with that knowledge is the only way to free it from tyranny. The European university must bow to the American university. The history of America, from the Incas to the present, must be taught in clear detail and to the letter … Nationalist sentiment must replace foreign sentiment. Let the world be grafted onto our republics, but the trunk must be our own. And let the vanquished pedant hold his tongue, for there are no lands in which a man may take greater pride than in our long-suffering American republics … It was imperative to make common cause with the oppressed, in order to secure a new system opposed to the ambitions and governing habits of the oppressors. The tiger, frightened by gunfire, returns at night to his prey. He dies with his eyes shooting flames and his claws unsheathed. He cannot be heard coming because he approaches with velvet tread. When the prey awakens, the tiger is already upon it. The colony lives on the republic, and our America is saving itself from its enormous mistakes – the pride of its capital cities, the blind triumph of a scorned peasantry, the excessive influx of foreign ideas and formulas, the wicked and unpolitical disdain for the aboriginal race – because of the higher virtue, enriched with necessary blood, or a republic struggling against a colony. The tiger lurks again behind every tree, lying in wait at every turn. He will die with his claws unsheathed and his eyes shooting flames.

Martí's *Nuestra América* <www.cubaminrex.cu/josemarti> has become an icon of postcolonial literary studies but Martí's legacy, like Bolívar's, is being reappropriated by new nationalist generations in Latin America.

also provided attractive conditions for foreign investors. It was the state, particularly in Brazil, that created a heavy industrial sector and used exchange controls to divert resources from the agro-export sector to the new industrialization. State intervention was also decisive in organizing the growing working class into trade unions that controlled workers as much as they mobilized them in support of the government. In some extreme cases, such as oil-rich Venezuela, the state was almost totally responsible for the creation of a national industry, keen to avoid disaster when the wealth of oil would dry up. It should be clear now why we can call this whole historical period one of national-statism.

The nation-statist model of socio-economic development emerged under the aegis of a new world power, namely the United States. The postwar wave of US investment in Latin America was directed primarily towards the manufacturing (and petroleum) sector, whereas British investment was directed more towards public utilities and agriculture. This led to a veritable internationalizing of the internal market as the internal consumer market within Latin America became a more important factor. A new international division of labour was emerging in the 1950s and especially in the 1960s, which involved sections of traditional industrial production relocating in developing countries. This led to a renegotiation of the 'internal' conditions of dependency, creating a 'compromise state', as it were, between the landed oligarchy and the new industrialists and, of course, the new imperialist interests. The latter promoted industrialization, albeit as part of a dependent development in so far as technological and financial dependency remained in place even though the classic neo-colonial agro-export model had been superseded.

There was one group of countries that industrialized strongly in the 1950s and 1960s. Brazil showed a strong and continuous developmental drive from the 1930s onwards, not even broken by the military regime after 1964. A close collaboration between the public and private sectors prevailed and the development of agriculture was at least adequate. Argentina had industrialized even earlier, but in the postwar period entered a stop–start economic cycle and continuous political instability as weak civilian governments alternated with anti-industrializing military regimes at times. Investment levels were always low and economic policy-making continuity suffered owing to the political instability. In Mexico industrialization was based solidly in the public sector and protectionist barriers throughout this period. Chile and Colombia had strong export sectors (copper and coffee respectively) but did achieve serious levels of industrialization within their more open economies. Political stability was a mark of both these countries, at least until the 1970s.

In the countries mentioned above a pattern of industrialization and consolidation of the internal market led to considerable social diversification. The social division of labour was accentuated and the working population increased exponentially. A new political 'pact of domination' also emerged with the incorporation of the commercial and industrial elites into the management of the state. The urban middle classes and even the urban 'mass' were also now active players in the political process and no longer silent spectators as under the oligarchic state. Consumption increased markedly in all these societies with the early emergence of 'consumer society' patterns. Industrialization with growing consumption was designed to 'incorporate' the majority of the population into national society and the political process, and was largely successful in this endeavour, especially under the banner of developmentalism (*desarollismo*) and populism. It was the state that provided the fundamental matrix that made this model successful, in organizing the factors of production, carrying out industrialization functions itself where necessary, and creating a credible national administrative apparatus.

There was another group of countries, however, where industrialization and social transformation were much slower and weaker. The Andean countries – Ecuador, Peru, Bolivia, Paraguay – and the countries of Central America all fall into this category. Here the old primary-export model continued to hold sway and there was no real degree of social diversification and development. Where industrialization did take place (as for example in Peru), it was very closely linked to and subsidiary to the primary sector. In Bolivia the tin economy was never used to energize the rest of the economy through investment and diversification. Paraguay is a case apart in terms of stagnation mainly because it was ruled by the socially and politically retrograde regime of General Stroessner from 1954 until 1988. In economic corruption Stroessner's Paraguay was matched only by Somoza's Nicaragua. In the rest of Central America, modest economic growth in the 1960s (in part tied to the development of the Central American Common Market) did not disturb the fundamental pattern of the agro-export economy and social domination by a conservative agrarian oligarchy.

In most of the above countries the domestic market was not so central to development in so far as the 'enclave' pattern still predominated. Diversification of the economic and social structure was scant and understandable when one considers that the five most important agricultural products accounted for three-quarters of exports in Central America, for example. There was considerable modernization of the agricultural sector in the 1960s, but this simply created more landless peasants and hence more potential for political unrest. In Guatemala where there had been a progressive regime in power since 1944, the US-backed 1954 counter-revolution showed how the traditional landed oligarchy could effectively absorb the industrialists and defuse any potential their sector might have to transform society or politics. Both economic and political power were highly concentrated and there was an almost total social exclusion of the urban masses. Dependent capitalist development and the 'personalist' state which prevailed in most cases (Costa Rica being a clear but almost unique exception) led to considerable social tensions and the eruption of the revolutionary upsurges in the 1970s and 1980s.

Another version of national-statist development is, of course, that of Cuba which since the 1959 revolution that brought Fidel Castro's regime to power has pursued the option of a centrally planned economy. In the first decade of the revolution there was a move to institute a centralized system of planning backed by technical aid from the Soviet Union. The social achievements of the revolution were considerable and the 'slavery of sugar' was to some extent broken through industrialization. However, failure to meet the 1970 sugar harvest targets led to a certain degree of reorientation towards more 'rational' capitalist work methods. Essentially the revolution was being 'institutionalized' in political terms with some degree of democratic process tempering the Fidelista leadership. The emphasis on market mechanisms increased after the collapse of Soviet socialism, but the social gains of the revolution were doggedly defended. In terms of Cuba's role in Latin America its influence was greatest during the guerrilla upsurges of the 1970s and 1980s (in Central America) but has since waned as an alternative pole of attraction from the capitalist model 'made in USA'. What will happen in Cuba after Fidel is very much an open question today and one on which hinges the normalization of USA–Cuba relations.

There is still much academic and political debate on the causes of the collapse of the national-statist development model in Latin America. Among the supporters of the neo-liberal turn in the 1980s it has become an article of faith that this earlier period was irredeemably flawed. These negative perceptions centre around a view of inefficient, corrupt, inward-looking (that is, parochial) development sponsored by a self-serving and/or not very intelligent political class. In reality, while it had its negative points it also had its positive aspects including, for better or worse, the definitive urbanization and industrialization of Latin America. If there was one basic flaw it was more in terms of the contradictions which were emerging in the 1960s between the growing aspirations of the popular masses (who actually believed the nationalist-populist messages) and the needs of the associated-dependent economic model which required a controlled if not cowed working class. The need for an internal market to buy its products could not go as far as these consumers actually becoming empowered citizens.

ilitary Authoritarianism

The collapse of democracy came first in Brazil with the 1964 military coup putting an end to the populist political cycle that had begun with Vargas in the 1930s. A succession of populist presidents culminated in João Goulart who came to office in 1962 as Vargas's political heir. Nationalist rhetoric from above and peasant/labour union mobilization from below seriously rattled the propertied classes and they appealed for military intervention. The military doctrine of National Security made the armed forces prone to see 'communist subversion' in any form of social protest and they duly obliged in 1964. This was probably a different coup from those which followed in the 1970s in so far as it maintained a strongly nationalist economic development project and allowed a limited space for political parties to continue operating. In spite of the 1968 'coup within a coup', which hardened the level of repression, the Brazilian military authoritarian regime was more pragmatic than others in Spanish America, which goes a long way to explaining the longevity of the regime which only decided to allow for (indirect) elections in 1985 and then only under carefully controlled conditions.

In the 1970s a wave of military regimes had overtaken the continent; while in 1960 there had been only four military governments by the mid 1970s the military governed most of Latin America. The myth of the democratic middle class promulgated by modernization theory had now been laid to rest. Far from being a solid bulwark against authoritarian upsurges from the old oligarchy, or the military, these sectors were in the forefront of military intervention as in Pinochet's landmark 1973 military coup in Chile. It was now more common to read of theories of the 'middle-class military coup' (see Nun 1967). In this they were different from the nineteenth-century *caudillo* (strongman) military interventions, or even from the mid twentieth-century conservative interventions by the military. This wave of military dictatorships – supported by the most 'modern' sections of the propertied classes linked to the world market and much of the middle class – saw themselves as revolutionary in that they would cleanse society of all the evils of communism, materialism and atheism and build a new stable authoritarian political order.

The military interventions in Argentina in 1966 and 1976, respectively, are clear examples of the 'new' military dictatorships in Latin America. The 1966 coup led by General Onganía put an end to a cycle of weak civilian regimes caused by the political proscription of Peronism by most regimes after the military coup which overthrew Perón in 1955.

Onganía envisaged a lengthy period of office – some 20 years at least – to rival that of General Franco in Spain whose corporatist state he greatly admired. In spite of considerable repression of workers and students in particular, there was a veritable explosion of popular anger in the 1969 *Cordobazo* (named after the provincial city of Córdoba where the rising began). The Onganía regime retreated into shock and was replaced by a less ambitious general who began the process of Peronist legalization which culminated in Perón's return from exile in 1973. The Peronist interlude was to be brief and did not lead to the consolidation of democracy. Perón himself died in 1974, barely a year after assuming the presidency, and was succeeded by his widow, Estela Martínez de Perón, who presided over an ignominious civil war between the right wing and the left wing of Peronism which paved the way for a return of the military in 1976.

The 1976 military coup in Argentina established what was to soon to become the bloodiest regime ever in Latin America. Repression of the workers' movement and of critical intellectuals and professionals generally was ruthless. Within a few years some 20 000 people had 'disappeared' (a new macabre euphemism) presumed dead (for the military ideology see Box 2.3). The military set about an ambitious plan of economic rearticulation to meet the needs of the international economy, political repression and the creation of social quietism through terror. The military rejected any time limit to their mandate, saying '*La junta no tiene plazos, sino objetivos*' (the Junta has no fixed term, only objectives). These objectives were largely met at the economic level and the political repression was certainly effective. However, in the face of mounting discontent (and even divisions among its supporters), at home the Junta launched the infamous 'recovery' operation on the Malvinas (Falklands) Islands in 1982 with disastrous results. Defeat by the British task-force was followed by political defeat in Argentina and the very rapid and definitive return to democratic rule by 1983.

In Chile, General Pinochet came to power in the bloody military revolt against the Salvador Allende government on 11 September 1973. A democratically elected socialist or social-democratic government was overthrown brutally in a coup widely described at the time as fascist in inspiration and methods. The fear felt by the dominant classes, and wide layers of the middle class as well, was real enough without the need for CIA campaigns highlighting the 'communist' threat represented by Allende. In fact the Communist Party, part of Allende's governing Popular Unity coalition, was a voice for restraint and moderation on the left. Pinochet overthrew not only Allende but the whole Chilean democratic

---

Box 2.3   The military dictators of Argentina speak, 1976–8

When General Videla came to power in Argentina through a military coup in 1976 he declared that: 'One historical cycle has ended ... another one begun ... The enemy has no flag or uniform ... nor even a face.' In 1978 he stated that: 'In Argentina, political prisoners don't exist. No one is persecuted or constrained on account of his political ideas.' However, Videla later admitted that:

> We must accept as a reality that there are missing persons in Argentina. The problem is not in ratifying or denying this reality, but in knowing the reasons why these persons have disappeared. There are several reasons: they have disappeared in order to live clandestinely and to dedicate themselves to subversion; they have disappeared because the subversive organizations have eliminated them as traitors to the cause; they have disappeared because in a shootout with fire and explosions, the corpse was mutilated beyond identification; and I accept that some persons might have disappeared owing to excesses committed by the repression.

The dictatorship's 'interior minister', General Harguindeguy, spelt out more explicitly how:

> Those who in one form or another have been responsible for the blood that flowed in our country should, in the course of their own

---

system (a model across Latin America for many decades) which he, and his supporters, blamed for creating the 'populist' conditions in which a reformer like Allende could come to power. Pinochet's regime, based on widespread repression and the exile of a whole political generation, had set as its objective the wholesale transformation of Chilean society – a capitalist revolution – to definitively 'inoculate' the country against any re-emergence of the communist 'virus'.

In 1974 the Pinochet regime's 'Declaration of Principles' affirmed that theirs was going to be no mere transitional regime, and democracy was blamed for all the country's ills. The capitalist revolution proceeded apace with Chile being an early model of the 'monetarist' approach to economic development (see Chapter 3). However, the vague Catholic-inspired corporatism advocated by Pinochet (with echoes of Francoism) was not consolidated. Essentially, the pre-existing party loyalties were re-emerging and the democratic reflexes of the country proved to have been dormant but far from dead. In 1977 the regime advanced a plan for

→

self-criticism, consider themselves marginalized from the national future. I will repeat once more what I am so tired of saying: political parties ... have no place in the Argentina of the future. Those whose electoral calculations and pacts brought us to crashing failure cannot today raise their voices to advise, nor even debate ... those who were incapable then of rising to the level of their responsibility ... step aside and let themselves be replaced by new men who have better ideas and more strength.

For Rear Admiral César A. Guzzetti it was a case that:

The social body of the country is contaminated by an illness that in corroding its entrails produces antibodies. These antibodies must not be considered in the same way as [the original] microbe. As the government controls and destroys the guerrilla, the action of the antibody will disappear ... This is just the natural reaction of a sick body.

It was Ibérico Saint Jean, the dictatorship's governor of the province of Buenos Aires, who spelt out most dramatically what the regime really would have wished to do: 'First we will kill all the subversives, then we will kill their collaborators, then ... their sympathizers, then ... those who remain indifferent; and finally, we will kill the timid.'

Source: Freitlowitz (1998): 20–32.

a severely restricted and exclusionary form of democracy; however, a 'Pinochetismo without Pinochet' was to prove unattainable for the regime. What the democratic parties of the left and the centre (which probably now regretted its support for Pinochet in 1973) agreed on was a policy of *concertación* (agreements) rather than confrontation. This political elite pact (which safeguarded the dictator's role after elections) was rewarded with democratic elections in 1990 duly won by a centre–left coalition.

The cases of Argentina and Chile (along with Uruguay which saw a similar coup in 1973) gave rise to a vast literature on what was seen as a new 'bureaucratic-authoritarian' type of state (see, for example, O' Donnell 1999a). For O' Donnell, the 'bureaucratic-authoritarian' (BA) state responded to the failure of the import-substitution model in the new context of economic internationalization which now required a 'deepening' of economic integration. There was a necessity, too, for authoritarian measures given the activation of the masses during the populist regimes which accompanied the import-substitution development model. This approach has since been criticized as a model. There was no general 'need' to 'deepen' dependent development, the degree of popular activation was variable, and each of the military regimes was quite distinctive in its origins and their logic. However, this analytical tradition is still useful in that it seeks relationships between the structure of society and political processes, and between the transformation of the international global economy and the national dependent development process. As with all theoretical models it needs to be tempered perhaps by close observation of particular cases and their variations.

Mexico's authoritarian political regime did not involve the military in government, nor did it fit the BA model in any real way. However, Mexico has for long been characterized as non-democratic, even being called in Spanish a *dictablanda* (soft dictatorship). Essentially the political machinery of the post-revolutionary party the PRI (Institutional Revolutionary Party) was able to control the electoral process through patronage if not through fraud. The trade unions were an integral part of the 'revolutionary' state apparatus and did not really articulate an independent social voice. While elections were held regularly and the press was free, the political ethos was undoubtedly authoritarian, verging on the totalitarian given the PRI's almost complete monopoly over power. This was to change gradually after the 1968 massacre of students while Mexico hosted the Olympics. From then on opposition forces emerged, social discontent became much more open, and the contradictions of the many years of PRI rule began to show. In 2000 an opposition party, led by the pro-USA 'anti-politician' Vicente Fox, actually won the elections and even took office without resistance.

Colombia and Venezuela also had political regimes which were hardly democratic, but nor were they BA states. In both countries political elite pacts had been formed in the late 1950s that allowed for a stable formal political process. Venezuela from around 1973 to the late 1980s appeared to be a veritable model of democracy, but as Peeler has shown, all was not well because 'this party system was so efficient in mobilising votes and concentrating them to produce democratically elected governments that worked, that this provoked the very backlash that undermined it' (1998: 170). Indeed, so institutionalized had the system become, and resistant to healthy change, that it became known as the *partidocracia* ('partyocracy'). In Colombia the flaws of the political settlement became most obvious in the 1980s as the country settled into a long civil war and the rise of an absolutely massive drugs trade. Though not disposed to seize power directly on the whole, the armed forces of both countries have played (and continued to play) a major role in keeping social discontent under control and thwarting radical political challenge. There was probably nothing inevitable about the military authoritarianism period in Latin America. It certainly cannot be put down to some innate Hispanic 'authoritarian character', or to genetic flaws in Latin American democracy. Nor can we really accept, as it once was in Latin America, that dependent development *necessarily* leads to authoritarian political rule. In the democratic period that has since opened up (see next section), stable political rule under democratization has proven productive in terms of the governance of Latin America's republics. What is clear is that this period was a true watershed in the contemporary history of Latin America. Military intervention responded, in different ways of course across the continent, to overcome or to seek to overcome the contradictions unleashed by the long postwar national-statist phase of development. The military period changed the whole socio-economic structure of the continent (see Chapter 3), took Latin America squarely into the arena of globalization and also taught the societies of Latin America the great value of democracy, albeit in its imperfect regional manifestations.

Democratic Openings

Perhaps the most dramatic democratic opening in Latin America occurred in Argentina in 1983 as the military dictators retreated owing to the double impact of defeat in the 1982 Malvinas/Falklands military adventure, and growing unpopularity and discontent at home. The military had hastily declared a self-amnesty for themselves on the human-rights issue and then retreated to barracks. The middle-class Radical Party put up a candidate, Raúl Alfonsín, who helped greatly in deepening the democratic ethos in Argentina. He declared that 'Radicalism is more than an ideology, it is an ethic. It is the struggle against the corrupt, immorality and decadence.' The choice for Argentina was a stark one between democracy and a return to the past, to chaos, to violence. Alfonsín's image of honesty and decency swept away the Peronists who had as an unfortunate electoral slogan, *Volveremos* (We shall return), that called forth dark memories of their 1973–6 period in office and the subsequent dictatorial nightmare. With Alfonsín the element of political will (to transform, to reform, to work with an ethical reference point) came to the fore and revalued democracy for a long time to come.

In Chile there was none of Argentina's dramatic settling of accounts with the ex-military rulers, as when Alfonsín put the Junta on trial and actually imprisoned them. However, Chile's first two post-dictatorship administrations of Patricio Aylwin (1990–4) and Eduardo Frei (1994–9) achieved a significant transformation; they certainly moved far beyond Pinochet's aspiration for a 'protected' or 'tutelary' democracy. While authoritarian enclaves remained, not least Pinochet's own protected position, democracy in terms of the electoral system was consolidated. On the economic front, while there has been an undoubted level of continuity with the neo-liberal policies of the old regime, there has also been a much greater emphasis on 'growth with equity'. Social policy became much more inclusionary and social life a whole lot more consensual than it had been during the long Pinochet years. As Chilean economist Osvaldo Sunkel puts it:

> Besides its ethical bases, the elimination of poverty, the attenuation of inequalities, the quest for equity and the opening up of an attractive horizon of opportunities are imperative requirements for the consolidation of democracy and, the strengthening of a dynamic and modern economy. (Sunkel 1993: 11)

Brazil's transition back to democracy was even more 'managed' than the Chilean case. The military regime had begun to decrease tension (*distensão*) as far back as 1975, but it was not until 1985 that an electoral college had been allowed to elect a civilian president, Tancredo Neves. However, after waiting 21 years to become president, Neves died just before assuming office. He was succeeded by his deputy José Sarney, who had been leader of the pro-military party. Though this was hardly an auspicious beginning, democracy was consolidated and direct elections led to the presidency of a political outsider, Fernando Collor de Mello, in 1990. However, he was only to last 2 years in office and left through a process of impeachment after serious corruption accusations. By now the leftist Workers' Party was making a serious bid for the presidency and was already in charge of some key cities and some provincial governorships. Political competition was alive and well. The 'decompression' engineered by the military had been successful and there was even talk of Brazil becoming a 'boring' country, which might be no bad thing for democratic consolidation.

The second half of the 1990s in Brazil were remarkable owing to the two presidential terms of Fernando Henrique Cardoso, the dependency sociologist turned democratic politician. He took office in 1994 after defeating Luis Inácio 'Lula' de Silva of the Workers' Party by some

Box 2.4   Fernando Henrique Cardoso: sociologist and president of Brazil (1995–2002)

Cardoso is widely regarded as the originator of Latin American dependency theory and has written lucidly on the politics of the region since the 1960s. Between 1964 and 1968 he was exiled in Chile by the ruling military regime in Brazil. Some of his most original work dates from that era including the famous *Dependency and Development in Latin America* (written with Chilean historian Enzo Faletto). His analysis of the Brazilian regime and its contradictions in the 1970s and early 1980s took him into politics. He served as a senator for 9 years and helped construct a centre–left coalition against military rule. He was minister for foreign affairs and, later, for finance in the early 1990s and was, finally, elected president in 1995 and re-elected in 1999. For his critics he had turned his back on dependency theory and embraced neo-liberalism. But his recent writings on globalization and democracy can also be seen as bringing together his early academic work and later political experience in a type of third-way politics:

> Globalization has become a sort of fashionable buzzword: Quite often said; seldom with the same meaning. It is in fact one of those far-reaching concepts that are used by different people to explain facts that are of a completely different nature ... Hand in hand with economic globalization goes a change in the role of the State. Globalization means that external variables have an increased bearing on the domestic agendas, narrowing the scope for national choices ... [and] has left less room for widely differentiated national strategies with regard to labor, macro-economic policy ... Globalization has changed the role of the State in another dimension. It has completely shifted the emphasis of government action, now almost exclusively laid on making the overall national economy develop and sustain conditions for competitiveness on a global scale. And all this ... at a time when democratic values and a strengthened civil society compound the demands for change ... This is no easy task ... But there is no alternative ... By reallocating its resources and its priorities to education and health in a country with sharp social contrasts such as Brazil, the new State will be contributing to something it failed to do in the past: to promote equal opportunity at a time when qualification and education are a pre-requisite not only for finding a job, but also for increasing the degree of social mobility. (Cardoso 2001: 244–7)

25 percentage points. Cardoso had been finance minister under the interim presidency of Collor de Mello and the successor regime of his deputy, Itamar Franco. His economic plan had been successful in bringing down inflation and in helping to reactivate the economy. The orientation towards the regional common market, the MERCOSUR (see Chapter 9), was

much stronger and Brazil was emerging clearly as the leading power in Latin America. Cardoso was re-elected and continued his mandate until 2002, when 'Lula' finally attained the presidency. For some commentators Cardoso had betrayed his radical roots in merely seeking to reform the basic neo-liberal direction set by the dictatorship. Thought it is too early to tell, it would seem, however, that Brazil's economic development has been set on a more sustainable course and political democracy has been strengthened to the extent that another military coup today seems inconceivable.

The Southern Cone (including Brazil) was where the military dictatorships had held sway most clearly, but now by the turn of the century democracy had been consolidated in the subregion. Democracy is, of course, subject to various and confusing definitions. We could say that 'true' democracy does not exist given the daily violations of the law (see Chapter 4). However, we could also take up Przeworski's definition that 'The process of establishing a democracy is a process of institutionalising uncertainty, subjecting all interests to uncertainty' (Przeworski 1986: 58). No one group's interests can be guaranteed, in other words. In this sense democracy has been consolidated in the Southern Cone as witnessed in the deeply conflictual but still managed process at the end of 2001 as Argentina's economy collapsed. It is well to remember that democracy is a process and not a one-off event at elections. It is also clear that democracy requires political imagination and that imagination was something that was not exactly encouraged in the long night of the military dictatorships.

In Central America the democratic openings of the 1990s were of a quite different nature in so far as they followed on from a period of revolutionary war. In El Salvador the FMLN (Farabundo Martí Front for National Liberation) had posed a serious threat to the regime in the 1980s and governed a substantial part of the national territory. In 1990, partly as a result of the post-cold-war era emerging and the collapse of the Sandinista regime in Nicaragua which had supported it, the FMLN was able to negotiate a peaceful settlement with the government. Since then the FMLN has made substantial electoral gains, although not in the presidential elections. Nevertheless, a fragile democracy is being consolidated. A similar story can be told for Guatemala where the URNG (Guatemala National Revolutionary Union), although not as strong as the FMLN, had considerable backing from civil society, particularly the indigenous peoples, and was able to negotiate a peace settlement with a particularly murderous state. Even in these fairly extreme cases democracy could be built especially when foreign intervention ceased to be an issue.

In the Andean countries democratic consolidation was threatened on various fronts. Bolivia has suffered from an on–off democratization process since 1977, and the post-1980 military regime was even worse than its predecessors. A highly repressed, demoralized and socially disarticulated country does not offer a good setting for democracy, which at best will be a fragile affair. In Peru a similar situation prevailed, associated also with the vigorous insurgency of Sendero Luminoso and the effects of the personalist and authoritarian regime of Alberto Fujimori from 1990 to 2000. Emerging as a populist response to social disorder, Fujimori implemented a ruthless neo-liberal plan and political repression. In 1992 he carried out a unique *autogolpe* (self-coup or palace coup) to give himself even more draconian powers. As to Colombia, the much-vaunted political stability of the country was bought at the price of a systematic exclusion of the insurgent left, which, after the events of 11 September 2001, were faced down by a merciless US-backed military repression. Democracy is unlikely to flourish in this context either.

The prospects for democracy in Mexico are always difficult to assess in this country which, as they say, is 'so far from God, so near the United States'. The longstanding electoral dominance of the PRI was shaken in the 1990s and then overthrown in Vicente Fox's remarkable presidential victory in 2000. The emergence of a strong middle class less tied to the state and the 'revolutionary' traditions lies behind this shift. Mexico is now a member of the OECD (Organisation for Economic Development and Co-operation), the 'club' of the advanced industrial societies. This, however, is largely due to Mexico's growing economic integration with North America through NAFTA (the North American Free Trade Association) and does not reflect some magical overcoming of dependent development. Nor is Mexico immune to the problems of drugs, money-laundering and organized crime generally. In the 1990s Mexico began to rival Colombia in terms of the development of a 'mafiocracy' which saw the benefits of the alternative global economy then emerging. In the wake of the financial crises of the 1990s, Mexico is emerging as a post-revolutionary state, more integrated with globalization but not necessarily more democratic.

To sum up, then, on the basis of our brief review of the historical context in which contemporary Latin America operates, what are the prospects for democracy today? Chapter 5 will examine both the achievements and limitations of the new democracies since 2000, in particular the apparent 'left turn' in recent years. One of the main issues at stake is whether democracy can be consolidated (or even maintained) when social inequality is steadily increasing (see Chapter 6). A study by

Karen Remmer (1991) examined the political impact of the economic crisis in Latin America and concluded that:

1. Democracies have coped with economic crises at least as well as the dictatorships did;
2. Economic crises in the 1980s did undermine democracy but did not lead to political extremism; and
3. Regular elections enhanced the capacity of political leaders to deal with economic crises.

In short, democracy is attainable in Latin America and, in spite of some disenchantment (*desencanto*) with it after the democratic openings, it is still valued by most people. Democracy is possible but it also needs to be constantly strengthened and, indeed, deepened by extending political democracy to the social and economic terrains where huge levels of inequality conspire against democratic consolidation.

The main factor constraining the full social, economic and political democratization of Latin America is the belief (or ideology) that there is no alternative to neo-liberal economic ideas. The horizon of possibilities are, indeed, very limited if we take as a given the IMF (International Monetary Fund) policies and practice. At best this leads to 'adjustment with a human face', which means that some more money will be given to education and training. However, within various community movements, political organizations and cultural movements there are alternative strategies for development emerging (see Chapter 7). Latin America has a rich history of successful as well as failed economic development, political democratization and social transformation experiences to call on. The present and the future of Latin America will, almost certainly, be informed by its history and not just imposed by the rules and context set by globalization.

3
Political Economy

The political economy of a region is a crucial determinant for the well-being, or otherwise, of its inhabitants. Latin America, more often than not, hits the international news when one of its countries experiences a financial crisis: Mexico in 1994, Argentina in 2001, maybe Brazil next? Yet at the last turn of the century many of the countries of Latin America seemed to have considerable economic prospects ahead of them. This chapter traces the broad outlines of the region's political economy, commencing with an overview of 'dependent development' as both a concept and a reality. We then move to the post-Second-World-War phase of state-led industrialization under generally nationalist and populist (Chapter 2) political regimes. This is followed by the emergence in the 1980s of the neo-liberal 'new economic model' based on pushing back the state and opening up to the world market. Finally, we consider whether there are alternative economic strategies to the dominant model, an issue that has become particularly pressing after the collapse of the 'new economic model' in Argentina.

Dependent Development

The dominant theoretical explanation for Latin America's development or underdevelopment is the US import known as 'modernization theory'. It assumed that capitalist expansion worldwide was and is an essentially benign process; capital and technology could be 'diffused' from the advanced industrial nations to the rest for the benefit of all concerned. The diffusion of innovations and 'entrepreneurship' to the most 'backward' corners of the world would gradually transform them into 'modern' societies based on the principles of liberal democracy. The key to development was seen as integration into the world system and the adoption of Western values (not to mention capital). Progress might be slow but it would inevitably 'trickle down' from the West to the so-called underdeveloped (or in more polite parlance 'developing') world, and from the cities to the rural areas of the latter. This optimistic scenario did not, however, materialize in practice.

From within Latin America, the modernization perspective was contested from the 1960s onwards by what became known as the 'dependency theory', although its proponents usually called it a perspective or approach. It was argued that 'dependence is a *conditioning situation* in which the economies of one group of countries are conditioned by the development and expansion of others' (Dos Santos 1970: 761). Where modernization theory saw integration with the world economy as beneficial and a prerequisite for development, the dependency approach (at least in its popularized versions) saw it as wholly detrimental and inimical to true development, which could only occur through 'de-linking' with the world economy. According to dependency writers, integration, far from leading to political democratization, would inevitably mean that the local proponents of Western values would rule only through repression. This was a structuralist approach – focused on the unequal structures of the global economy – and a historical one, deeply conscious of the brutal colonial past and detrimental neo-colonial present of regions such as Latin America.

Against the extreme 'development of underdevelopment' approach associated with Andre Gunder Frank – for example, the notion that things can only get worse – Latin America experienced considerable growth (or development) in the twentieth century. It is estimated that the continental per capita income (earnings per person) increased at least fivefold between 1900 and the year 2000. Against the 'stagnationist' approach of Frank and others, it is now clearly recognized in Latin America that dependency and development can go hand in hand and are not mutually incompatible. Nor can we counterpose 'external' causes of dependent development to 'internal' causes around social class formation and political struggle. It may be best to think of dependency 'theory' as a methodology: a lens through which to examine the political economy of Latin America. It may be well to consider the conclusion of Cardoso and Faletto that:

> The originality of the [dependency] hypothesis is not in its recognition of the existence of external domination – an obvious process. It is in the description of the forms and the effects of this type of dependence in classes and state with reference to past situations.
> (Cardoso and Faletto 1979: 174)

Dependent development in Latin America rested on an ever-increasing integration with the world economy. From 1850 onwards most countries in Latin America entered a phase of considerable dynamism based on 'outward-oriented' growth. Capital poured in – Argentina had received $3.2 billion of direct foreign investment by 1914 – and so did labour, with immigrants making up nearly half the working population in the case of Argentina. As Rosemary Thorp writes about this period: 'Growth was at the heart of the stimulus to infrastructure and urban development that gradually began to build a national market' (Thorp 1998: 88). Political institutions were created – from central banks to legal codes – and societal structures were built, from schools to trade unions. This growth and the expansion of the internal frontier was, of course, highly exploitative. Nor was it always successful even in its own terms. For every Argentina, which in 1914 was one of the richest countries in the world, there were many more small, sugar-producing economies that created precious few institutions and did not diversify.

Integration with the world economy in turn rested on what has become known as the 'commodity lottery'. The export of primary products – be they minerals, coffee, cattle or whatever – could have different effects. Some products lent themselves naturally to 'forward linkages' into the rest of the economy, such as cattle which could be processed in various ways, but others – such as bananas for example – did not. Also, 'backward linkages' demanding inputs from the rest of the economy were created by some products such as nitrates that required machinery to extract, but not with others such as guano (bird droppings) that were simply gathered (on the rise and fall of guano see Box 3.1). As Bulmer-Thomas notes, 'The geographical and geological diversity of Latin America meant that each republic had only a limited choice of commodities to export' (1994: 15), but there was also a lottery in terms of whether a product can be substituted by synthetics (for example, cotton) or whether international competition becomes fierce (as for sugar) or not. All in all, this was not a very stable or predictable basis for political/ economic development.

Bulmer-Thomas in his wide-ranging economic history of Latin America since independence argues that 'The commodity lottery and the mechanics of export-led growth have been important determinants of success or failure in Latin America's economic development since independence but so has the economic-policy environment' (1994: 17). We certainly cannot ignore the issue of agency and political choice as too many 'structuralist' accounts tend to do. There is clearly good economic policy and bad economic policy, but there is also a constraint imposed on the type of decisions which can be taken. A subordinate, dependent economy does not have the same span of choices that a hegemonic

Box 3.1   The rise and fall of guano

The rise and fall of guano (the excrement of seabirds) is a good illustration of what the 'commodities lottery' has meant for Latin America. It shows how fragile a base for economic development natural resources are. Guano became recognized as a fertilizer in the middle of the nineteenth century, and exports from Peru, to Britain in particular, took off rapidly. The Pacific coast of South America was also rich in sodium nitrate which too was readily accessible. Along with the phosphates-rich guano these became major exports for the Andean countries. But they also caused conflict such as the War of the Pacific towards the end of the century that saw Chile taking over Bolivia's rich nitrate fields and causing that country to become landlocked from then on. Chile's dependence on natural nitrates was beneficial in the short term, but created a quasi-colonial economic relationship with Britain as well as a distorted economic development process. If that was not bad enough, a German scientist, on the eve of the First World War, discovered how to produce nitrates artificially, and virtually overnight the mainstay of the Chilean economy collapsed. Similar stories of a 'commodity lottery' can be told for sugar and tin, and one day no doubt will be told for coca.

dominant power has. There is also the issue of 'path-dependence', which is why this chapter necessarily must go back to the mid nineteenth century. It is not just that 'history matters', but also the way in which, if a country or region embarks on a certain course, the costs of reversal become very high. Economic structures and institutional arrangements become entrenched and thus act as a heritage that is hard to shake off. Outward-oriented growth is a clear example of this.

Economic policy was created by the economic and political elites or ruling groups in each country. They were part of a political system during the heyday of integration with the world market that has become known as the 'oligarchic state'. In each country a faction of the dominant economic groups tended to become hegemonic, based on the most important export commodity. Thus in Argentina there was a group based on cattle and wheat production, in Brazil it was the coffee-producers and in Chile the mineral-producers. These were not feudal ruling classes in the sense that they opposed modernization or even industrialization, which was often encouraged as a supplement to the main agro-mineral export orientation; they did, however, act as a political oligarchy in the sense that power was concentrated in the hands of a few wealthy families.

As Cardoso and Faletto note in their landmark study of 'dependent development' in Latin America: 'Politically, "oligarchic" domination in Latin America had begun to crumble before the 1929 world depression' (1979: 76). That is to say, the political economy of Latin America cannot be explained totally (or even predominantly perhaps) by external events. The way the social and political order was reorganized depended crucially on the nature of the socio-economic structure in each country. New social groups – 'middle classes' in some ways – had been emerging since the turn of the century and were now seeking political expression. Where the dominant economic sectors were under national control, as in Argentina where powerful landowners held sway, there was considerable success in incorporating these middle sectors into political life. In other situations, such as Central America, characteristic of the 'enclave economy', the demand for political participation by the urban middle class could more readily lead to peasant uprisings and were therefore dealt with predominantly by repression.

The engine of export-led growth and the stability of the oligarchic state both began to falter around the time of the First World War. For the world economy as a whole, the period running from 1914 to 1945 has been described as 'an age of dislocation and an age of experiment' (Thorp 1998: 97). Nowhere is this more true than in Latin America, where two world wars and the Great Depression of the 1930s led to great dislocation but also provided the spur to begin a process of industrialization which would utterly transform the political economy of the region. While even the larger economies were still heavily trade-reliant in the 1930s and industry was only incipient, there had been considerable diversification taking place by the end of this period. The constraint on imports caused by the dislocation of the world wars and the Great Depression led to a considerable degree of import-substitution industrialization. This relative boom even allowed some countries such as Mexico and Brazil to settle their foreign debts, crucial for integration with the world economy and financial markets during the long postwar boom.

In 1945 as the Second World War was coming to a close the world was a place very different from what it had been just 30 years previously. Where once Britain clearly dominated the global trade and capital markets, now the United States was emerging as a clearly hegemonic power, based on mass industrialization and the powerful dollar. Whereas in 1914 three-quarters of overseas investment was in portfolio terms (for example, through financial investment), and only a quarter was in direct production, by 1945 these ratios were just about reversed. That in essence encapsulates the difference between the British era of imperialism and the new USA-dominated era of neo-colonialism or dependent development. Henceforth the internal markets of Latin America would be internationalized and domination would occur not just through the 'enclaves' of petroleum installations or banana plantations. This 'new' dependency in Latin America led inevitably to a realignment of internal political alliances, as the old landed oligarchy, the new industrialists, foreign capital and the workers in the factories and the fields struggled to situate themselves in the new dispensation.

State-Led Industrialization

After 1945 the Latin American state began to move from its role as 'nightwatchman' (an overseer but not a player) to one of active intervention. The state began, in the larger countries at any rate, to actively foment industrialization. The working class generated by this process of industrialization posed a potential problem for the dominant order and this encouraged moves towards political institutionalization. A *laissez-faire* attitude towards the state – typical of the oligarchic period between 1850 and 1914 – had little purchase in the new era. The new dominant state ideology of 'developmentalism' (*desarollismo* in Spanish) combined Keynesian economic policies, a strong degree of nationalism and varying levels of populist rhetoric. The new ideology possessed a strong vision of history as progress and a notion that social development depended critically on industrialization. Whereas the oligarchic state had focused mainly on social order, the *desarollista* state also understood that the state needed to act as an agent of social integration.

Today many economists and political observers look back on the period of state-led industrialization as one of unrelieved mistakes. The blinkers of neo-liberalism, however, seem to have hidden from these critics the very real achievements of this period. As Rosemary Thorp finds: 'Latin American economic performance during the three decades that followed the Second World War was outstanding' (Thorp 1998: 159). Indeed, between 1945 and 1973, the continent's gross domestic product grew at 5.3 per cent per year, an unprecedented record. Equally significantly, the manufacturing sector had now become in a very real sense the 'motor' of the economy's growth, achieving an overall weight in the economy of over a quarter by the end of this period. The rapid industrializers included the Southern Cone countries of Argentina, Chile and Uruguay, along with Brazil and Mexico. Colombia and Peru came

> **Box 3.2   The national-statist popular sociopolitical matrix (1930–90)**
>
> | *Matrix elements* | *Characteristics* |
> |---|---|
> | Development model | National industrialization, strong state role |
> | Links to international economy | Import substitution industrialization |
> | Civil society | Social actors based on work, social class or political affiliations |
> | Ideology/Culture | Nationalist, populist, politically focused |
> | Politics | The compromise state, weak institutions |
> | State role | National development model, focus of collective action |
> | Modernity concept | Western, industrial, people-oriented, political |
> | Risks | Political instability, ideological polarization, dependence on foreign capital |
>
> *Source*: Adapted from Garretón *et al.* (2002: 9).

in more modestly and later, but the other Andean countries and those of Central America tended to lag behind, still following the agro-export model.

The period of state-led industrialization has also been characterized as one of 'inward-oriented' growth. The countries embarked on this path prioritized the development of the domestic market rather than export promotion. A light consumer industry dedicated to servicing this market was followed, in the 1960s, by the development of heavy industry. By the late 1960s Argentina, Brazil and Mexico could be characterized as 'semi-industrialized' countries with Chile and Colombia not far behind. The development needs of the national economy also led to increased opportunities for employment, with a massive growth of white-collar and industrial employment. A certain degree of income redistribution occurred during this period with the middle and working sectors of the population gradually improving their situation. The incorporation of the broad masses into the production and consumption systems also helped generate considerable popular support for the state.

As noted above, many countries did not, in fact, adopt the state-led or inward-oriented development model after 1945. Indeed, these were the majority where the 'commodity lottery' still prevailed and the economy's futures were linked to a handful of primary-product exporters. Examples would be the tin producers of Bolivia, Cuba's sugar magnates and the banana barons of Honduras. Here, the pre-existing level of industrialization was simply too weak to act as a springboard for a new *desarollista* model. Furthermore, the old economic elites retained their full power and were unwilling to share it with a new industrial elite, let alone the working masses. The whole economic and social infrastructure of these countries remained geared towards servicing the agro-export economy. For some economists this model was seen as successful in so far as these countries saw their share of world trade increase, actually overtaking that of the semi-industrialized set of countries by 1960. For the people, however, there were scant benefits except in those fortunate countries like Venezuela where the benefits did lead to a degree of social development.

The debate between inward- and outward-oriented growth during the postwar period is still hotly contested. For Bulmer-Thomas the first period is seen as an 'aberration' and 'the timing of the model could hardly have been worse' (1994: 288) given that the world economy was then going through a period of unprecedented expansion. The inward-looking nature of development during this period is seen as inevitably feeding inflation. With hindsight many mistakes in economic policy-making have been identified, and this is a key determinant for successful development as we have argued above. Politicians certainly promoted industrial job-creation as a means to securing patronage and votes. Public indebtedness may also have been exacerbated by corruption. However, the retrospective critique of the state-led industrialization remains somewhat abstract and ahistorical. This strategy was not just an economic policy but also a nation-building strategy, as not only roads, steel plants and central banks needed to be built but the very social structure of an industrial society had to be created, right down to providing the protection and support necessary for the creation of an industrialist class.

The *desarollista* state was a key element in the inward-oriented economic development model. In Brazil, for example, government participation in fixed capital formation more than doubled between 1947 and 1960, reaching almost 50 per cent of the total if we include mixed government enterprises. It was this important state sector which laid the infrastructure which made possible the boom of the Kubitschek period (1956–60) where a 'great leap forward' sought to advance Brazil 'fifty years in five'. It was this decisive intervention by the state which laid the basis for the 'associated-dependent' model of development as foreign capital moved into Brazil, as elsewhere, from the mid 1950s onwards. Whereas direct foreign investment in Brazil was $52 million in 1954, the figure had reached $139 million in 1956 and then continued rising. This foreign investment was directed at the most dynamic sectors of the economy – cars, chemicals, petroleum, machinery and electrical sectors for example – which depended on a stable state infrastructure.

The model was also, to varying extents, based on a 'populist' state, where the myth of the providential person comes to substitute for the ideological relationship which social consensus is usually based on. In 1945, Perón in Argentina created a social movement which has lasted until the present day, and Vargas in Brazil during the 1950s also represented the charismatic leadership typical of populism, calling himself the *pai dos pobres* ('father of the poor'). These movements, over and above their particular features, represented a type of compromise state in which the inward-oriented alliance of industrialists and others coexisted uneasily with the landowners and other old regime elites. The point at this stage is to note that the populist state was oriented towards popular participation and a degree of social and economic redistribution. A stark reminder of this is that coinciding with the rise to power of Perón in Argentina, the share of wages and salaries in the national income rose from 44 per cent in 1943 to 60 per cent in 1950. These gains would be wiped out by the new economic model of the 1970s.

Eventually the postwar economic model was 'exhausted' or was overcome by its contradictions. The phase of 'easy' import-substitution seemed to be over by the late 1960s and had lost much of its dynamism. There was now, according to some authors, a need for 'deepening' the process of industrialization through vertical integration, which would necessitate greater control over labour costs and hence an end to populism. But this view has been contested as an explanation for the rise of the military dictatorships in the 1970s. Whatever the case may be, the import substitution model was no longer dominant or accepted by the majority of the dominant classes. Certainly there was a turn away from the internal market by these to embrace the external market. In this sense the unequal distribution of income which prevailed in Latin America considerably narrowed the internal market and thus the scope for further import-substitution industrialization.

One of the seemingly 'technical' economic debates of this period (1950s–60s) still resurfaces regularly today. The 'monetarists' who took their inspiration from the 'Austrian school' of von Hayek and others focused on a few policy instruments such as the control of money supply, the reduction of the government deficit, the elimination of subsidies and the freeing of prices. Tackling the growing inflation rate was presented as the main issue and 'sound money' as the main remedy. For the 'structuralists', associated with the Economic Commission for Latin America (ECLA) set up by the United Nations in 1947, inflation was rooted in the economic structure. Thus certain 'structural' bottlenecks needed to be addressed around the availability of foreign exchange, the supply of imports, and food supply. Only conscious government action could remedy the structural failures of the market. For example, the failure of most countries in Latin America to engage in a thorough land reform and redistribution of resources – in stark contrast with Korea and Taiwan for example – acted as a significant 'structural' impediment to agrarian modernization and development.

Finally, of course, economic models are determined politically and they do not fail or succeed because of some technical economic debate. The end of the inward-oriented *desarollista* populist state came at various times. In Brazil a military takeover in 1964 put an end to democracy (as well as populism) but retained an industrializing strategy. In Chile in 1973 General Pinochet violently overthrew the elected regime of Salvador Allende and launched a severe 'free-market' model. In Argentina, the 1976 military coup put an end to a whole cycle of developmentalism and democracy, launching the most clear-cut and vicious of the 'new' economic models, ironically pointing towards a return to the old pre-1930 agro-export model. Basically, in reality the economic debate between the structuralists and the monetarists was settled by tanks in the streets. However, this period is today being re-examined and the neo-structuralists (see the section 'Beyond Neo-Liberalism' below) are now urging for some of its good features to return, especially given the catastrophic collapse of the 'new economic model' in Argentina in 2002.

The New Economic Model

In 1973, General Pinochet was bombarding government house in Chile, putting an end to Salvador Allende's experiment in socialist democracy (as well as his life), and also launching a new economic model which was to have significant international impact. The Chilean economic model engineered by the so-called 'Chicago Boys' (Chilean economists trained at the University of Chicago) was the right wing's answer to dependency theory and was to inspire some people in the West, for example Margaret Thatcher. The 'Chicago Boys' acted as a key link between the international capitalist elites and the Chilean military project to carry out a veritable 'capitalist revolution'. What was striking about the political economy of Chile after 1973 was 'the simultaneous deterioration of employment, wages, per capita consumption, and other social indicators that measure the population's access to housing, education, and health, as well as the skewing of consumption by income strata' (Foxley 1983: 48). This Chilean model was, in many ways, the precursor of what was to become known as the 'Washington Consensus' in the 1980s, albeit with a more legitimate political face than that provided by General Pinochet.

In Argentina the 1976 military coup sought to put an end to the whole cycle of inward-oriented development under a populist state that had begun under Perón in 1945. Martínez de Hoz, the architect of the new economic strategy, came from an agrarian oligarchy background and was intimately linked to the international financial elites. The main beneficiaries of the new model – based on wholesale repression of the working population and all forms of political dissent – were to be agro-industry, the financial intermediation sector and key dynamic industrial sectors integrated into the world economy. A new political economy was being forged through a broad economic, political and social restructuring process. It was not simply a question of turning the clock back to the 'golden era' of pre-1930 based on agrarian exports; what was being sought by the architects of the new economic model was a stable and profitable international division of labour led by the financial sector, which was by then turning into the key international economic sector and promoter of what was becoming known as 'globalization'.

The political economy of monetarism following the early Chile and Argentina cases was to become dominant in the 1980s across Latin America. Monetarism was to achieve undisputed ideological hegemony over the old structuralist and import-substitution theories and strategies. The new monetarists differed from their 1950s counterparts in their much stronger long-term component compared with the earlier version's emphasis on short-term adjustment policies. They also had the undoubted advantage of being able to rely on authoritarian regimes to push through unpopular measures, and the added legitimacy provided by the likes of the Thatcher and Reagan governments in the UK and USA respectively, which were to advocate monetarism aggressively. The main tenets of monetarism are deceptively simple. The market should work unimpeded to allow the free determination of prices; the state should withdraw from its regulatory functions; the national economy should be opened up to international trade; and both the capital and labour markets should be deregulated.

The debt crisis in Latin America, which came to a head in 1982, led to a generalization and a deepening of the new economic model. While Mexico's financial crisis was the most dramatic event of 1982, Latin America as a whole was severely affected and by the end of the year virtually every country was seeking a renegotiation of its foreign debt. The need to generate a greater trade surplus to cover the debt-service payments now became the paramount issue. The new development model – a modernization approach for the era of globalization – was dubbed the 'Washington Consensus', although it was never truly consensual. Be that as it may, we can analyse the now consolidated model under four main headings:

1. *Trade liberalization* – that is to say the dismantling of tariff and non-tariff barriers to trade;
2. *Privatization* – to sell off state assets thus reducing state 'interference' with the market;
3. *Financial reforms* – to promote greater integration into the international capital market; and
4. *Labour reforms* – to introduce 'flexibility' to lower the cost of labour.

It is this package of measures, taken as an integrated whole, which constituted the cornerstone of economic 'reforms' carried out in the 1980s.

Following the Southern Cone trade liberalization programmes of the late 1970s, most other countries in Latin America began to free up their trade regimes during the second half of the 1980s. According to the Inter-American Development Bank, the average level of tariffs in Latin America dropped from 42 per cent in 1985 to 14 per cent in 1995 (IDB 1997: 42). Non-tariff restrictions had affected 38 per cent of imports in the pre-reform period, but by the 1990s were only affecting 6 per cent of imports. Crucially from the point of view of foreign investors, most regulations seeking to prevent capital outflows were also removed during this period. In terms of results, the opening up of trade has led mainly to increased imports and not to a significant boost in exports as had been hoped for. The decade of trade liberalization has led to a collapse of many national-owned small and medium enterprises, and those dedicated to the internal market. ECLA argues that 'the current trade regime should be modified by integrating it to an industrial development strategy, rather than relying on imperfect market forces alone' (Fitzgerald 1996: 50).

Privatization, according to the Inter-American Development Bank, 'has been the most visible component of the strategy to reorganize the apparatus of the state and simplify government activities' (IDB 2000: 45).

The 755 sales and transfers to the private sector that occurred in Latin America between 1988 and 1995 represented fully half of the value of all the privatizations occurring in the developing world. Nearly half of these sales were in the area of utilities where the possible gains were seen to be greatest. A fifth of the total sales were of banks which were obviously fostering the financial reforms dealt with next. Along with the ex-communist states of Eastern Europe, Latin America would be a leader in the great privatization drive of the 1990s as promoted by neo-liberal globalization. As Rosemary Thorp notes, 'Privatization now became widespread. Very few countries stood apart from the process ... In the course of 10 years, the shape of the Latin American economy was profoundly changed' (Thorp 1998: 227). The long-term results of this shift are not clear, but in the short term it boosted the public coffers and helped allay the endemic fiscal crisis of the state.

Financial reform was meant to be more than financial liberalization as practised in the 1980s. The idea was that institutional independence and greater regulation would improve the banking system. While modern banking regulation systems were set up in most countries in the course of the 1990s, the main emphasis was on the freeing of the operation of financial markets. This led to reducing reserve rate requirements and the freeing of interest rates. For the Inter-American Development Bank, 'smoothly functioning financial markets can stimulate growth in a variety of ways' (IDB 1997: 57) but they can only point to a modest 0.5 per cent growth as a result of the financial reforms. Much of the impact of the financial reform has been at the ideological level, and thus much has been made (as Margaret Thatcher in Britain did) of the effect of privatizing public enterprises in creating a spread of shareholding and the emergence of a 'people's capitalism' (*capitalismo popular*). For the international banker, Latin America would also appear to be a more 'finance-friendly' place in the 1990s than it had been in the nationalist-populist era.

The labour reform aspect of the new economic model is one of its central planks in terms of restructuring society, but it is also little studied. It is a neo-liberal belief that undue 'rigidities' in the labour market can hold back investment and hence growth, and there was a concerted bid across Latin America – but led by countries like Argentina where repression was fiercest – to dismantle the historic gains of the labour movement. What greater labour 'flexibility' meant in practice was much greater freedom to 'hire and fire', the elimination of many labour rights, and an increase of 'informal' forms of occupation. The last, more 'flexible' patterns of working outside the formal labour market, was supposed

Box 3.3   The neo-liberal, market-driven sociopolitical matrix

Matrix element	Characteristics
Development model	Market-driven, open economy, minimal state role
Links to international economy	Free financial flows, no national regulation
Civil Society	Citizens as consumers, previous social actors (such as workers) weakened, new social movements
Ideology/Culture	Individualism, lifestyle above politics, competition over cooperation
Politics	Generally weakened, markets as decision-makers, powerful economic groups prevail
State role	Should deliver market reforms, then withdraw, macroeconomic management role but not for distribution
Modernity concept	Individualist, technocratic, rationalist, the USA as ideal
Risks	Dependent on international trade, disarticulation of society, no general legitimacy

Source: Adapted from Garretón *et al*. (2002: 95).

to absorb some of the unemployment created by the trade/financial reforms, but there has been little sign of this. The net effect of the labour reforms has been to create a more fragmented working population and a more confident employer class, even though the latter still complain that labour legislation needs to be urgently 'modernized'.

The 'new economic model' was to utterly transform the socio-economic structures of Latin America. It is one of those moments of transition when a whole region embarks on what is, in essence, a revolutionary transformation. There would, henceforth, be a new matrix setting the parameters of economic debate and policy-making, and political choice would be severely restricted in so far as the 'economic model' was perceived as untouchable. There was a widespread feeling that the 'magic of the market' would sweep away all of the obstacles to economic growth. While the social devastation caused by the new economic model was all too evident, there was still a widespread acceptance of this social cost because the model promised, and for certain periods delivered, macroeconomic stability and laid at rest the dread of hyperinflation which when it did manifest itself had devastating consequences. Of course, there was always the paradox that an economic model purporting to free the market from the state had to use the full power of the state to carry out its measures.

While the social impact of neo-liberalism is analysed in detail elsewhere (see Chapter 6), we cannot avoid the issue here in so far as it was such a major component of the political economy of the new economic model. The key 'social indicators' for Latin America as a whole show a clear enough pattern in the changes that occurred in the 1980s (Figures 3.1 and 3.2). Wages went down and poverty increased steadily and dramatically. The jobs that were kept were increasingly in the informal sector. Even the World Bank, when looking back in the mid 1990s at a decade of structural reforms in Latin America, was forced to conclude that while 'macroeconomic imbalances have been corrected ... nevertheless the economic results are unsatisfactory' (World Bank 1997: 33). It seemed a case of 'all pain, no gain', as the Bank admitted.

Nor did the 1990s fulfil the World Bank's ambition that Latin America would be transformed from a continent of economic despair to one of hope. The percentage of the population living in poverty in Latin America was higher in 2004 (44 per cent) than it was in 1980 (40 per cent). Although many countries did display better economic growth rates in the 1990s and even increased social expenditure, this did not significantly alter income distribution patterns. Overall, as Pedro Sáinz, in a paper for

Figure 3.1   Social indicators: unemployment and poverty, 1980–90

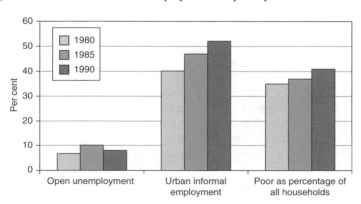

Source: Based on Thorp (1998: 221).

Figure 3.2   Social indicators: wages (as percentage of 1980 value)

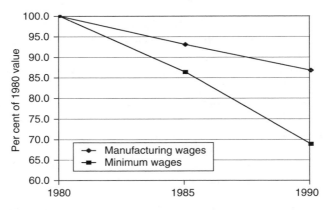

Source: Based on Thorp (1998: 221).

the IDB, puts it, this period of intense economic restructuring and social change in the 1990s had not (as of 2004) led to improvements for the population. Rather, 'this period of transformation saw large-scale foreign actors gradually increase their economic and political power in Latin America, with negative consequences for domestic economies, especially in terms of increasing income inequality and rising poverty' (Sáinz 2006: 11). The era of globalization has meant for Latin America foreign takeover of key industries, increased economic vulnerability and instability, and a continuation of the pattern of long-term economic stagnation.

Beyond Neo-Liberalism

For over a decade Argentina had been seen as the success story of neo-liberalism in Latin America. The peso was even 'pegged' to the US dollar through the Law of Convertibility of 1991. Towards the end of 2001 the whole model collapsed and an interim president (there were four in as many weeks) declared: 'For many years in Argentina they have made us believe that amid this new world order, there is only one possible economic model. This is a complete falsehood.' The government had run out of companies to sell ('privatization'), wages and employment could be squeezed no further ('labour reform') and the link with the dollar ('financial reform') meant that exports could not be placed abroad as they were too expensive. A succession of IMF

(International Monetary Fund) stabilization programmes ended with the largest sovereign debt default ever. When the military withdrew to barracks in 1984 they left behind a legacy of a $46 billion foreign debt, and when President de la Rua sought to raid the country's pension funds in late 2001 to service this debt even the IMF knew this was a step too far and the whole neo-liberal edifice collapsed.

The story of the rise of neo-liberal ideas in Latin America is fairly well known. The military dictatorships that came to power in Chile in 1973 and Argentina in 1976 launched this process but then it was generalized after the 1982 debt crisis as noted above. With the rise of globalization – an increased international integration of economic systems – the shift towards the world market seemed natural enough. After the fall of the Berlin wall in 1989 and the collapse of the Soviet Union a few years later there was no longer an alternative path available for developing economies. It was a question of either participating in the global economy under the rules set by the powerful nations or dropping out of the race altogether. The 'de-linking' from the world system that had been advocated by some extreme proponents of dependency theory in the 1970s did not now seem a particularly attractive option. By the mid 1990s the 'new economic model' seemed to rule unchallenged but in reality it was already riven by contradictions and questioned even in the corridors of power.

The new economic model continued to have widespread tacit acceptance – if not enthusiastic support – because of the perceived failure of the old national-statist model and the very real continued danger of lapsing back into hyperinflation. Also, quite crucially the consolidation of the economic model coincided with a generalized turn towards democratic political rule across Latin America. Economic 'reform' and political democratization appeared to go hand in hand. It was not simply the case that the neo-liberal recipes were 'better'; they reflected also the failure of competing models and the widespread, fervent desire not to return to the 'bad old days' of military rule. In reality, of course, the much vaunted 'magic of the market' was not able to sweep away all the obstacles to economic growth. The social costs also became too high for society to bear. For a whole period, though, the cracks were papered over and the new economic model was taken for granted across the political spectrum, somehow seen as the natural horizon of everyone's political aspirations.

Clearly, even in the early 1990s there were in fact different ways in which developing economies could participate in the globalization race. As Korzeniewicz and Smith argue, 'embryonic and fragmentary efforts are already underway in Latin America that make it possible to visualize a "high road" to economic growth, hemispheric integration and globalization' (Korzeniewicz and Smith 2000: 29). One way to encapsulate the high-road/low-road distinction is through a comparison of Pinochet's Chile (1973–89) and the post-Pinochet political economic strategies. While it has been common to hear that the new economic model launched by Pinochet has been continued by the democratic regimes, the facts are not so simple. Certainly the outward orientation continued as did the basic reliance on market mechanisms. However, there is a world of difference between Pinochet's absolute exploitation of the population and encouragement of cut-throat competition and the various democratic governments' attempts to link competitiveness with social development and an expansion of the internal market based on a certain degree of wealth distribution. This can perhaps be seen as neo-liberalism 'with a human face', but it is still not the same as Pinochet and much more like a neo-structuralism which seeks to recover what is still relevant in the 1960s–70s ECLA model of inward-oriented development.

Nor was the 'Washington Consensus' as monolithic and consensual as most of its critics seemed to believe. By the late 1990s the World Bank was explicitly discussing how to move beyond the Washington Consensus; there was a growing feeling that democratization in the region needed to be consolidated. The first-generation economic reforms should now, according to the World Bank, be followed by a new focus on the social and institutional agenda of the region. When the region's political leaders met in Chile in 1998 to discuss the social and institutional failings of the free-market model, it was the president of the Bank himself who coined the expression of a new 'Santiago Consensus'. World Bank President James Wolfensohn declared prophetically in 1998:

> If we do not have greater equity and social justice, there will be no political stability, and without political stability no amount of money put together in financial packages will give us financial stability. (Cited in Higgott 2000: 131)

So, even the architects of the Washington Consensus were having their doubts about the long-term viability of the model.

If the economic mainstream, in the shape of the World Bank, was rethinking the Washington Consensus, so the left was rethinking its own alternative economic strategy. For a long time it was sufficient simply to oppose the recipes of the 'new economic model', focusing on such dramatic issues as the foreign debt. However, wherever the left achieved any degree of political influence such as in Argentina, Brazil, Chile and

Mexico a more viable economic strategy needed to be developed. To that end a group of influential political intellectuals and leaders from across the continent gathered in Buenos Aires in 1997, a meeting from which emerged the Buenos Aires Consensus. While intended as a full frontal attack on the Washington Consensus this position took globalization for granted and argued that monetary stability was the *sine qua non* of any economic policy. However, they reclaimed the ECLA tradition in arguing for the need for much greater endogenous (inward-looking) growth and for as much emphasis on welfare as on growth. In parallel with the Inter-American Development Bank they argued for the need for better institutions to achieve some local regulation over the market.

Perhaps a more radical and certainly more 'applied' experience comes from Brazil where the radical Workers' Party had run key cities and regions for some time. In the southern city of Porto Alegre the Workers' Party has, since 1998, governed the city and sought to put forward practical alternatives to neo-liberalism. In particular the city's 'participative budget' exercise has been dubbed an 'experience in direct democracy without parallel in the world' (Cassen 1998: 3). In its rigour and its breadth this way of involving citizens directly in drawing up the city's budget is truly remarkable. Going far beyond previous exercises in 'municipal socialism', this participative budget planning has achieved deep popularity among Porto Alegre's 3.5 million citizens. There is active engagement of these citizens in deciding budget priorities from education to transport, from health to crime, and this all feeds transparently (and with accountability mechanisms) into the budget for the following year. When Workers' Party candidate Luís Inácio 'Lula' de Silva became president this was a chance to see whether there was a real alternative to neo-liberalism's total reliance on the market (see Chapter 5).

Indeed it is the very question of market sovereignty that is being increasingly drawn into doubt as the new economic model shows its flaws. In the post-Washington-Consensus era, the questions of the market and the state have come to the fore again. The interventionist state of the *desarollista* era (see the section 'State-Led Industrialization' above) may have been superseded by what some call the 'competition state', but nothing indicates that the market can regulate itself. As Lechner points out 'the state and the market follow different rationalities, therefore there is no sign that one can substitute for the other' (1999: 23). For Lechner, with the demise of the *desarollista* state and the failure of the new economic model to kill off the state, there is now a pressing need to construct a new type of accountable democratic state. To seek the harmonization of the goals of economic growth and social equity may be an

66

Box 3.4   The Porto Alegre alternative

Porto Alegre in Brazil is a city that has promoted a new kind of radical local democracy. A key element in this was the 'participatory budget' pioneered by the Workers' Party local government from the late 1980s onwards. It was from Porto Alegre that the Workers' Party 'way of governing' developed. They followed the old Marxist dictum 'to each according to their need' but set in the framework of modern city management. For example, while in the rest of Brazil the pressure was on in the 1990s to privatize public services, Porto Alegre built what is considered the best public transport system in Brazil. There are serious limits to what the participatory budget can achieve within the limits of one city and even in Porto Alegre itself this phase has now come to an end. But, nevertheless, Porto Alegre really did show direct democracy in action as some of the grassroots participants recall:

Silvio: In my opinion the most important thing the PB [Participatory Budget] has brought to the whole population is the question of popular participation. When it began 15 years ago, in a very different political situation, which all of us can remember to some extent, the people were mere spectators. There was a lot of paternalism on the part of many politicians, who carried out public works as a way of winning support for their own interests, not those of the community. With the arrival of the PB people began to become protagonists of political change. By organizing themselves they began to see the changes – sewage, paving – and I think it's an example of popular participation for the whole world. People have become agents of change. Change, transformation, are for me, the best words to define the PB.

Edimar: Before the community did mobilise, but the projects were decided on in the council chamber, behind closed doors. Now they know what the community is demanding. They don't just imagine what the community might need; they have to follow what particular communities are demanding. It changes people's attitude to politics. Before they'd just go 'Nah! That's just politics, just party stuff.' But now they begin to fight, and they realise that if they want a particular thing they need to get involved, politics or not. So poor people, who didn't have much knowledge, begin to understand how things work and get more involved in the movement, first to win something for themselves but also to help others. So they learn a sense of solidarity.

Source: Bruce (2004): 9–11.

objective that goes back to the 1950s, but it still remains the main issue in contemporary Latin American political economy. The crisis in Argentina at the end of 2001 saw all the above elements combined in dramatic ways. It was civil society out on the streets, banging pots and pans in a noisy protest against the government's proposed austerity measures, which brought it down and with it the post-1976 new economic model. It was not only trade unionists and poor people but also the once affluent middle classes – now becoming the 'new poor' – who were protesting vigorously. While the US and European banks and governments demanded that Argentina must 'honour its commitments' in terms of its foreign debt, the emergency government in Argentina had other priorities. To avoid an economic meltdown a moratorium (delay) was declared on its foreign debt and the *peso* was devalued to facilitate exports. Rather than pay foreign bankers interest, the government said it would create jobs. President Duhalde, a fairly orthodox supporter of the late General Perón, even began to look back wistfully to the economic strategies Perón advanced in the 1950s driven by state-led industrialization and providing for the local market. A sustainable recovery for Argentina certainly meant abandoning the 'new' economic model.

When ex-President Cardoso of Brazil was a radical sociologist in the 1970s, he once said that 'dependency' was what people called imperialism when they did not want to lose their Ford Foundation grants. From his later perspective it is unlikely that he held a more benign view of the world system as he struggled to make sure Brazil did not follow the same path as Argentina. Today dependency theory is not part of mainstream academic debates, but what it described is still part of the picture. Globalization has certainly created development or at least modernization for many parts of Latin America, but few would dispute that this has been dependent development. Foreign domination as 'conditioning situation' (as the dependency definition had it) for Latin America is, if anything, more all-embracing than it was in the 1970s. Certainly no one sensible would argue for 'delinking' from the world economy today, but the search for a non-dependent model of development is once again back on the agenda. Sustainable development cannot be dependent and nor can it ignore the 'social question', such as people's welfare.

The new populist left presidents such as Chávez in Venezuela and Morales in Bolivia (see Chapter 5 below) are posing once again the option of more traditional nationalist-statist models of development for the continent. National control of mineral resources (oil and gas) is seen as essential for national development. It would be wrong however to assume that there is an inherently anti-imperialist political economy emerging, since in these countries as elsewhere the dense web of international economic relations and institutional frameworks still prevails and is, indeed, not really challenged in its essentials. The more pragmatic left presidents of Chile (Bachelet) and Uruguay (Tabaré Vazquez) have opted for a more consensual relationship with the international economic order while prioritizing social reform at home. This model has been quite effective in its own terms and has proven to have a stabilizing effect in terms of democratization. For their part, the radical economic reforms once articulated by the Porto Alegre alternative and others referred to above have not taken root and have on the whole not received mass popular support. Within an emerging democratic order the wish for economic stability and no return to the populist-era hyperinflation still acts as a restricting factor in terms of viable economic alternatives.

4
Governance

Government in the era of globalization is more complex than it once was: from the 'outside' powerful economic forces constrain decision-making and from the 'inside' the state finds itself 'hollowed-out' by the neo-liberal reforms (see Chapter 3). We thus increasingly talk about 'governance' that implies a process of steering (rather than dictating) society and the economy. This chapter thus addresses, in the first instance, the elements and contemporary forms which the electoral and political party systems have taken across Latin America. We next address the way the law has operated, or not operated, to govern society and to provide the 'rule of law' deemed necessary for democracy to prosper. We turn then to the role of the state bureaucracy in administering society, from state-led industrialization up to today. Finally, we critically examine the role of the NGOs (non-governmental organizations) that, to some extent, have filled the gap created by the 'hollowing-out' of the state in the era of free-market rule.

Electoral and Party Systems

Latin America may have an international reputation for political instability, but in fact there are many countries characterized by stable electoral and party systems. Since the collapse of the dictatorships in the 1980s due to international pressure and domestic resistance, democratic rule has been consolidated virtually across the continent. Indeed, as the *Cambridge History of Latin America* acknowledges: 'The countries of Latin America (Brazil excepted) share with the United States the experience of being the oldest continuous republics of the contemporary world' (Hartlyn and Valezuela 1998: 63). Though many of these republics would prove vulnerable to military intervention as we saw in Chapter 2, it would be quite wrong to think in terms of 'banana republics'. This pejorative term did, indeed, reflect the reality of some small countries in Central America during the 1950s when they were practically colonized by US international giants like

United Fruit, but the reality in Latin America as whole is more prosaic, as we shall see.

Most of Latin America's republics can be characterized as 'polyarchies' (participation is high and power dispersed among competing organized groups), that is to say they are regimes based on competing political elites which recognize the need to place some limits on their power. Except in tokenistic forms, mass participation, as in a classical democracy, is resisted. Fundamental structural change to address the pressing needs created by deep social inequalities (see Chapter 6) is also resisted. On the positive side, polyarchies are said to have free and competitive elections, as well as the freedom of expression and of association that makes these possible. Of course this model does not apply across the board. Latin America's oldest polyarchy, Costa Rica, is followed by Chile and Uruguay since the end of military rule, and then we have Colombia and Venezuela with well-established political systems. Most other countries qualify according to some criteria of polyarchy but not others. However, the Dominican Republic, Haiti, Peru and, for some observers, Mexico do not fulfil basic criteria such as transparently free elections.

It is often said that a fundamental flaw in Latin America's electoral systems is the prevalence of 'presidentialism', defined as undue powers for the executive branch of government as compared with the legislative and judiciary. On the face of it, it would seem clear that, all other things being equal, a parliamentary democracy would be more likely to sustain stable democratic regimes than a presidential democracy. However, we must note that we are not comparing two 'pure' systems, one based on presidential pre-eminence and the other on parliamentary pre-eminence. Nor are all presidentialisms the same: President Pinochet is not the same as Costa Rica's president. The 'strength' of a presidency may come from different sources and it is not always bad. Nor when presidents seek to alter the law to allow for re-election is it always for the wrong reasons: Peru's President Fujimori was not the same as Brazil's President Cardoso. A balanced assessment of the debate would probably conclude that 'presidentialism has not *generally* contributed significantly to the problems of democratic governance and stability although ... it may have done in specific cases' (Mainwaring and Shugart 1997: 1).

Another major factor seen to thwart full democratic consolidation is the prevalent political culture, which some observers see as flawed by its Catholic Hispanic authoritarian origins. The classic contemporary study of political culture was Almond and Verba's *The Civic Culture* (1963), which was firmly in the tradition of the modernization approach of the 1950s (see Chapter 3). What it sought to do was draw out a direct link between microlevel political attitudes of individuals and macrolevel regime types. There were many problems with this study, including the restriction of its surveys to urban areas, the limitation of quantitative methods in political analysis and the lack of any sensitivity to regional variation. Essentially this approach was based on the assumed superiority of the US norm taken as the benchmark for all other societies. It was, furthermore, deeply ethnocentric in the way in which it sought to 'blame the victim', as it were, in seeing the problems of Latin America's democracies as solely the result of the pathological authoritarian belief systems of Latin Americans.

Since the heyday and subsequent rejection of the US-centric notion of civic culture, the concept of political culture has returned to Latin American studies of democratization. Even from within the dependency tradition there is now a renewed emphasis on the role political culture plays in relation to democratization. It entails a move beyond the structuralism that sees a direct link between economic conditions and political outcomes, to recognize the vital importance of attitudes and 'culture'. Following the collapse of the military dictatorships there was an aftermath of authoritarianism in the general political culture that needed to be addressed. While survey research is still notoriously unreliable, and hugely impacted by the mass media of course, it does give us access to what different segments of the population believe in and aspire to in relation to the political processes of their society. Democratic attitudes may not create democratic societies, but they would on the face of it seem to be a necessary prerequisite.

Perhaps the best way of 'unpacking' the nature of democracy in contemporary Latin America is not, however, through examining formal criteria and a pre-given benchmark. If we turn to the nature of political parties in the region a better, more nuanced understanding of Latin American democracy may emerge. To consolidate democracy it is generally held that political party systems should be institutionalized as a bulwark against a resurgence of authoritarian regimes. Liberal democracy is defined precisely in terms of the regular and predictable (hence institutionalized) functioning of electoral and party systems. What the political parties allow for, at least in theory, is a competition for millions of individual votes that become collective decisions on how societies are to be governed. What we have for Latin America is a very useful index of institutionalization (versus 'inchoate' party systems) based on the following criteria: the regularity of party competition; the development by parties of stable roots in society; the legitimacy of the electoral and party systems in the eyes of citizens; and the relative solidity of party organizations (Mainwaring and Scully 1995: ch. 1). Taking these four criteria as a basis to construct a composite index of institutionalization, Mainwaring and Scully arrive at the conclusions drawn out in Table 4.1.

We must note that only the first criterion, namely regularity of party competition, can be measured at all reliably, with the rest having to be based on informed judgement at best. We also need to be aware that this Table 4.1 is based on data for the 1980s and 1990s and thus ignores the often vital long-term historical perspective, as well as critical developments since, of course. However, the table does allow us to draw up a general picture of the variations in terms of political institutionalization across Latin America. There is a striking variation between, on the one hand Chile, Costa Rica and Uruguay, as highly institutionalized systems, and the relatively inchoate (or poorly institutionalized) systems which prevail in Brazil and the Andean countries such as Bolivia, Ecuador and Peru. One need not conclude that institutionalization is good for democracy, but it does seem clear that an inchoate party system is detrimental to stable democratization. In the weakly institutionalized system there is far greater scope for the emergence of the populist and authoritarian leader with a personalistic appeal to voters who do not have a strong, stable party system to relate to. On the other hand, we could argue that party systems can become too institutionalized, as arguably happened in Venezuela where a sort of 'partyocracy' to some extent took the place of democracy.

Electioneering in Latin America today is quite different from what it was even a decade ago. Where once the party machine and mass rallies

Table 4.1   Party system institutionalization in Latin America

Country	Institutionalization index
Costa Rica	11.5
Chile	11.5
Uruguay	11.5
Venezuela	10.5
Colombia	10.5
Argentina	9.0
Mexico	8.5
Paraguay	7.5
Bolivia	5.0
Ecuador	5.0
Brazil	5.0
Peru	4.5

Source: Mainwaring and Scully (1995: 17).

Box 4.1   Television and the rise of Collor de Mello

Today, most election campaigns in Latin America are as slick as any in North America or Europe. The 'media massage', the opinion-poll manipulation and the spin doctors all play their part. Television is clearly the preferred medium. But in the late 1980s all this was relatively new when a supposedly obscure provincial governor in Brazil, Fernando Collor de Mello, was catapulted into the presidency by the media and television in particular. The elections of 1990 held under the provision of the new democratic constitution of 1988 were the first full elections for nearly 30 years.

Collor came from one of the smallest and poorest provinces of the north-east and his rapid rise in popularity surprised all in the affluent, dynamic south-east of the country. The media became interested in this politician who seemed to attract the anti-politician voter. Beneath the innocent exterior there was a well-oiled Collor machine with well-paid advisers and analysts on hand. As he gained in popularity, financial interests, in particular the media magnates, came on board in spite of Collor's populist message. A crucial supporter was Roberto Marinho of the *Organizacões Globo* communication empire that accounted for three-quarters of the total television sector.

In many ways television from then on 'made' Collor into a president. The media ably marketed his glib anti-corruption message, which was ironic given that in a few years' time he would be impeached for gross financial misconduct. But for the time being Collor appeared as a 'Mr Clean' who would wipe out corruption and bring in an economic revolution. His admiration for Britain's Prime Minister Thatcher gave some indication of what his economic programme would be. But his message was vague on economics and focused on an ill-defined 'renewal' of Brazil. As one analyst put it:

> In a country with more TV sets than connections to tap water supplies and with so many people living in conditions of poverty, Collor made use of this his acknowledged skills as a broadcaster to spread his message. TV and radio connected him directly with the voters. After only one appearance on TV, his popularity rating nearly doubled. To present himself as a charismatic character and disguise his origins and links to the 'forces of evil' [big business] he had chosen to counter, mass communication was his 'ideal tool'. (Valença 2002: 120)

prevailed, it is now the 'spin doctors' and the 'focus groups' which hold sway. In the 1989 elections in Brazil, Collor de Mello came from an obscure provincial governorship via his control of an important television company, Rede Glóbo, to the presidency of the country (see Box 4.1 for details). Public meetings become less important as TV campaigning takes centre stage but they do not disappear, especially in rural areas. A more important effect perhaps is the decline in disciplined and accountable political parties and their mass membership; politics tends to become more volatile as the mass media element becomes dominant. Even in Chile where traditional party structures are still quite strong the mass media, and TV in particular, became key features in elections since 1989. However, even with the very active and central participation of US and UK election 'advisers', the right wing failed to make a comeback and the instant appeal of the TV screen was matched by more traditional rallying of social forces.

Another fundamental transformation of party politics has been in relation to the role of women. During the dictatorships party politics were suspended and this had been a predominantly male domain. Many women's organizations sprang up in defence of human rights, often around 'non-feminist' concepts of motherhood (the Mothers of the Plaza de Mayo, for example – see Chapter 7). With the process of democratization came a certain politicization of gender, as organized women sought to pursue a gender agenda in the new democracies. Women came to the fore in many countries: in Nicaragua the 1990 elections led to the victory of Violeta Chamorro over the Sandinistas' Daniel Ortega who had a fighting-cock as his campaign mascot, and in Brazil in 1994 the leftist Workers' Party had two women senators elected including the influential Benedita da Silva, a black woman from a Rio de Janeiro shanty-town. Overall, though, as Lievesley argues, the aim of the new democracies

> has been to manage women by appropriating the language of the women's agenda, incorporating their concerns into party and government programmes promising legislation ... and enabling individual women to rise to political prominence, albeit in order to control them. (Lievesley 1999: 142)

The election of Michelle Bachelet in Chile (see Chapter 5) may represent a shift away from patriarchal politics, but only time will tell.

The (Mis)Rule of Law

The rule of law (in Spanish *estado de derecho*) is generally deemed a prerequisite for democracy and good governance. It means, above all, that basic civil rights should apply equally to the whole population. All citizens should have access to justice on an equal footing and without impediment; the due process of law should be a universal given. So, when the dictatorships were pushed back in the 1980s many hoped that a new flourishing of the *estado de derecho* in Latin America would banish forever the fear of a return to authoritarian rule. The tyrants were overthrown and democracy would ensure that the law was sovereign. In practice the grim realities of social inequality and technocratic politics prevailed. Disenchantment with the political process was generalized but nowhere more so than in relation to the manifest failure in most countries to provide a genuine *estado de derecho*. Such was the reversal that an influential collection of essays on the matter could title itself the '(un)rule of law' (Mendez *et al.* 1999).

The rule of law in Latin America has been honoured more in the breach than in its observance for many decades. The long night of the dictatorships created a culture of impunity among the powerful then that has not been easy to overcome. Jean-Paul Brodeur reports that in a gathering of specialists on the law in Latin America, 'The fact that aggressors of all kinds could harm their victims without having to answer for their behaviour before the criminal courts was perceived ... as a major source of scandal' (Brodeur 1999: 81). To be economically secure and socially powerful often means to be literally above the law. There is a deeply ingrained culture among the powerful that obeying the law is a duty only for the poor or the stupid. To pay taxes or in other ways be part of the legal framework of society would in fact be seen as a criminally insane thing to do, at least voluntarily. The feelings of this social class can be summed up in the words of a successful business person in Argentina who declared proudly that 'To be powerful is to have [legal] impunity' (cited in O'Donnell 1999a: 312).

The transitions to democracy in the 1980s and 1990s occurred in the shadow of fear as well as impunity. State terrorism and the authoritarianism that pervaded all layers of society created a profound and corrosive feeling of fear. This was not just the fear of a clearly identified danger against which the individual could pursue a rational course of action. The forced 'disappearance' of thousands of citizens, the arbitrary arrest of others and the censorship of all forms of independent action and thought created a generalized and undifferentiated climate of fear. The only response, apart from denial, was anxiety or flight, but certainly rational defence was all but impossible. So, the transitions to democracy had an overarching degree of fear associated with them. As Torres-Rivas writes, from a Central American perspective but more generally relevant, 'Fear, when it ceases to be personal and subjective and envelops large areas of society, has unpredictable social and political effects on the behaviour of the group' (1999: 295). It is certainly highly corrosive in relation to the rule of law.

Violence also remains an overwhelming reality in Latin America even under nominally democratic regimes. The experience of violence has been ubiquitous and endemic for the poor in Latin America, and not only under the dictatorships. State violence is not so much pathological as the norm, so will clearly not disappear the day after democratic elections are held. This is a structural form of violence, not just random acts of illegality. It is a violence which feeds on, and itself reinforces, poverty, poor housing, ill-health and a generalized feeling of insecurity. Again citing Torres-Rivas: 'It is a form of violence that manifests itself especially in the loss of a culturally acquired sense of respect for oneself and others, and thus in a feeling of indignity, impotence, loss of worth' (1999: 2871). Clearly in this situation the 'rule of law' has little meaning and a cynical attitude towards it can naturally be expected. To turn towards crime or a minor role in the drugs trade is also a perfectly natural response for those caught up in this negative spiral of fear, violence and insecurity.

Political democracy, which now prevails across the continent, has not created a truly civil democracy where the rights of the citizen are scrupulously observed. The rights of the powerful to flout the law are certainly protected. Tax evasion, money-laundering, child labour, slave labour and even drug-trafficking are not consistently seen as legitimate targets for law enforcement agencies. On the other hand, these agencies do often see it as their role to protect the rich and powerful from what are perceived as 'dangerous elements' in society, usually from among the poor and underprivileged groups in society. In Argentina, for example, one can be detained for a month for 'drunk and disorderly' conduct and even cross-dressing. In Venezuela, usually seen as a paragon of democratic virtue, the law allows for imprisonment for up to 5 years of those deemed a threat to society. As to the rule of law, Pinheiro notes bitterly that, 'In Latin America, police officers see the rule of law as an obstacle to, rather than an effective guarantee of, social control' (1999: 59). Thus they literally take the law into their own hands as we shall see.

One of the most salient facts of the (un)rule of law in Latin America, seen from abroad, is the indiscriminate and unpunished killings of street children in Brazil, Guatemala and elsewhere. It is considered quite normal for shopkeepers to seek the physical elimination of homeless children who detract from their activities. This 'social cleansing', usually carried out by the police after hours, is not restricted to specified 'perpetrators' but applied to whole social categories of outcasts such as

Box 4.2   War in the Favelas

In 2004 Brazilian culture received a boost when the film *Citade de Deus* (City of God), Fernando Mierelles's depiction of gang wars in the *favela* (shanty-town), received four Oscar nominations. This harrowing fictional account became an even more dramatic reality in May 2006 when open warfare opened up in São Paulo – Latin America's largest city – between a major criminal gang and the police. For days on end police stations and patrol cars were machine-gunned, police officers were killed and scores of buses and banks were torched. In São Paulo alone over 120 people were killed and many more injured. There were outbreaks in other cities and across the prison system. In the end the state governor negotiated a settlement with the gang or 'family' concerned, the PCC (First Command of the Capital) and its notorious imprisoned leader Orlando Mota Júmor, otherwise known as Macarão (Noodles).

At one level this was simply an open expression of the covert war between organized crime and the state with citizens as innocent bystanders caught in the crossfire. However, there was more to it, given the widespread corruption emerging in Brazilian political life. There was a widespread feeling that the state often colluded with the large armed criminal organizations in preying on the misery of the *favela* dwellers. It is worth noting that the main criminal organization Comando Vermelho (Red Command) emerged in the early 1980s during the military dictatorship after interaction in the prisons between political and criminal prisoners. Its motto was 'Peace, Justice and Liberty', and it attracted a strong popular and cultural following. It is part of the political system as much as corruption is part of politics. One angry commentator put it thus: 'How many bursts of the PCC's machinegun fire will it take to silence the electoral rhetoric and the pseudo-theory of these other indirect accomplices of organized crime in São Paulo and Brazil as a whole?' (Benoit 2006: 4).

street children or gays. In Mexico the killing of political opponents is also considered routine and is carried out with the collaboration of the state authorities. The regime of impunity for those engaged in violence on behalf of the state means that judges and journalists who might expose this lawlessness are often cowed into silence by more acts, or threats, of violence. This violence breeds corruption and a further deterioration of any concept of a legitimate democratic order. The general complicity or indifference of society, from the poor as well as the rich, means that this threat to the barrier of law is very hard to tackle.

The way many Latin American societies deal with their prisoners is also scandalous from the perspective of the rule of law. The indiscriminate use of torture not only violates basic human rights but means that often the 'wrong' people are in jail. Thus it was reported in the mid 1990s that 90 per cent of homicide investigations in Rio de Janeiro produce insufficient evidence to lead to trial. Lack of due process continues in the prisons where inmates are treated with total disregard for their human rights. In 1992 the military police raided the house of detention in São Paulo, killing 111 inmates of whom 84 were awaiting trial. In Peru the brutal suppression of three prison rebellions in 1986 was so brutal that they attracted considerable international attention. The Inter-American Court of Human Rights found, predictably given the evidence but also surprisingly, that the government had violated the right to life and the right of habeas corpus. Most ill-treatment, brutality and killings in prisons rarely reach the public eye, however, but represent a continuous drain on the rule of law and the prospects for a civil democracy.

At a more 'structural' level we must also note the persistence of torture in many countries, now routinized as a means of dealing with 'ordinary' criminals. Torture is deemed to be pervasive in Mexico but is also common in many parts of Central America, in Peru, Paraguay and Venezuela and even in supposedly more properly democratic Chile and Uruguay. In Brazil the reforming chief of the civilian police admitted in 1995 that 'torture has long been a common practice of the Brazilian Police ... society has accepted torture as a just punishment for common criminals and a legitimate means of obtaining information' (cited in Chevigny 1999: 53). While the use of torture has certainly declined overall since the days of the dictatorships, its 'normalization' in dealing with ordinary crime goes squarely against the project of establishing an *estado de derecho* (state of law) in Latin America. This is but one particularly salient area where what the law says (torture is not, of course, 'legal') and what the law does are two quite different things.

Another 'structural' feature of the (un)rule of law exists in the rural areas in dealing with the poor and landless. According to Brazil's Pastoral Land Commission, there were 1730 killings of rural workers and their supporters between 1964 and 1992, but only 30 of these cases ever reached the courts (Pinheiro 1999: 7). The killing of Chico Mendes in 1988 was but the most salient internationally of those carried out with impunity by Brazil's landowners. President Cardoso pledged to stop these killings when he assumed office in 1995, but in his first year there were 74 deaths in rural conflicts. Human-rights organizations were hardly surprised as they knew that the state military police and other law enforcement officials were involved in these killings. So, as Roger Plant argues, for the rule of law to mean anything to the rural poor, not only must governments find a way to bring the landowner's armed bands under control, they must also create a situation where those who barely have access to a subsistence living can 'feel that there is some scope to improving their situation through use of the legal system' (Plant 1999: 101).

Finally, then, what is to be done to overcome the (un)rule of law in many parts of Latin America? Exhortations from abroad have had little effect in structural terms although they can help expose particularly salient abuses. The arrest of Chilean dictator General Pinochet in London in 1998 did have a salutary effect in reinforcing the notion that human rights are not negotiable. In a more general sense, though, we need to understand that the law, as O'Donnell explains, is 'a dynamic condensation of power relations, not just a rationalised technique for the ordering of social relations' (1999a: 323). Full civil citizenship can come about only through a challenge to the poverty and inequality which prevails in society (see Chapter 5). The law, which enshrines certain formal rights, can help to empower individuals and social movements, but these rights can reflect only the general power relations in society. Two positive features now exist, namely the internationalization of human rights (after the Pinochet case) and the gradual overcoming of the legacy of fear left behind by the dictatorships.

Bureaucracy and Administration

Political governance entails not only a system of political parties and the rule of law, but also the organization of a state able to administer the national territory and its population. By around 1930 there was a clearly recognizable 'modern' form of state in the Southern Cone countries, while most countries in Central America (with the exception of Costa Rica) had but a rudimentary form of state administration. In between came countries like Brazil, Colombia and Mexico where state development was uneven geographically and in terms of its functions. From 1930 onwards, Brazil and Mexico in particular moved very decisively towards a 'modern' form of state, achieving perhaps the most coherent and important state bureaucracies in the whole region. By comparative international standards – let alone 'Third-World' standards – the republics of Latin America achieved an early and sustained consolidation of the state. The period of state-led industrialization, from the end of the Second World War to the early 1980s was to further strengthen that capacity.

The global depression of the 1930s had already created the need for increased state intervention in Latin America, but in the 1950s import-substitution industrialization (see Chapter 3) led to the formation of what can be called a 'developmental state'. The overwhelming need to achieve economic growth led to the state assuming a *dirigiste* (leading, steering) role, given the absence of a strong pre-existing industrialist class. This was a nationalist state committed to national-based economic development. It could be authoritarian but it could also be redistributivist in terms of economic resources, which helped build up an internal market. The developmental state stood between the international system and the national society, mediating its influence; it could be protectionist where necessary, establishing tariff barriers to allow incipient national industries to be sheltered from undue international competition. The developmental state was usually committed to political stability and had a long-term vision not entirely unlike that of the 'command economies' of Eastern Europe.

The administration of the developmental state was run on classic 'bureaucratic' lines. The pre-1930 'oligarchic state', based on an agro-export economy, had relied on patrimonialism to administer the national territory, that is to say the public and the private patrimony was undistinguished.The bureaucratic model of state administration, on the other hand, makes a crucial distinction between the *res publica* (public body) and private property. A bureaucracy is based on a professional civil service which has rational administrative systems based on impersonal and legal criteria. In practice the state bureaucracy in Latin America expanded to serve as a source of employment and of patronage. Rational policy-making and meritocratic promotion thus coexisted with more negative characteristics. What is not in doubt is that the state expanded considerably in the postwar period, as we can see in Figure 4.1.

As the crisis of the state-led industrialization model became apparent, so too did the shortcomings of the bureaucratic model. Nationalist-statist industrializing and essentially democratic politics came abruptly to an end with the Pinochet coup in Chile in 1973. What Pinochet and his technocratic elite were actually opposed to was politics *per se*. As Veronica Montecinos explains, 'The Chicago Boys led to a vast rationalisation and technocratisation of government, arguing that the use of scientific methods should replace the previous irrational and obsolete models of decision-making' (1998: 130). The previous model was seen as bureaucratic (which it was) and excessively democratic (which it was not); politics and politicians were all seen as corrupt and inefficient. Henceforth the language and ideology of economic rationality would

Figure 4.1   Public employment as a percentage of total employment, 1950–80

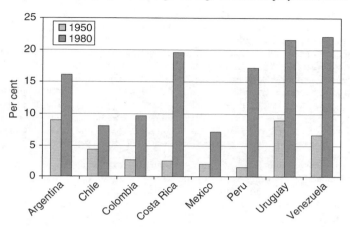

Source: Whitehead (1998): 398.

rule supreme. As the Pinochet 'revolution' took hold the values of market and private initiative took deep root and by the end of his period even democratic politicians would be saying that 'The principle of efficiency as a political value has been accepted' (cited in Montecinos 1998: 136).

The 1980s saw the rise of the 'technocrat' as manager of the nation's destiny in much of Latin America. Society had become, to some extent, depoliticized and decision-making would be based on 'technical' criteria. At this time, the state was selling off many of the state enterprises and ceding many of its functions to market mechanisms. The promise to the population was that consumption would now take the place of politics. To make this dream of the technocrat come true, outside support was to prove vital. As Barbara Stallings notes:

> technocrats who had long argued for more open economies and a bigger role for the private sector suddenly found increasing backing from the outside. They could count on political support from the United States ... and intellectual reinforcement from the IMF and the World Bank. (Stallings 1992: 84)

The crucial 'external' determinant of the technocratic-led, neo-liberal revolution was thus the need to maintain or regain investor confidence in the Latin American 're-emerging markets' as they were being called.

The 'first generation' of state reform was often managed by military dictatorships, but it continued under the democratic regimes of the 1990s.

Box 4.3   The 'Chicago Boys'

This group of Chicago University of Chicago economists inspired by Milton Friedman's free-market rhetoric were to play a key role in implementing General Pinochet's economic policy in Chile following the 1973 coup. Their objective was to reverse the national-development, inward-oriented economic model that had prevailed until 1973. To implement this new market-friendly model and submission to the interests of global finance a strong state (General Pinochet) was necessary. The cohesion and power of the 'Chicago Boys' has become legendary and a key reference point for neo-liberal economic theory subsequently. As O'Brien puts it:

> They were thus able to act as a 'vanguard party' of a sector of capital. Backed by leading sectors of the Chilean capitalist class, and international capitalist agencies and US business interests, they argued for a revolutionary overhaul of the Chilean economy and society. (O'Brien 1985: 151)

The experience of the 'Chicago Boys' shows clearly how the new economic model emerged on the basis of a strong state prepared to subdue social resistance and dispense with the niceties of the democratic process. In the longer term they paved the way for a thorough 'technocratization' of economic and political decision-making in Latin America. After the restoration of democratic rule in the 1980s the economy in particular was seen as an area where technical, even scientific, criteria would prevail. Large sections of the population now distrusted politics as a whole – not least because they had seemingly led to catastrophes like the Pinochet coup – and they preferred to trust these seemingly disinterested technocrats who followed in the footsteps of the Chilean economists educated at the University of Chicago in the USA.

Thus politicians like Menem in Argentina and Fujimori in Peru were elected on 'populist' platforms but soon turned to fairly extreme neo-liberal policies. By this stage the external context (that is, globalization) meant that there was effectively no alternative to the new economic model. Neo-liberal technocrats like Domingo Cavallo in Argentina and Hernán Buchi in Chile had become so popular as economy ministers that they looked like credible presidential candidates. Even Cardoso in Brazil, though an intellectual and not a technocrat, reached the presidency in 1995 via a successful term as finance minister. The new-found popularity of the technocrat was based largely on fear within society: fear of hyperinflation which occurred in various countries and threatened the whole social fabric, and a fear of return to military rule if the technocrats and their economic rationality were not allowed to prevail.

The 'second generation' of state reform in the 1990s was an integral part of the mechanisms whereby Latin America became part of the globalization revolution. The state-centred development model of the 1950s–60s had given way to the market in the 1970s–80s. Privatization of much of the state had occurred and the 'bloated' bureaucracy had been thinned out. In Argentina the national government employed 900 000 people in 1990 but that figure was down to 300 000 in 1996. Education and health services in particular were decentralized and/or privatized. This leaner state was not, however, more efficient and the World Bank Report of 1997 was dedicated specifically to 'reconstructing' the state (World Bank 1997). Why, after a decade of 'dismantling' the state would it need reconstructing? Essentially the social fabric of society was threatened, as was democratic governability. Furthermore, as Cardoso noted very clearly:

> reform could never entail (although it *did* in practice) destruction of the administrative and political decision-making systems, much less to a lessening of the state's regulatory capacity or of its power to steer the process of change and to set its course. (Cardoso 1999: vii)

Brazil's state reform of the 1990s was particularly significant in that it came late but was also pursued within a clear intellectual agenda. Bresser Pereira, the minister in charge of the state reform in Cardoso's Brazil, explains that:

> The current reform is based on the concept of managerial public administration as a response not only to the grave crisis of the state that marked the 1980s but also to the process of economic globalisation. (Bresser Pereira 1999: 115)

Compared with the classic bureaucratic form of public administration, the 'managerial' model emphasizes decentralization, delegation of authority, a reduction of hierarchies and an ethics based on serving the needs of the citizenry rather than the organization. Transforming public administration along managerial lines was to prove both popular and efficient. The purpose was to increase the legitimacy of government, not to destroy the administrative apparatus. It was also designed to make the state more efficient in dealing with the challenges posed by globalization rather than to meet the agenda of international investors.

The process of state reform in Latin America during the 1990s was a crucial political issue. It redefined the relations between state and society and reconfigured power relations across the continent. Previous attempts at administrative modernization never had quite such a fundamental impact. The whole model of development and the nature of the region's insertion into the world economy has changed. This transformation is much more in keeping with the postulates of dependency theory than the mainstream modernization approach to development. For the latter there is a straightforward 'functionalist' logic that to modernize society trained technical personnel are required. The assumption that modernization is a one-way process is flawed, however, and under the military regimes many basic administrative functions (tax collection and maintenance of electoral registers, for example) fell by the wayside. A dependent development approach, which recognizes the interplay between external factors and internal political processes, seems to better explain the rise of the neo-liberal technocracy.

So, where is the state in Latin America going in the twenty-first century? The current debate is all around the supposed negative characteristics of the state: what it cannot do, what it should not do. It is now becoming clear that there is a need to discuss in a positive way what the state should do. To put it in a nutshell: less is not necessarily better in terms of a state. The hollowing-out of the state by the measures sponsored by the new economic model has left a dangerous void, and it is clear now that the market cannot achieve many things, least of all a modicum of political stability and social integration. Economic globalization has made the tasks of democratic government more difficult, particularly in regions such as Latin America still locked into situations of structural dependency. The pressing needs of governability require a strengthening of the capacity of the state to ensure that the general needs of society are fulfilled. As President Cardoso of Brazil put it: 'To reform the state does not mean to dismantle it' (1999: vii).

NGOs: Filling the Gap

A reader of this book in the West would, in all likelihood, first have come across Latin America through the activities of an NGO or non-governmental organization. The NGO worldview seemed attractive to many in the West as they became engaged with the 'Other' from the South. A bland definition of the NGOs was that of 'associations formed within civil society bringing together individuals who share some common purpose' (Turner and Hulme 1997: 200). But in practice many NGOs and their supporters were imbued with the radical spirit of the 1960s and believed in a 'third way' between capitalism and what passed as socialism in the East. The very word NGO came to spell activism, commitment and empowerment. The NGO was to represent civil society and it was to promote globalization 'from below'. In an age of materialism NGOs promised an idealistic perspective unsullied by party-political concerns. As yet the they had not been touched by the reality of power politics and their own vulnerability to the democratic deficit critique.

Though the origin of the NGOs in Latin America goes back to the 1950s, they really began to flourish in the area during the 1970s under military dictatorships. The non-governmental organizations of this era, whether in the Southern Cone or in Central America, were in fact *anti*-governmental organizations. Many radical intellectuals were driven out of the universities and established independent 'think tanks' which received international funding from various US and European foundations. As Lehman and Bebbington explain: 'Research centres in need of funding and grass-roots movements connected, and thus gradually ... became a link between the people at the grass-roots and the international development community' (1998: 257). The latter were understandably reluctant to channel development funding through unsavoury political regimes and thus the research centres became key conduits. The development community meant at first some of the major international NGOs but gradually national governments and eventually the World Bank saw the advantages of developing a more 'progressive' development delivery agency.

What happened then in the 1980s with the NGOs was a certain confluence between their anti-statist project and the hollowing-out of the state by the neo-liberal technocrats. In part the NGOs were facing the dilemmas of any social movement posed between the need to remain faithful to its objectives and the advantages of institutionalization. It was also part of the price of success in so far as the NGOs had gained considerably in influence and prestige which they now wanted to bring to bear in a more coherent way. Thus, a pioneering general meeting of Latin American NGOs in 1987 declared that:

> In terms of relations with other social actors, the relationship with the state has been accorded priority, based on the assumption that the division between civil society and the state should not be seen as absolute. (Cited in Landim 1996: 214)

While the NGOs pledged themselves to a continuous role of criticism and denunciation of injustices, they argued that they were 'in a better position than state entities for developing creative proposals that responded to the most fundamental social problems' (ibid.). Precisely at around this time the state was beginning to retreat from some of its traditional roles in managing society, and the NGOs were presented with an opportunity (as well as the danger of co-option, of course).

The possible role of the NGOs in 'filling the gap' left by the retreating state was taken up explicitly by the World Bank in the 1990s. It was clear that, on the ground, development NGOs in particular were beginning to fulfil some of the functions vacated by the state in the neo-liberal 'revolution'. The World Bank became very concerned with the role of 'civil society' in holding together the atomized individuals (consumers) created by the neo-liberal transformation. They began to see the need for structural adjustment 'with a human face' to avoid the worst effects of social disintegration and political instability. What the World Bank economists began to do was to foster the concept of 'social capital' to complement the neo-liberal strategy, arguing that:

> Social capital is the glue that holds societies together and without which there can be no economic growth or human well-being. Without social capital, society at large will collapse, and today's world presents some very sad examples of this. (Cited in Fine 2001: 158)

The NGOs would be seen as an integral element in this drive to create some degree of social cohesion and make up for the retreating state.

From a progressive standpoint the apparent co-option of the NGOs by neo-liberalism was deeply disturbing, and for some writers the NGOs in Latin America are now openly 'in the service of imperialism' (Petras and Veltmeyer 2001: 128). These writers argue that while the World Bank and the IMF set the macroeconomic agenda for imperialism, 'the NGOs come into the picture to mystify and deflect the discontent [created] away from direct attacks on corporate/banking power structures and projects' (ibid.). They supposedly misdirect people's anger into apolitical micro-projects and meaningless 'political education' which distract attention from the real enemy: imperialism. From this negative perspective the NGO is purely an ideological smokescreen and, even worse, a useful foil for the dirty work of neo-liberalism. These critics even argue that in their own terms of alleviating poverty there is, in fact, 'a direct relation between the growth of NGOs and the decline of living standards' (ibid.: 129). It will be important now to see whether this negative prognosis is more accurate than the starry-eyed idealism espoused by some NGO supporters.

The role of NGOs in Latin America today is a complex one and varies across the continent: it certainly cannot be reduced to either panacea or stooge of imperialism. There are well over 15 000 NGOs active in Latin America but these are of many different types. Reflecting the origins of many members in the radical church (especially but not only the Catholic church), most NGOs saw themselves 'serving' the people rather than their own ends. They are oriented towards strengthening civil society and not building a particular political party (although links with political parties exist, of course). However, as 'hard funding' dried up in the late 1980s there was a turn towards 'soft' funding such as research consultancy work. Here the criticism is that many NGOs foresook their radical origins and adopted the agenda of the international funders. Where once they might have researched and helped organize the poor in a shanty town, now they were doing bland research on *civil society*, 'social capital' or whatever issue was prominent on the international development agenda. From serving the poor they went to serving the World Bank, as it were.

Yet this picture is not valid across the board. For Chile and Argentina, 'the language of the international alternative development subculture is still there, but it has become domesticated, it has lost its dissident edge' (Lehman and Bebbington 1998: 260–1). In both countries activists who worked with grassroots organizations in the shanty towns, especially among women who have, since the restoration of democracy, entered local and national government in many cases. Such a shift often spells a decline of NGO activity as leadership people leave and the emphasis on mobilization declines. Yet it would be too simple to simply read it as 'co-option' or even 'betrayal', as some critics portray it. In the first instance, mobilizations do not continue forever and, sooner or later, administration must take over if social problems are actually going to be dealt with. Second, there is evidence that the NGO *modus operandi*, in terms of emphasizing local self-management and so on, has been transferred into the arena of local government. In this sense political governance is shifting towards a more inclusive and participatory model.

In Brazil, however, the NGOs are not nearly as close to the state as they are in the other Southern Cone countries. The state has not really sought to co-opt the NGOs, or their leaders, and thus these have preserved much of their grassroots orientation or *basismo* as they call it. The discourse of the NGOs continues to be hostile to the bureaucratic way of working of the state, and what it sees as the 'clientelist' way in which it operates. It opposes political patronage, with a strong emphasis on mass mobilization, and links with radical political parties and church groupings remain strong. The Brazilian NGOs have been very successful in bringing to the fore the big issues after the restoration of democracy, namely the persistence of violence and hunger. The Brazilian state itself, though, especially after the Bresser Pereíra reforms (see p. 83), has also been able to reform itself and taken a leaf out of the NGO book at times in developing ways of working in society which are not clientilistic. This is particularly true at local government level where the leftist parties have a strong presence.

In Mexico, again, the situation is different, with the state being porous and flexible enough to find room for NGO-type strategies from within. In Mexico, the NGOs have been neither co-opted nor able to carve out the political space their counterparts in Brazil have. A well-consolidated state, with considerable (if declining) political legitimacy owing to its revolutionary origins, is not easily dislodged by an NGO. One example is Solidaridad, the major poverty alleviation programme in the mid 1990s that deployed considerable resources in a bid by the technocrats and the modernizers to displace the more clientelist patterns. As Lehman and Bebbington note:

> those who would dismiss Solidaridad as 'merely' a modernization and centralization of patronage are rushing too hastily to judgement and are also being too judgemental, for the program has borrowed more than one tactic from the NGO culture. (1998: 264).

The complex relations between NGOs and the state are examined in Box 4.4 through a brief case-study. Civil society can be activated and motivated by an enlightened state keen to modernize administration methods, and NGOs are not the only bodies that can do this.

If the state reforms were part of the Washington Consensus drive to restructure Latin American society, the NGOs may be an integral element in the post-Washington-Consensus era. The proponents of globalization now speak of civil society and even empowerment, and the NGOs are a vital part of this new strategy, becoming the preferred vehicle for service provision as against the state. The rise of the NGOs is due directly to the failure or the refusal of the state to fulfil its traditional roles. But we must consider the verdict of Laura Tedesco, for whom, 'In reality, NGOs are a manifestation of the retreat of the state rather than its solution' (Tedesco 1999: 138). If that is indeed the case then the problem of democratic governance will continue. It certainly seems unlikely that NGOs will succeed where the traditional state bureaucracy and administration (see the previous section) have mainly failed. The NGO was originally an unambiguous expression of society's needs; now it is advocating methods much closer to market-based strategies for development and a mode of governance seemingly at ease with neo-liberal globalization.

Box 4.4   NGOs and politics

The non-governmental organizations (NGOs) are not really anything of the sort; they are more likely to be quasi-governmental organizations like the famous 'quangos' in Thatcher's Britain. Some are still civil society organizations 'representing' the poor and oppressed, but many are simply private organizations adopting an NGO banner to obtain funding. In the era of neo-liberalism and the attack on the state sector, the fact is that NGOs were promoted by the international financial institutions as a means to undermine the state so as to promote the market, not the poor.

In Mexico, after the 1985 earthquake, the NGOs emerged as a powerful force in the reconstruction effort. In spite of their heterogeneity they acquired a strong presence which the government inevitably sought to co-opt. Dialogue with the NGOs was a way of bringing them on board by the ruling party. The government sought to iron out the legal problems of NGO participation in state schemes and offered them funding on a competitive basis. Though not necessarily fooled by this show of goodwill, the NGOs inevitably began to work with the government, which even created a state council for the NGOs.

John Shefner described the Jalisco NGO experience in 1990s Mexico, from which we may derive interesting lessons on NGOs and politics more generally:

> In general RAMAS [Mutual Support Network for Social Action formed by the NGOs in 1992] members believed that the intention of PRONASOL [the government's National Solidarity Programme] strategy toward NGOs was co-optation. They relied on their political sophistication as long-term NGO leaders and members of the opposition and on the shared solidarity among their co-workers to resist government manipulation and exploit available resources where they could. As much as they believed in their own capabilities to escape co-optation, however, they doubted other organizations' abilities. RAMAS members were responding to the dual effect of Mexican neoliberal policies, which have forced the retreat of the state from some social arenas, opening opportunities for new political participation by NGOs and popular organizations alike. At the same time, the economic devastation wrought by these policies limited the resources of these organizations and their constituencies in ways that made them even more vulnerable to the offerings of state patronage. All this happened at a time when the volume of international funding of local NGOs in Latin America was in sharp decline. As a result, less money became available to Mexican NGOs traditionally dependent on this support. The institutionalized access to resources, however limited, thus became even more valuable for them. It remains one of the most directly successful strategies of the Mexican corporate system. As Eckstein writes, bringing relevant groups into the resolution of political crises defuses a wider challenge to the state. This state effort has been recreated in the SEDESOL [Secretaría de Desarollo Social – Social Development Secretariat] strategy of working with NGOs, although it is as yet unclear how successful it will prove to be. (Shefner 1998: 121)

5
Politics

Democratic politics in Latin America is now thriving as never before. In 2006 alone there were 12 presidential elections and another 3 legislative elections in Latin America. Free elections, a free press and thriving political parties signal the consolidation of democracy. The first section of this chapter examines the nature of that consolidation process through a number of key case-studies that can be seen as indicators of more general trends. However, there is also considerable disenchantment with democracy, which is seen not to deliver social and economic advances in many cases. We examine the basis for this disenchantment by looking at recent Brazilian politics in particular. Then we turn to what many observers have called a 'left turn' in Latin American politics with the rise of Hugo Chávez in Venezuela and Evo Morales in Bolivia, for example. Finally, we turn to the challenges faced by democratic politics in contemporary Latin America, including widening rates of inequality and corruption.

Consolidation

Today democracy seems everywhere in Latin America to be a durable form of politics. As Centeno puts it: 'Voters and parties are playing by the system, losers are accepting defeat, and winners can feel reasonably confident that they will finish their term' (Centeno 2006: 48). The threat of a military coup seems remote in most countries, particularly in the Southern Cone where they were a feature of the 1960s and 1970s. In so far as democracy can be measured – and the United Nations Development Programme has advanced a methodology to do just that – the average Electoral Democracy Index (where zero is no electoral democracy and one is the maximum level) has risen rapidly from 0.28 in 1977 to 0.69 in 1985 to 0.93 in 2002 (UNDP 2004: 33). In terms of the development of political citizenship we thus find an optimistic scenario. Rather than take Latin America as a whole – and it is hard to see what 'Latin American politics' might be as a species over and above the very

Box 5.1   First woman president: Michelle Bachelet (Chile)

Born in 1951, Verónica Michelle Bachelet Jeria became president of Chile in 2006, the first time a woman had achieved that office. Bachelet – a surgeon, paediatrician and epidemiologist who has also trained in military strategy – served as both health minister and defence minister under outgoing socialist President Ricardo Lagos. But this is not simply a case of political continuity within the Socialist Party machine. Michelle Bachelet is a separated mother of three and an avowed agnostic, and thus not an obvious establishment figure in conservative Catholic Chile. Furthermore, Bachelet's father was an Air Force general who was detained after the 11 September 1973 coup under charges of 'treason' that meant he had not turned against the Constitutional government of Salvador Allende. He died under torture, then Bachelet herself and her mother Ángela Jeria Gómez, an anthropologist, were also detained and tortured at the notorious Villa Grimaldi centre before going into exile.

With General Pinochet dead and buried in 2006, in the wake of corruption as well as torture charges pending, while one of his victims has become president, there has been an historical shift in Chile. Bachelet was an extremely popular and efficient minister, and will no doubt prove likewise as president. There are political factors that explain her victory, not least the remarkable stability achieved by the Concertación political alliance since Pinochet left the scene in 1989. Furthermore, the women's movement had been making steady inroads into the political system since the 1980s. There is, however, a wider set of cultural factors at play explaining Bachelet's victory. Basically, while she was the candidate of the ruling party, she was also an outsider in the political system, with a clean, incorruptible image and a perceived distance from normal routine political machinations. '*Vota Mujer*' (Vote Woman) was a slogan that took root far beyond the traditional catchment area of the socialists. The cultural construction of gender during Bachelet's campaign took on an entirely positive and unifying tone. Her victory marks a cultural sea change in Chile – and Latin America as a whole – in terms of closing the gender gap.

distinct regional patterns – we will now focus on countries where the general patterns are most sharply developed.

Chile

A positive view of electoral democracy is nowhere demonstrated more than in Chile in the years since General Pinochet ceded power to electoral politicians in 1989. When Michelle Bachelet was elected president of Chile in early 2006 this was the fourth victory in a row for the multi-party coalition Concertación formed in 1988 to oppose Pinochet's plebiscite. She is a woman and a radical socialist, so could logically be a subject of our 'Left Turn' section below, but what is most remarkable is the continuity in Chilean politics that she represents and how this has favoured democratic consolidation in post-Pinochet Chile. But as Patricia Navía argues: 'Without having the idea of *change* as a central component of her campaign, the continuity that she represented would not have sufficed for a victory' (Navía 2006: 9). Compared with her predecessors Bachelet perhaps might be described as the representative of a situation of change within continuity.

The first Concertación president, Patricio Aylwin (1990–94), was a moderate Christian Democrat who talked about giving neo-liberalism a human face, as did his successor Eduard Frei Jr (1994–2000), also a Christian Democrat. This is, of course, the political party that encouraged Pinochet to overthrow Allende in 1973 or at best stood to one side. While the Washington Consensus was adhered to, poverty rates in Chile were reduced from 40 per cent to 20 per cent during this period. Ricardo Lagos was the Socialist Party President from 2000 to 2006 and he also maintained a conservative fiscal policy and signed a free-trade agreement with the United States. However, as one commentator put it: 'Ambitious and well-designed programs to promote access to health, education, and infrastructure development have radically transformed Chile under Lagos, who is leaving office with approval ratings of more than 60 per cent' (Navía 2006: 10). This is truly a remarkable period of political stabilization, showing how a conservative economic policy is not incompatible with progressive social policies. Democracy in Chile was the beneficiary.

The Chilean political parties have played an exemplary role in consolidating democracy and an extension of citizenship. The right-wing parties in Chile are no longer Pinochetista and offer a government option that would not now be destabilizing. There is now an argument that PR (proportional representation) should return to encourage greater political pluralism. While it partly exacerbated the political crisis of the 1970s, in today's consensus-style politics it is unlikely to do so. Another issue on the agenda today is the need to strengthen the culture of rights in Chile. As Angell and Reig put it: 'State behaviour especially after the military government, has been characterized by a culture of secrecy and relatively little opportunity for citizen participation outside elections' (Angell and Reig 2006: 497). Bachelet is committed to creating greater levels of transparency and accountability in Chilean politics and to promote the growing 'rights revolution'.

Argentina

Argentina is a country that suffered a great deterioration of the democratic process under the long presidency of Carlos Menem (1990–99) and demonstrates most clearly the downsides of adherence to the Washington Consensus. The massive economic crisis that led to a virtual collapse of the economy in 2002 is perhaps unprecedented since the 1930s and was a signal for rethinking of economic policies across Latin America. Considering that background the political process has shown a remarkable capacity to recover. The first reaction to the economic implosion of December 2001 was an almost total rejection of party politics. '¡*Que se vayan todos*: let them [politicians] all go!' was a popular slogan that took root way beyond the left groups or even the popular classes. The political process had lost all credibility among the people, who saw their life savings evaporate while foreign banks seemed forewarned to withdraw from Argentina in time. The incompetent and corrupt political class was seen by many to be responsible for the country's sorry state in 2002.

There was a succession of caretaker governments in 2002, trying to maintain some semblance of institutional continuity, albeit with little conviction. Towards the end of that year two out of three voters surveyed agreed with the concept of doing away with the political class altogether and nearly half said they would not vote (even though it is obligatory) or would cast a blank vote in the event of an election (Sanchez 2005: 459). Government in Argentina was worse than fragile and popular hostility towards politicians had risen to unprecedented levels. Thus when 'normalizing' elections were called for April 2003 much more was at stake than which political party would take office. In the event two politicians from the dominant Peronist Party were put forward: Carlos Menem looking for a triumphant return despite his major role in causing the debacle and Néstor Kirchner – a seemingly marginal governor from a province in Patagonia.

The 2003 presidential race was lacklustre in the midst of a general mood of apathy and resignation. The radical alternativist political groupings such as the unemployed movement (the famous *piqueteros*, after the pickets or barricades they erected on highways) made a big push for a boycott of the contest. While around a fifth of voters abstained (about the same proportion as in the 1999 elections), the proportion of blank votes collapsed to 25 per cent, the lowest since democracy was regained in 1983 (Sanchez 2005: 468). The prospect of a Menem victory certainly caused much disquiet and in the end Kirchner won in the first round when Menem withdrew from the second round, thus seeking to deny him political legitimacy. The party system did not collapse as it did in Venezuela, for example in the 1990s. Kirchner became the unlikely leader of political recomposition and the consolidation of democracy in Argentina, a role that goes a long way to explaining his enduring high rates of nearly 75 per cent popular approval.

Mexico

In the year 2000 Mexico broke a 70-year-long period of one-party rule that opened the way to greater democratization of the political system, which brought it more in line with the rest of Latin America. Vicente Fox was not the Partido Revolucionario Institutional (Institutional Revolutionary Party) and thus pluralism could be consolidated. Fox declared that corruption was the 'evil of all evils' and an era of transparency was promised. Progressive intellectual Jorge Castañeda was appointed foreign minister and even though he resigned in 2003 this was the first time a progressive intellectual was appointed to such a senior role in Mexico. Fox also dealt with the ongoing, if faltering, Zapatista insurrection in an intelligent, co-optive manner. Nevertheless, soon after the 2000 election it became clear that Fox's Partido Acción Nacional (National Action Party) had financed its electoral campaign illegally through the flimsy 'Friends of Fox' front organization. The drugs trade also continued to prosper under Fox as did its links with the political order.

The head of Mexico's Federal Electoral Institute wrote just before the 2006 presidential elections that denied leftist candidate Andrés Manuel López Obrador victory that the Institute 'has become on of the foundations of political stability and ranks among the public institutions with the highest levels of public confidence' (Ugalde 2006: 20). However, that was not the case when thousands of calls were made for a vote recount to ascertain whether the leftist candidate's defeat by a few hundred thousand votes out of a total electorate of 41 million was fair. Certainly there was considerable evidence of irregularities and a ballot-by-ballot recount would have been the only way for fairness and transparency to be evident to all. In these circumstances it seems disingenuous for the head of the Federal Electoral Institute to have said that 'Today electoral fraud is a thing of the past ... and vote counting procedures are well established and respected' (Ugalde 2006: 19). Democratic consolidation in the Mexican sense is really not incompatible with a strong role for money in the political process.

The cases of Chile, Argentina and Mexico all illustrate in different ways the very real achievements of democratic consolidation in Latin America but also its fragility and limitations. Relatively weak political institutions combined with crippling levels of economic inequality do not help democratic consolidation. It is certainly true that the classic military coup is a thing of the past. Haiti's coup of 1991 is the exception that proves the rule and Aristide eventually returned to office anyway. The attempted coup in Venezuela in 2002, seemingly backed by the United States of America, lasted two days before the coup-makers retreated. Likewise in Paraguay and Bolivia in 2000 and Bolivia in 2005 military interventions or their plotting were brought swiftly under control. It may not seem much to say that democratic consolidation means there was not a military dictatorship but this negative achievement is actually of major significance given the continent's history.

Disenchantment

In some ways it was probably inevitable that some degree of disillusionment or disenchantment would emerge as citizens realized the political limitations of actually existing democracy. Following the first flush of enthusiasm for the new post-authoritarian regimes, *desencanto* (disenchantment) was bound to set in as it did, for example, in post-Franco Spain in the late 1970s. If Spain's carefully managed transition to democracy resulted in a crisis of the parties, it is not surprising that in Latin America, with a much graver economic situation, there would be disillusionment with democracy. A report by the United Nations Development Programme found that nearly half of Latin American's citizens in 2002 would be willing to support an authoritarian government if it solved the country's economic development (UNDP 2004: 52). The course of political democratization in Latin America will not necessarily run smoothly.

Brazil

Luís Inácio da Silva, otherwise known as Lula, became president of Brazil in 2002 with a handsome majority, after running unsuccessfully as the Partido dos Trabalhadores (PT or Workers' Party) candidate in the 1989, 1994 and 1998 elections. Lula had pledged to maintain the existing economic policy and his finance minister later put this in terms of

Box 5.2   First worker president: Luís Inácio Lula de Silva (Brazil)

Born in Caetés (Pernambuco) in 1945, 'Lula', as he became known early in his career, became the thirty-ninth president of Brazil in 2002 and was re-elected in 2006. In 1956 his family of smallholders moved to the city of São Paulo where he began to work as a press operator in an automobile parts factory. He very rapidly became involved in what was then an incipient illegal trade union movement, rising rapidly through the ranks. In 1978 Lula was elected president of the Steel Workers' Union of São Bernardo do Campo where the main auto plants of Ford, Mercedes, Volkswagen and others were based. This was the period when the new unionism burst onto the political scene with several mass strikes that also served to create a political opening for democratic opposition to the dictatorship. In 1980 Lula helped found the Partido dos Trabalhadores (PT), a left-wing workers' party, and in 1983 he helped form a new rank-and-file, non-state-oriented union association, the Central Única dos Trabalhadores (CUT). In 1984 Lula led the PT onto the massive Diretas Já (Direct Elections Now) campaign demanding direct-vote presidential elections. Lula himself won a seat in congress in the 1986 elections.

The 1990s were really for Lula marked by a series of unsuccessful bids for the presidency, first in 1989, then in 1994 and in 1998. In the 2002 campaign Lula issued his famous *Carta ao povo brasiliero* (Letter to the Brazilian People) that represented a pledge to maintain the outgoing president's commitment to negotiate the economic policies with the International Monetary Fund. This is not the place for an assessment of Lula's record in office but it is generally recognized that he forsook the early radicalism of the PT for a more moderate social-democratic outlook, and radical nationalism gave way to conciliatory positions *vis-à-vis* the international economic agencies. Not many go as far as Petras and Veltmeyer, who state that: 'If Cardoso is an orthodox neo-liberal, Da Silva's regime is a Taliban neo-liberal one' (Petras and Veltmeyer 2005: 75). Be that as it may, there was considerable expectation that the post-2006 Lula regime would take a more radical stance. For his part, Lula declared during the campaign that: 'If I win these elections then the integration of South America will have won.' He also promised to move forward to ease income inequality in Brazil so that the country 'can take a leap in quality in the world of politics, economics and business'.

'you don't change the treatment during the illness' (cited in Sader 2005: 70). Be that as it may, the financial and business sectors were reassured that there would be no default on the foreign debt (then under way in neighbouring Argentina) and that the 'battle against inflation' would not cease. Agrarian reform – a crucial issue for the PT's rural partner the Movimento dos Trabalhadores Rurais Sem Terra (MST or Landless

Peasants' Movement) – did begin but it had ground to a halt after a couple of years with a backlash from landowners. The PT had effectively transformed itself from a workers' party into an effective party of government.

The achievements of Lula's first period in office were considerable and Lula's oft-proclaimed 'priority of the social' was no empty slogan. This element included land reform, the Zero Hunger initiative and extension of the government's *Bolsa Família* (Family Fund) as part of anti-poverty programme. A National Plan for Agrarian Reform (ANRA) was launched and made significant inroads, especially in terms of rehousing rural families in spite of continued social movement criticisms. As to the Family Fund, it has been extremely successful even if it is hardly radical, representing an adaptation of President Fox's scheme in Mexico. However, in the end the verdict of Emir Sader (among many) is damning: 'While some good initiatives have been proposed on social issues, these have been largely stymied by the Finance Ministry's rigid fiscal austerity; as a result, the government's social record has been disastrous' (Sader 2005: 72). A democracy that does not put food on the table is bound to create disillusionment.

In 2005 the Workers Party's re-election seemed assured: they were no longer a fringe opposition but, rather, the new *status quo*. However, a major corruption scandal then broke out involving Lula's closest advisers. It seemed that there had been a wholesale buying of deputies' votes by the government through the *mensalão* (monthly big payment). The PT then tried to quash party representatives' support for a congressional investigating committee but it was to no avail and the extent of the financial scandal soon became public. Lula's popularity slumped and the opposition forged ahead. Yet by 2006 Lula had regained ground, helped by a popular attitude that '*rouba mas faz*' (they steal but they do things). The disillusionment on realizing that the PT was much like any other corrupt political party was counterbalanced by a strong feeling among the popular classes in particular that Lula's government had at least tried to improve their situation.

Lula always signified the promise of radical change against the interests of the dominant *status quo*. In 2002 this election was seen as an historical turning point, a move by the citizenry of Brazil from a pro-establishment to an anti-establishment modality. In fact, 'the PT was never a revolutionary party, and its radical rhetoric was always tempered with respect for the democratic rules of the game and a considerable dose of pragmatism' (Panizza 2004: 471). In neither 2002 nor 2006 was a fundamental political alternative being offered: both leading contenders converged at a broadly social-democratic centre. The language of 'change' was more than outbalanced by the commitment to stable economic governance. Thus ex-President Cardoso had no problem in actually endorsing his successor, the once radical leader of São Paulo's metalworkers. This is a mark of a certain political stability, and disenchantment is only an issue for those who were enchanted by Lula's radical political packaging in 2002 in the first place.

Uruguay

In much smaller Uruguay, a country of 3.5 million people – of whom half live in the capital Montevideo – the leftist Frente Amplio coalition finally attained the presidency in 2004 after unsuccessful attempts in 1994 and 1999. The Frente is a broad front ranging from ex-Tupamaro guerrillas to moderate Christian Democrats but its main founders were the communists. Its leader Tabaré Vazquez had been mayor of the dominant capital city Montevideo since 1989 and had acquired a reputation for sound progressive management not unlike the Porto Alegre Workers' Party (PT) administrations in Brazil. As mayor of Montevideo, Tabaré Vazquez articulated a strongly anti-neo-liberal stance, leading the campaign against the proposed privatization of the state-owned oil company ANCAP in 2003. Under Vazquez there was also a strong move towards decentralizing local government and increasing citizen participation in the political process.

Uruguay had suffered directly from the knock-on effects of the economic crisis of 2002 in Argentina with unemployment rising dramatically in what was once considered 'the Switzerland of Latin America'. Elected on a wave of popular discontent with neo-liberalism, Vazquez has kept his radicalism mainly rhetorical since assuming office. So while on the one hand he has re-established diplomatic relations with Cuba, he has also signed an investment protection accord with the USA and moved towards a unilateral free-trade agreement that would jeopardize Uruguay's role in MERCOSUR. Such is the regime's thirst for foreign investment that Vazquez is backing a controversial plan to build two enormous wood-pulp mills on the Uruguay river (border with Argentina) against environmentalists' protests. Jorge Castañeda draws a blunt conclusion:

> [T]his government is, in substance if not rhetoric, as economically orthodox as any other. And with good reason; a country of 3.5 million

inhabitants with the lowest poverty rates and the least inequality in Latin America should not mess with its relative success. (Castañeda 2006: 6)

General

While Brazil and Uruguay are clear-cut cases of disillusionment setting in when progressive governments seem to backtrack and return to the neo-liberal model, the question of why change seems to be so hard to achieve is a more general one. Colombia, for example, has a well-oiled party political setup and regular elections, but this world seems far removed from the ongoing armed conflict with leftist political formations and major drug syndicates as well. Thus Álvaro Uribe who became president in 2002, when seeking re-election in 2006,

> has been conspicuously frugal in his pronouncements and has avoided explicit statements about what his goals are for a second term, other than the vague claim that his re-election will ensure continuity for his programs to handle the armed conflict and the economy. (Crisp and Botero 2006: 24)

In the event Uribe was re-elected to rule Colombia until 2010, receiving 62 per cent of the vote.

In the Andean countries there is a similar disenchantment with democracy as a meaningful political domain. Citizens vote but they have little confidence that elections, or parliamentary politics itself, will deliver meaningful change. Political institutions are weak while at the same time there are high-stakes conflicts over natural resources for example. As one commentator in Bolivia puts it:

> A longstanding practice of excluding large sectors of the population from all real influence in politics, despite the existence of formal democracy, has produced a crisis of belief in democracy, affecting both governing bodies and the party system. (Salman 2006: 163)

While democratization in the last two decades has been largely a success story we cannot just take its consolidation at face value without considering its very real limitations and the consequent disenchantment with democracy in general in many parts of Latin America.

There are good reasons why democracy often elicits a bored rather than an engaged response, and a general lack of confidence that it can oversee significant reforms. In a very interesting research exercise involving ex-presidents and other high-ranking politicians in Latin America, the UNDP uncovered some of the reasons for this scepticism. These political leaders all agreed on the achievements of democratization but also its limitations in terms of spreading social rights (UNDP 2004: 60). They also feel either that political parties have been abandoned by the citizens or the other way round. But most significantly these political leaders emphasize that: 'The imposition of restrictions by de facto power centers has been a longstanding problem in Latin America' (UNDP 2004: 62). Less euphemistically, they are referring to the business and financial elites who, especially in alliance with the mass media they often control, can set serious limits on democratic politics and social reform.

Left Turn

Since the year 2000 there have been eight victories by leftist parties or coalitions in presidential elections. The Southern Cone countries and Brazil all currently have left-wing governments, as do of course Bolivia and Venezuela. In 2006 there were unexpected victories by the former Sandinista leader Daniel Ortega in Nicaragua and Rafael Correa in Ecuador. That year was also marked by the favoured leftist presidential candidate Andrés Manuel López Obrador in Mexico being considered by his supporters to have been prevented from becoming president only by electoral fraud. This left turn represents a serious shift away from Washington-Consensus-style economic policies. It also marks a break with the politics of fear when the prospect of a military backlash would have stopped many voters making a choice for left-wing politicians. But it is important to distinguish very clearly between the populist leftism of, say, Hugo Chávez in Venezuela and the more traditional social-democratic leftism of Michele Bachelet in Chile, for example.

Venezuela

Hugo Chávez, Chavismo (as his movement is known by some) and the 'Bolivarian Revolution' that he has proclaimed is seeking the mantle of independence hero Simón Bolivar, present one of the most divisive issues in contemporary Latin American politics. For his supporters (see Gott 2001), Chavismo is a progressive movement for social and political reform that supersedes a long era of political cronyism in Venezuela. For his detractors (see Shifter 2006), Chávez is an authoritarian demagogue, an enemy of democracy and a threat to regional stability. Chávez had indeed taken part in an attempted coup in 1998 against the democratically elected government of Carlos Andrés Perez, but he was himself elected to office with a handsome majority in December 1998 and survived a coup attempt by opposition forces – backed openly by the United States of America – in 2002.

Even his opponents have recognized that

> Chávez's government ... has undertaken important social programs and launched workers' co-operatives in urban slums. Plans are underway to set up 'social production companies' that would ... seek to distribute earnings among workers and community projects. (Shifter 2006: 4)

The accumulated social deficit of the previous formally democratic regimes have left Chávez with a country which, while oil-rich, had two-thirds of its population living beneath the poverty line. In terms of the political style of Chavismo it is undoubtedly populist rather than social-ist, and the continuous involvement of the armed forces does not augur well for democracy. However, in terms of the accusations by the opposition and the United States of America it is clear that Chávez differed from his predecessors in that

> at no time did the 'authoritarian' Chávez government have recourse to authoritarian political measures ... The constitution was never suspended, no state of emergency was ever declared, private sector media broadcasting was never restricted, no leading opposition figures were arrested and Chávez did not use the series of destabilizing opposition actions to broaden the military base of his government, as critics suggested he would. (Buxton 2005: 335)

There is a separate question as to whether Chávez represents a viable left alternative for the rest of Latin America. For his supporters – especially for those abroad – optimism rules supreme. Others are more sceptical, for example Jorge Castañeda for whom Chávez, while

> he is making life increasingly miserable for foreign – above all American companies ... [and] is flirting with Iran and Argentina on nuclear technology issues ... does very little for the poor of his own country. (Castañeda 2006: 7–81)

Be that as it may, the relevant historical parallel for Chávez is not Fidel Castro, let alone Ché Guevara, but Juán Perón, the military/nationalist/populist leader of Argentina in the 1950s. In a broad historical sense

Box 5.3   Demagogue or democrat? Hugo Chávez (Venezuela)

Hugo Rafael Chávez Frías, born 1954, was elected Venezuela's fifty-third president in 1998. He promotes the 'Bolivarian Revolution' incorporating a particular Latin American brand of socialism. Chávez is a career military officer and was a key leader of the 1992 failed coup attempt against President Carlos Andrés Pérez. While the coup failed it brought Chávez into the limelight as founder of the Fifth Republic Movement committed to opening up the notoriously closed Venezuelan political system (*partidocracia*: partyocracy) and its associated corruption. It also pledged to address the high levels of poverty and inequality that persisted despite the phenomenal income provided by Venezuela's considerable oil reserves. When Chávez was duly elected president and took office in early 1999 the stage was set for a new phase in Venezuela's and Latin America's political history. His sweeping victories in the presidential elections of 2000 and 2006 sealed his position as a major figure in Venezuela's and Latin America's political history.

This is not the place to assess the record of Hugo Chávez as president of Venezuela. There is now a vast literature emerging on the topic that can be consulted but, ultimately, only time will reveal his legacy. For many in Venezuela and abroad, he is a dangerous demagogue who stirs up passions and acts in an autocratic way, playing irresponsibly with the country's oil wealth. He is seen as a threat to regional stability and a polarizing element in Venezuelan politics. For his followers and admirers at home and overseas, Chávez is a bold reformer who has empowered the poor and stood up to US imperialism. He is thus seen as truly in the tradition of Simón Bolívar,

→

Chávez has undoubtedly played a progressive role but he is clearly not a democratic socialist and his very personalist and particularistic movement is unlikely to serve as a role model for the rest of Latin America.

Bolivia

When President Evo Morales announced the nationalization of Bolivia's oil industry in 2006 this news had great resonance across Latin America, awakening memories of anti-imperialist movements going back to the 1930s. Morales, an Aymará labour leader with support among the indigenous coca leaf cultivators, had come close to being elected in 2002. But in December 2005 he became Latin America's first ever democratically elected indigenous leader after a period of intense political turmoil and anti-neo-liberalism mobilizations. The view from the

> 'The Liberator'. Whatever judgement is reached about Chávez (and to some extent the jury is still out) he has undoubtedly become a significant player in world politics in a much more provocative and visible way than, for example, Lula in Brazil. He certainly poses a serious problem for US plans in Latin America if nothing else.
>
> When Chávez addressed the United Nations in 2005 he had this to say:
>
>> Today in Venezuela we demand a new international economic order. But also essential is a new international political order. We cannot allow a handful of countries to unconstrainedly reinterpret the principles of international law, giving legitimacy to doctrines like preventive war. And do they ever threaten us with preventive war! They now call it the responsibility to protect us, but we have to ask who will be doing this protecting? How are they going to protect us? ...
>>
>> Permit me, in conclusion, to mention how our liberator, Simón Bolívar, spoke of world integration, of a world-wide parliament, a congress of parliamentarians. It is necessary to again take up proposals like this ... We will fight for Venezuela, for Latin American integration and the world. We reaffirm here in this hall our infinite faith in man, who today thirsts for peace and justice, and to survive as a species. Simón Bolívar, father of our country and our revolutionary guide, swore not to give his arm any rest, or repose to his soul, until America was free. We also will not rest our arms or give repose to our souls until we have contributed to saving humanity.
>
> *Source*: http://www.zmag.org/content/print_article.cfm?itemID=8756&sectionID=1

United States of America was troubled, not least by the fact that Morales had the firm support of the dreaded Hugo Chávez. But as one US commentator put it:

> Evo Morales's victory, 53.7 percent of the vote to Quiroga's 28.6 per cent amid Bolivia's highest-ever turnout and cleanest-ever elections, may indeed set back coca eradication programs and free-trade agreements. The victory is, however, a democratic revolution and the fulfillment of unmet promises from Bolivia's illusory revolution of 1952. (King 2006: 12)

Illusory or not, Bolivia's national revolution of 1952 led by the country's powerful miners' trade unions was a landmark event in Latin America as a whole. Morales is constrained by the country's poverty (the worst in Latin America), but the renationalizing of natural resources strikes deep chords in the country's majority population. Nor does attachment to a fairly hypocritical US anti-drugs campaign (a thin cover

Box 5.4   First indigenous president: Evo Morales (Bolivia)

Born in Orinoco (Oruro) in 1959, Juán Evo Morales Ayma became president of Bolivia in 2006, and at the same time the first indigenous president in Latin America. In 2002 Morales came a close second in the presidential race which was a great shock to the USA and Bolivia's traditional political parties. Morales was leader of a small left-wing party the MAS (Movimiento al Socialismo – Movement for Socialism) that espoused fairly orthodox anti-imperialist and anti-neo-liberal positions. For Morales himself the driving element of MAS and his followers is imperialism:

> The worst enemy of humanity is capitalism. That is what provokes uprisings like our own, a rebellion against a system, against a neoliberal model, which is the representation of a savage capitalism. If the entire world doesn' t acknowledge this reality, that the national states are not providing even minimally for health, education and nourishment, then each day the most fundamental human rights are being violated.

For Morales the US-sponsored Free trade of the Americas project is no less than 'an agreement to legalize the colonization of the Americas'. It was thus no surprise when on 1 May (Workers' Day) 2006 he signed a decree stating that all of Bolivia's natural gas reserves were to be nationalized. This move was backed by mobilization of the armed forces who moved into the oil fields. Major multinational oil firms such as the USA's Exxon Mobil Corporation, France's Total, Britain's BG Group Plc and Spain's Repsol were forced to renegotiate their contracts or face expulsion. Even Brazil's energy minister declared the move 'unfriendly', an understandable statement given that Petrobras (short for Petróleo Brasileiro SA) controls 15 per cent of Bolivia's gas reserves. Across Latin America this dramatic move evoked echoes of the 1940s and 1950s when the first wave of nationalist, industrialist and statist governments came to power. It was undoubtedly a popular move and cannot be reduced to a simple bid to please Hugo Chávez in Venezuela.

Evo Morales, before he became president, was leader of the *cocalero* movement, a loose federation of coca-leaf-growing *campesinos* who do

→

for anti-insurgency operations) cut much ice among the indigenous growers of the coca leaf. Castañeda, a liberal left intellectual and politician is sceptical of Morales and new leaders like him, arguing that:

> The populist left has traditionally been disastrous for Latin America, and there is no reason to suppose it will stop being so in the future.

→

not accept the US-led 'War on Drugs' as valid or legitimate. In their own words:

> For thousands of years the Andean people have used the coca leaf in their daily chores, to lift the stamina needed for the heavier tasks, to strengthen societal bonds in important moments in their lives, to safeguard bodily and spiritual health, and as a gift offered to their gods. The coca leaf has been a guardian of the deep relations of respect they keep with the land and the life that springs from it. Although rulers wielding power over the Andean realm had corrupted the use of coca as it best fit their interests, it was only after Europeans arrived that the use of the leaf was forbidden and that persecution of those using it began. Upon realizing that the coca leaf was part of the traditional religious practices, the catholic priests invoked the abolition of idolatries as an excuse to decree the end of the coca era ...

> In the twentieth century, the United States – invoking the United Nations' concern with drug abuse, and based on discriminatory scientific fabrications alleging it was coca that had turned the Andean man into a beast – had all the nation-states in the world sign the 1961 Single Convention on Narcotic Drugs. The document, amongst other things, made coca use a crime and demanded that the Andean peoples abandon it within 25 years from the date its provisions went into effect. As the Andeans continued to chew coca after that period elapsed, the US used a coca smoking epidemic, in the form of crack, as an excuse to start a War on Drugs, sending police and military forces to eradicate the coca fields, terrorizing the Andean peoples to this day.

> Ever since that fateful day in 1532, the Andean people have seen white men come by with books proclaiming the superiority of their creeds in one hand while, with the other, they clutched a stick to thrash the Indian who would not bow to that reality. Now that Mama Coca has led her people to sovereign power, placing the stick in their hands, the time has come for Europeans and their American breed to take out the leaf from their sacrilegious list, respect their own word in the UN Carta Magna, respect the sacred leaf, and respect the Andean peoples and their freedom of religion.

> '¡Causachun coca!' 'Long live coca!'

As in the past, its rule will lead to inflation, greater poverty and inequality, and confrontation with Washington. (Castañeda 2006: 8)

While confrontation with US plans for an immense free-trade zone stretching from Alaska to Patagonia is indeed inherent in the situation, it is less clear why such a dire economic prognosis is necessary. For one thing, the neo-liberal economic recipes are hardly in good shape and they are being rejected by one country after another, starting with Argentina following the economic collapse of 2001. Furthermore, it is surely politics that is paramount in deciding whether Bolivia emerges out of underdevelopment and political instability. Evo Morales and his 'EVOlution' reflect the growing confidence and maturity of the indigenous peoples of the Andes, a prerequisite for the building of effective democratic governance. Current moves to reform the Bolivian constitution through a wide-ranging constituent assembly may yet prove to be a milestone in Latin America's political history.

Cuba

Cuba has of course, the longest-lasting left-wing government in Latin America and is one of the few surviving socialist states in the world. It is not, thus, strictly speaking part of a 'left turn' but is still well worth examining, not least for what it means when it finally moves into a 'post-Fidel' era. In fact that began in 2006 when Fidel Castro became seriously ill and all powers were transferred to his brother Raúl, the head of the armed forces, who ruled through a more collegiate form of leadership than Fidel had. A collective leadership has, in fact, been in control for some years now. In that sense the debates around what will happen 'after Fidel' are rather apocalyptic and ignore the extent to which Fidel and the Cuban Revolution are very much part of Cuba's long nationalist history. From that long-term viewpoint, Soviet influence is only the last of a series of interventions – notably by the US and Spain – before those waxed and then waned. Cuba is now rejoining the Latin American mainstream, which in some sense reflects the end of a period in Cuba but also probably represents the start of a new period in Latin America based on more radical continental aspirations.

Cuba has gone through many economic and political phases since the revolution in 1959. There have been industrialization drives, sugar export priority phases, Sovietization periods, moral incentives priority periods, the 'Special Period in Peacetime' of the 1990s and so on. Foreign affairs had been extremely interventionist in Latin America and southern Africa until 1992, when Castro declared that

> Military assistance outside our borders is a thing of the past. The most important task is to see that the Cuban Revolution survives. Ahead we intend to live by accepted norms of international behaviour. (Cited in Gott 2005: 296)

This normalization or routinization of the Cuban Revolution was due to changing international circumstances and a certain exhaustion at home. After 40 years its achievements were still considerable, as Gott concludes:

> This was a Revolution that had not ended in fratricidal strife, but had endlessly turned out fresh generations of well-educated citizens ... possessed of a developed sense of patriotism, with pride in their country's long history and the achievements of its people. (Gott 2005: 320)

As the post-Fidel era begins, and socialism without a socialist world order to be part of winds down, so Cuba is returning to the Latin American fold. Cuba is no longer a total exception, governed by a different logic and a beacon of revolutionary change (or at least its promise). The imperatives of the globalized economy and the inexorable rise of the informal sector have overwhelmed an economic system that lost between a third and a half of its national income in the 1990s. As Centeno reflects in sombre mode: '[T]he saddest aspect of Cuba's return to Latin America is the disappointing realization that little has changed despite the promise and the hope of the Revolution' (Centeno 2004: 413). While the neo-liberal utopia of the Washington Consensus has reached its limits, the older socialist utopia that Cuba represented since the 1960s has also reached its own. We are now in a post-utopian or post-millenarian era of politics.

Challenges

Contemporary politics in Latin America are dominated by the twin tendencies of consolidation of democracy and disenchantment with it. On the one hand, these tendencies are likely to continue in so far as democratic party politics is 'the only game in town', while on the other, disenchantment is bound to set in given the massive challenges facing the construction of inclusive democracy in its full social, economic and cultural sense as well as in political or electoral terms. This section will examine precisely those challenges. Governments of the left are equally facing these macroeconomic and political challenges. As one recent article puts it:

> The constraints that Latin American governments – left-wing and centre/right-wing – face are formidable. Radical, drastic changes in macro-economic policies are likely out of the question given the weakness of public sector revenues and the commitment to trade liberalization and the free movement of capital flows. (Moreno-Bird and Paunovic 2006: 47)

Inequality

While it is true in a general sense that political democracy and social inequality are not necessarily incompatible, current levels of socio-economic inequality in Latin America undoubtedly act as impediments to democratic development. Today Latin America is the most unequal region in the world, where the richest 10 per cent of the population have more than 30 times the income earned by the poorest 10 per cent. In the 25 years since democracy began to return to the region these socio-economic disparities have actually increased rather than diminished. In 2003 nearly half (44 per cent) of the Latin American people were living in poverty, of whom a fifth were categorized as 'indigent' or extremely poor. Again practically half of the population (46 per cent) are working outside the formal employment sector, not protected by labour laws and open to all forms of exploitation.

In brief, the concept of social citizenship – that is belonging fully to society and participating meaningfully within it – simply does not apply to half of the population, that is to say some 225 million people. The British sociologist T. H. Marshall, an early theorist of citizenship and the welfare state, once argued that

> social citizenship covers the entire range, from the right to security and to a minimum of economic well-being to the right to fully share the social heritage and to live the life of a civilized human being, consistent with the dominant standards in society. (Marshall 1963: 74)

And those standards are today increasingly set by the global elite that a significant section of Latin America's better-off citizens are fully part of. The issue now facing Latin America is whether the consolidation of political citizenship and its normalization, as it were, will translate into the promotion of social citizenship without which full citizenship cannot be achieved.

Corruption

Centeno puts it in measured terms that: 'Corruption remains a problem and few democratically-elected presidents have left office without having raised eyebrows concerning their patrimony' (Centeno 2006: 49). There have been spectacular cases such as President Menem in Argentina and President Collor de Mello in Brazil where very public trials have ensued. It is the more structural and 'normal' levels of corruption that are probably more corrosive of the political process. The vast majority of well-off people consider it their duty to avoid paying tax, and the problem of the 'free rider' is massive. What little tax revenue does get through to the state leaks in myriad ways out into private and unaccountable hands. We do not need to take an ethnocentric view that takes Latin Americans as a particularly venal lot to recognize that corruption is an obstacle to full democratization.

The problem of corruption is not just a moral one but goes to the heart of how a democratic political system operates. As Gerardo Munck puts it:

> The political costs of corruption are high. Corruption breaks the link between citizens and their elected representatives, though the specific practices may vary. Candidates running for office may receive money under the table and later return the favour through government decisions. Officials in the executive or the legislature may get kickbacks in exchange for decisions regarding the privatization of state enterprises, the regulation of business or government procurement. Legislators may sell their vote to officials from the executive branch. In each scenario, state actions are driven by considerations other than the connection between voters and elected officials. (Munck 2006: 11)

It is easy to see in this context how corruption represents a challenge to democratic politics in Latin America. It is hard to conceive how honest reformist politicians might even be able to run the state for the benefit of all citizens in this setting. Corruption furthermore diminishes the law rather than stand as a common good. In short the development of civic citizenship is in practice impossible while corruption is endemic.

Institutionalization

'Democracy is built through politics. Yet politics also has major weaknesses, which have led to increased rejection of politicians in our society' (Dante Caputo, UNDP 2004: 18). This is not really about some ill-defined populism seen as a particularly Latin American vice. It is more related to the way globalization has dissolved long-standing relationships between the state, political parties and societies, in particular the synergies between them. The transnational market has not only influenced or shaped the socio-economic structures but it has also utterly transformed the very notion of politics in Latin America. Where the main driver of societies once was politics, now it is the market. Politics increasingly becomes 'marketized' and the citizen is replaced by the consumer. In the new, democratic Latin America, political parties are more necessary than ever to construct a political domain but these parties seem fragile and unstable.

Political parties today, as Garretón puts it, 'tend to lack representativity (of social sectors), they may mobilize and lead but they do not represent fundamental social interests' (Garretón 2004: 89). It seems as though most political parties wish to represent only themselves, in a very instrumental vision of what politics is. Yet political parties are the only bodies in contemporary society (apart, to some extent, from social movements) that can articulate social needs in the political sphere of government. It is political *institutionalization* that is weak today in Latin America. New social movements may spring up to represent social demands but there is a lack of coherent and cohesive political institutions to mediate between society and the state. New institutionalized channels of political representation need to be found and as the UNDP report on democracy puts it, 'There is need to give politics back its context and capacity for change' (UNDP 2004: 26).

Inclusivity

The spread of democracy across Latin America in recent decades has also led to an increased participation by women in the political process. Whereas in the late 1980s the average role of female participation in parliament stood at 8 per cent this proportion has doubled to 16 per cent today. While still extremely low this level does represent some movement towards inclusivity on the gender ground. And while gender exclusion continues to be a major challenge we could probably argue that it is the lack of inclusivity of ethnic minorities that is one of the most explosive situations in Latin America today. Roughly 10 per cent of Latin America's current population are indigenous descendants of the original Amerindian peoples, with much higher proportions of these 40 million people living in the Andean countries and Mexico. A further 30 per cent of the population are of African descent, mainly concentrated in Brazil and the Caribbean. But are they citizens in the fullest sense? As Donna Lee van Cott puts it:

> Hostility among peoples of diverse ethnic and cultural backgrounds, whether rooted in generations of conflict or precipitated by recent events, is one of the most serious challenges to the survival and quality of democracy. (Cott 2005: 825)

As indigenous people and other oppressed minorities have mobilized across Latin America in the last decade (Bolivia being but one example) so the limitations of actually existing democracy have come to light. While it could act as a destabilizing force this type of mobilization has in practice brought new values to the fore such as equality, difference and justice, in a way that has been both a challenge and an opportunity for Latin American politics. In 2002 in Brazil, for example, President Cardoso issued a decree establishing a National Affirmative Action Programme, a first in Latin America.

Conclusion

We can end with a quote from the UNDP report on democracy in Latin America: 'Never before have there been so many countries living under democratic systems and never before have Latin American democracies been so robust. But what has been achieved is not secured' (UNDP 2004: 24). Political democracy is being consolidated but the rule of law is partial at best (see Chapter 4) and there are serious social and economic problems (see Chapter 6) that will hinder its development. This democracy lacks vitality and dynamism, it is rather 'thin' and it is uneven in its development. Above all, the quality and durability of this new democracy is in question. While political rights have advanced greatly over the last decade the concept of social citizenship is quite under-developed. We can thus predict turbulent political times ahead, even if traditional socialist avenues seem to have lost their purchase on Latin America as elsewhere.

In a sense there is a dual crisis between actually existing neo-liberalism proving difficult to sustain in practice and the left unable to articulate a viable or sustainable alternative. There will probably be no return to the orthodox Washington Consensus model but neither does a return to the nationalist populist model seem likely either in the era of globalization. Latin America is in transition: it is the era of globalization but the nation-state still matters; it is the post-communist era but old socialist themes such as income equality also still matter. What does seem clear from this chapter is that the battle of ideas is not an abstract choice between different economic theories or models of democracy. In the recent political events we have analysed here we can now see politics in the traditional sense of competition between political parties matters. After the blanket of conformity imposed by the dictatorships in the 1970s and 1980s, civil society in Latin America is becoming repoliticized.

A progressive alternative to real neo-liberalism might be developed by critical intellectuals and articulated by leftist political parties but, arguably, without a mobilized civil society all this will not come to fruition. A cowed, disorientated and demobilized civil society will be a poor vehicle for progressive transformation of any kind. This is not a simplistic, utopian, or even ultimately a manipulative argument for a politics 'from below' to counter the dominant politics 'from above'. It is just that if we look at Brazil, Central America or Chile we see that where and when civil society has become activated, progressive or democratic alternatives are more likely to prosper. The World Bank certainly understands fully the importance of civil society in achieving social support for neo-liberal globalization and giving it a social 'front'.

Securing democracy is, or should be, a task that the whole of the political system and civil society shares. While there is considerable consensus on the need for political and civil rights in Latin America today the issue of social rights remains deeply divisive. While basic social needs are not guaranteed and the imperative of social inclusion in terms of employment, education, and so on are not even recognized then a democratic deficit will prevail. Even governments that have considered themselves progressive have, as we saw above, failed to have any effect on dire levels of poverty and inequality. Until that occurs there will not be that prerequisite for building democracy – a society consisting of full citizens.

6
Social Patterns

Having focused in Chapters 3, 4 and 5 on political economy, governance and politics, we turn now to society and the social patterns established between individuals, families and broader social groupings. We begin with some of the most salient social structures in Latin America that pattern the life of the individual. These include social classes, of course, but also a range of other social divisions. People also form social relations based on gender and 'ethnic-racial' divisions in society as well as the 'informal' political relationships characteristic of patronage and the *compadre* (godfather and/or mate) systems. The social transformation of Latin America took place under the twin impacts of industrialization (see Chapter 3) and urbanization, which are examined next. Finally, this chapter examines the broad parameters of poverty and welfare in contemporary Latin America, setting the scene for the study of social movements in Chapter 7.

Social Structures

Since the Second World War, the most significant change in the social structure of Latin America has been, undoubtedly, the effect of import-substitution industrialization. The simple overwhelming fact is that whereas agriculture employed over half the labour force in 1950, it provided work for less than a third of the total by 1980. The rise of industry was not quite so dramatic, although in most countries it accounted for a quarter or more of the working population by 1980. While some countries such as Argentina and Chile were already semi-industrialized in 1950, it is also significant to see how others leapt forward in this era. Thus, for example, Brazil's industrial workforce rose from 16 per cent to 26 per cent between 1950 and 1980, and in Guatemala the rise was from 13 per cent to 26 per cent (Merick 1998: 40).

Industrialization also led to a significant change in the gender composition of the labour force. In 1980, the overall female labour force participation rate in Latin America was 18 per cent, which was high compared, for example, with 8 per cent in North Africa but low compared with the 40 per cent or so prevalent in the North. This relatively low figure masks considerable regional variation, however. Equally we must note the very low female participation rate recorded in the agricultural sector which is belied by the participation of women in a whole range of activities, paid and unpaid, within and beyond the household. It is the rise of the service sector in the postwar period that accounts for the increase in the female participation rate as a whole.

Industrialization also led to a shift in the nature of migration, away from the predominant pre-1930 pattern of international migration to a greater preponderance of internal migration. Immigration slowed down during the international depression of the 1930s, and while it picked up again after the Second World War it never regained the importance it held in the 'golden era' between 1860 and 1930. Between 1950 and 1980 the urban population of Latin America grew at nearly 5 per cent per year and some 27 million people across the continent left rural areas to join the great human flow into the cities. The economic restructuring of the 1980s and 1990s slowed the pace of the rural–urban migration, but by that stage the city had absorbed the country in a manner of speaking. Capitalism and its consumption habits had penetrated the countryside and the market had erased any fundamental rural–urban divide. Furthermore, the proportion of people living in rural areas had declined so significantly by the end of the century that the pressure to migrate had greatly reduced.

In terms of the social divisions within Latin American society, the above processes led to major urban–rural differences, a gender division of labour and, also, a growing divide between the formal and informal sectors of the economy. For the working population the rural areas remained depressed; what was different by the 1980s was that things were not much better in the cities whereas in the 1950s they had provided at least a source of employment. By the 1980s it seemed clear that family-based farming was no longer economically viable as it had become squeezed out by a market-oriented agrobusiness sector. Kinship and community networks did allow the small peasant farm to survive in the Andean countries, but overall the picture was negative. Agricultural modernization may have helped exports but by the 1980s even the World Bank was realizing the depth of rural poverty in Latin America and the hugely uneven distribution of land and wealth in the rural areas. Not surprisingly, the 1990s were to see considerable social protest in the rural areas.

The great transformation of the Latin American social structure between 1950 and 1980 had a marked effect on women in particular.

Women formed the bulk of the rural–urban migration that marked this period. Work for women seemed more available in the cities, although in reality there were many more women working as domestic servants than as teachers. One indication of gender selectivity in urban–rural migration is that while in rural areas female-headed households accounted for 10 per cent of the total at most, in the cities this proportion reached 25 per cent on average. While urbanization increased female participation rates, the reality is that women remained segregated in the urban labour markets in spite of the changes in the occupational structure. As one study notes:

> Opportunities for women were restricted not as a result of competition in the labour market but by factors such as the possibility of combining domestic and extra-domestic work and by social norms which fixed which occupations were accepted as suitable for women. (Oliveira and Roberts 1994: 277)

Another great divide within the massive social transformation that occurred between 1950 and 1980 is that between the so-called formal and informal sectors of the economy. The latter is usually outside the law, deregulated and open to abuse. Informal employment is usually in small-scale enterprises operating in the pores of the formal economy as it were, to which it is totally complementary, providing cheap inputs and much-needed flexibility. The informal sector provides refuge employment for low-income social groups, from street selling to recycling, from shoeshining to prostitution. If in the 1950s and 1960s it emerged largely owing to rural–urban migration and the creation of a labour surplus in the cities, since the 1980s it has been more of a response to structural adjustment policies. Across Latin America the share of the workforce involved in the informal sector increased from 16 per cent in 1970, to 20 per cent in 1980 and to over 30 per cent in 1990. Informalization, as it is called, is a true mark of dependent development in the era of globalization.

When it comes to identifying the broad social grouping that emerged out of the postwar social structures of Latin America, we could do worse than begin with consideration of the capitalist middle and working classes. Following a breakdown of data for social classes carried out by Alejandro Portes, we can produce a broad picture of class structure as shown in Figure 6.1. In the urban areas the informal-sector workers clearly prevail, although there is a reasonable small-business sector and an influential if quite small professional class. What is most significant for the rural areas is that if we include small farmers in the working

Figure 6.1   Social classes in Latin America, circa 2000 (as percentage distribution of the economically active population)

Source: Based on Petras and Veltmeyer (1998: 166).

classes these comprise fully 80 per cent of the economically active population and the rural capitalist class is very small indeed.

The urban capitalist class is smaller than average in countries like Bolivia and Ecuador where it accounts for only 2 per cent of the population, but larger in the Southern Cone countries where it reaches 6 per cent. This sector is often linked through commercial and financial networks to the transnational capitalist class. The free-market reforms since the 1980s have deepened the divisions between these capitalist sectors oriented to the foreign market and those dependent on producing for the internal market. The privatization of large swathes of the state sector has also created a new class of very wealthy people across Latin America. Clearly these social sectors have a major influence on local politics even when they do not, on the whole, play an active role themselves. Most of this class is now more attuned to the vagaries of the global system than to the prospects of their own country. The middle classes on the whole support the project of the capitalist class, except in times of economic crises when they become impoverished and choose to throw in their lot with the working classes.

The working classes or labouring poor of Latin America are extremely diverse in their composition. This mainly reflects the very uneven development of the continent where the most 'advanced' forms of employment coexist with the most 'primitive'. The 'modern' sector working in factories, much like anywhere else in the world, seemed to be inexorably growing in the 1960s and early 1970s, but contrary to the postulates of the modernization theory this trend did not continue and by the 1980s it was the 'informal' sectors and often illegal activities which were clearly on the rise. In the 1980s, 4 out of every 5 new jobs created were in this unofficial sector of the economy, and these were as likely to be in the drugs trade as in the much-touted microenterprise sector. The changing social structure of the working population has had a clear political impact, and in particular we have seen the relative decline of the more traditional forms of association such as trade unions which depended on relatively stable industrial development.

The social structures described above should, of course, be conceived in a dynamic way as they are clearly not static, and since the 1990s in particular have been undergoing rapid change. Nor do individuals and social groups just exist passively in the various slots to which they are assigned by the social structures and, as we shall see in Chapter 7, Latin America has seen more than its fair share of dynamic social movements that have had, in turn, a major impact on the social structure through political action. Social classes are not formed solely as economic groupings, in so far as it is clear that a whole range of other factors, including gender, 'ethnic', cultural and generational factors go into the making of social class. Another way of putting this is to say that social structures do not exist separately from the social relations in society, and we are now seeing the dynamic or relational aspects of social patterns in Latin America.

Social Relations

The social relations of gender cut across all the above social structures to the extent that a 'gender-blind' analysis of contemporary Latin

Box 6.1   '*Si Evita viviera*' (If Evita still lived)

Eva Perón (1919–1952) was and is an iconic figure in Latin American and international socialist, feminist and cultural circles. Much ink has been spilt over whether 'Evita', as she became known, would have become a member of the armed Peronist movements of the 1970s who took on her husband General Perón and his authoritarian entourage. There is, however, another intriguing but fraught question, namely Evita's relationship to feminism then and now. During the first Peronist period in office (1946–55) women entered the labour force in large numbers. But it was the political mobilization of women under Peronism that was one of its most remarkable characteristics. Eva Perón stands as a powerful symbol of the changing position of women during this momentous phase of Argentina's political history. What were her views on women?

In one of her earliest statements (1950) Eva Perón was clear that women in Argentina could and would now define themselves as more than wives and mothers:

> The history of our people and the history of all the peoples of the world demonstrates that women have been in the vanguard of all the great collective movements, shoulder to shoulder with their men, with their sons, demanding their rights in each historical period ... the *descamisadas* of October symbolize our women, committed to production, conscious of their social rights and ready to defend them against all the oppressors and against all oppression.

Delia de Parodi, the first woman in the House of Deputies, and later vice-president of that body, declared that the changing status of women during the Peronist period was 'the revolution in the revolution'. In a speech to the Peronist Party, Eva Perón articulated recognizably

→

America would simply miss the mark. The over-arching concept said to dominate gender relations is machismo and its less well-known counterpart 'marianismo' (which refers to the alleged virtues of the Virgin Mary). Machismo is a particular social and cultural construction of maleness around the supposed virtues of the breadwinner, the head of family and the dominant partner in all gender relations. Women who follow the precepts of marianismo will, by contrast, demonstrate inexhaustible reserves of patience and humility, and will willingly sacrifice themselves for their families. The traditional model of family assumed by the machismo/marianismo pair allocates to men the public arena of business and politics and to women the 'private' arena of family and

→

feminist themes when she declared that

> Women are doubly victimized by all injustices. In the home they suffered more than the rest of the family, because all the misery, all the desolation, all the sacrifices were monopolized by them so that their children would not suffer. In the factory, they suffered from the power of their bosses ... Women have not been mere spectators of the social drama. We have been actors and we will be in the future with even more intensity. We demand a part in the struggle because we have suffered as much or more than men.

Yet Evita was clearly acting in a subordinate role to Juán Domingo Perón whom she recalls thus in her memoirs:

> We married because we loved each other, and we loved each other because we wanted the same thing. In different ways, we both had wanted to do the same thing; he, knowing well what he wanted to do; I, by only intuiting it; he, with intelligence; I, with the heart; he, cultured and I, simple; he, enormous and I, small; he, the teacher and I, the student. He, the figure and I, the shadow.

Later she implored women to remember that

> It is not necessary to scorn man, because he lends his intelligence (to the struggle) and we our hearts, so that together with intelligence and feeling, we will be able to collaborate, as we are right now, supporting General Perón to construct a happier, more just and more sovereign homeland.

So Evita was and is a feminist figure but she was also a product of her era and her social situation.

Source: Hollander (1974).

children. This is a powerful image of the power relations inscribed in gender relations but to what extent is it just an ideology of domination?

The machismo model like the theories of patriarchy (male domination) generally tends to be a rather broad brush. While recognizing gender inequality most scholars are now somewhat more discriminating. Thus Sarah Radcliffe (1999) points to a whole range of ways the machismo model oversimplifies gender relations in Latin America. First of all it is an ideology which does not apply to all social classes or ethnic groupings universally. Clearly within the upper and middle classes the role of women is quite different from those living in urban or rural poverty, where household economy needs do not allow for an exclusively private role. Then also for black and indigenous social groups these gender and family ideologies can appear quite alien. In the Andean countries, for example, Quechua-speakers may have unequal gender relations but they do not follow the machismo–marianismo model at all. Finally, it would be wrong to assume that a model such as this has not been impacted on by social change (including globalization) and the growing political impact of feminism in its liberal and 'popular' variants alike.

It was Chile's dictator General Pinochet (*de facto* president, 1973–90) who most clearly articulated the authoritarian view of gender relations in Latin America:

> Woman, from the moment she becomes a mother, expects nothing more in terms of material things: she seeks and finds the purpose of her life in her child, her only treasure, and the object of all her dreams.

For the whole era of the military dictatorships the role of women in society was defined through a local variation of the Nazis' '*kinder, küche, kirche*' (children, kitchen, church) that sought to push women back into the home. In reality women became more and more active in the public arena in defence of human rights and democracy (see Chapter 6). Ironically, in terms of the *kinder, küche, kirke* ideology, it was often the direct need to defend their families which motivated women to resist the dictatorships publicly, as with the Mothers of the Plaza de Mayo, formed to protest the 'disappearance' of their children at the hands of the military junta in Argentina.

Another cross-cutting set of social relations are those established by race and/or ethnicity, both problematic categories but which reflect an ever-present reality in Latin America. The intermingling of indigenous American, European Caucasian and black African peoples in Latin America has created a class/ethnic set of social relations sometimes referred to as the colour–class system. There is a widespread myth that slavery in Latin America was somehow more 'gentle' than its North American variant, a view promulgated by the Brazilian historian Gilberto Freyre (1951) but one which has widespread support, especially through the notion of racial democracy (see Box 6.2). There is another tendency to view indigenous people and blacks in a similar 'structural' situation when, in fact, the history and social situation of the two group-ings is quite distinct. The counterpart to this view of 'equivalence' would be to totally separate Amerindians and Africans, the first to be situated in terms of ethnicity and ethnic relations, and the latter in terms of racism and race relations. The social relations of 'race/ethnicity' are in fact considerably more complex.

Black and indigenous identities cannot be seen as primordial and are always relational, that is to say constructed in relation to the broader society. They are quite distinct, one social category derived from African slaves, the other from various indigenous American peoples. In relation to the concept of 'nation' it is more common, as in Colombia, for blacks to be seen as an integral (if distinct) part of the nation while indigenous people are seen (and may see themselves) as a distinct national category. Racism by white society may be more pronounced towards indigenous people than towards blacks in many countries. These social relations cut across those of social class but they are not separate of course. Even the ways social groups are integrated into society differ, with blacks being subject to slave labour and indigenous people not, partly owing to different European conceptions of their 'ethnicity'. To move beyond reductionist explanations we can follow Peter Wade, for whom 'the emphasis is on the multiple ways in which people may identify differences and sameness, struggle, mobilise and make alliances and enmities' (Wade 1997: 24).

While the social relations of 'race' and 'ethnicity' are deeply inequitable and oppressive in many ways, the myth of 'racial democracy', particularly in Brazil, took deep root. There was a belief that race relations were more 'open', more tolerant, especially compared with the segregation and lynchings of the United States. The Brazilian historian Gilberto Freyre was instrumental in developing this rather rosy view, but it was supported by many other writers. However, a set of famous UNESCO (United Nations Educational, Scientific and Cultural Organization) studies in the 1970s decisively 'undermined the idea of a racial democracy in Brazil and, in some cases, detailed many aspects of how racism worked in a non-US, non-"caste" system' (Wade 1997: 571). The case of Cuba is also interesting because the 1959 revolution pledged itself to ridding the country of racism against its sizeable black minority. For a long time there was official denial that racism could exist as a source of oppression separate from socio-economic discrimination. However, since the fall of the Berlin Wall in 1989 there has been a growing recognition that social relations based on 'ethnicity' could have an autonomous existence.

The last set of social relations to be considered here are also political relations, even more obviously than the two considered above. Personalism, as against technical, apersonal relationships, permeates social and political relations. At a social level there is *compadrazgo* (a sort of colleague or 'buddy' contract) that is a ritual form of pseudo-kinship often exercised through the godparent relationship common to

Box 6.2   Race and equality in Brazil

There are many in Brazil, and internationally, who have an intuitive understanding that race relations in that country are not as inequitable as they were, for example, in the Deep South of the United States. The myth of racial democracy in Brazil is a widespread and persistent one, not even rebutted by the rise of Afro-Brazilian social movements since the 1980s. Racial categories in Brazil are quite ambiguous, with many arguing that it is impossible to know 'who is really black' given the degree of inter-marriage since the colonial period. While there may be some confusion as to who is 'biologically' black in terms of phenotype, when we take the broad categories of 'white' and 'non-white' the level of inequity and dis-crimination is truly staggering. The 'non-white' category would thus include the 'brown' category that includes mulattos, morenos, mestizos and pardos, all terms going back to the era of slavery. As Dos Santos explains:

It has been the great pride of Brazilians to affirm and promote the sup-posed racial democracy in which they live, especially compared with the abhorrent 'Negrophobia' demonstrated by their neighbours ... Talk of race and racism is still a social taboo and this is perfectly illustrated by the fact that 89 per cent of Brazilians polled by the Datafolha Institute ... agreed that their society was indeed racist, only 10 per cent of respondents admitted that they themselves were racist. (Dos Santos 2006: 31–32)

A break with this complacent orthodoxy only emerged under the presi-dency of F. H. Cardoso (who as a sociologist had analysed race and class relations in the 1960s), who publicly declared that discrimination was rife in Brazil. This admission was consolidated by President da Silva ('Lula') who set up a special secretariat in 2003 charged with promoting racial equality in Brazil.

many societies. As Tessa Cubitt puts it, for the *compadres* or ritual kin, participating as godparents in weddings or in religious education is necessary, 'but the relationship that is strongest and requires respect, warmth and the obligation to help at all times is the one between parents and godparents' (1995: 106). In the political arena, personalized social relations occur through 'clientelism' in which an unequal patron–client relation is balanced supposedly through an exchange of esteem and political support by the latter in return for the more powerful political patron or boss exercising power and influence on behalf of his grateful protégés.

While social and political relations in Latin America may have a par-ticular 'personalized' element, this can rarely be seen as unique. Political clientelism is often seen as a debilitating element in the bid to construct genuine political democracies in Latin America. The quality of democracy is seen to be compromised by the patently unequal relations implicit in the patron–client relation that is also seen as antithetical to universal suffrage. Clientelism is seen as corrupting since, at its simplest, it may involve an exchange of food or goods for votes. Democracy thus becomes part of the marketplace and its values rather than something special. Clientelism is seen to be a hangover from the days of oligarchic rule, and the era of populism when 'charismatic' leaders were seen to lead people astray with false promises. In reality the practice of clientelism and other forms of personalized politics are more complex in both their causation and their effects.

A recent study of poor people's politics in a Buenos Aires shanty town by Javier Auyero (2000) goes some way to providing a more realistic picture of clientelism. Certainly it plays a role, as do many forms of patronage, influence and political co-optation. Auyero prefers the term 'personalized political mediation' to describe the complex relation between political networks and the informal webs of reciprocal help set up in poor neighbourhoods to help make ends meet. Thus personalized political mediation occurs as a way of securing the political resources to simply survive. Certainly the problem-solving strategies of the poor are matched by the attempts by the political elites to control them and capture their votes. A dynamic understanding of this complex process cannot, however, be reduced to a simple undemocratic populist habit, but needs to consider how it has been recreated and restructured in the era of neo-liberalism to deal with the new poverty created by the structural adjustment programmes of the 1980s.

In the pages above we have carried out a quick survey of the social structure and some of the main social relations which impact on people's lives. In the era of neo-liberalism there has been a renewed emphasis on the individual and less on the social, with individual social mobility stressed as paramount and the 'identity politics' of gender and ethnicity also seen as more directly relevant to the individual than some broad social category. However, community and communal categories still keep coming to the fore. The community of poverty that is the fate for millions in Latin America creates a common structural/cultural identity, especially, but not only, in periods of economic crisis. The impact of globalization on social exclusion within and between countries is also bringing the national dimension to the fore again. Where one's nation-state stands in the new international division of labour created by globalization is perhaps the major determinant of someone's life chances today.

Urbanization

Whoever refers to industrialization in Latin America refers also to urbanization because the big cities expanded in the postwar period in a complex social process closely linked to import-substitution industrialization. The link was not as direct as in nineteenth-century European industrialization in so far as rural migration was also a major factor, but it certainly existed. And industrialization was linked to changes in the world economy (as seen in Chapter 3), so that urbanization can be seen as part of the dependent development process. Also particular to Latin American urbanization is the predominance of the main or primate city. Compared with other regions of the world, in Latin America the primate city dominates almost totally: in most countries its population exceeds that of the second-largest city at least three times, and in the cases of Buenos Aires and Lima that ratio rises to 10 times or more. The 12 largest cities of Latin America are listed in Table 6.1. The Brazilian predominance – 5 out of 12 – is noteworthy, but hardly surprising given the population of the country. The capital cities of Mexico (plus one other), Argentina, Peru, Chile, Colombia and Venezuela are also on the list.

Urban growth in Latin America was more rapid than that which accompanied Western Europe's industrialization. Even during Britain's urban explosion of the nineteenth century, annual growth rates never

Table 6.1   The 12 largest cities (conurbations) in Latin America, 2006

City	Population (millions)	Global ranking
Mexico City	19.24	2
São Paulo	18.61	5
Buenos Aires	13.52	9
Rio de Janeiro	11.62	15
Lima	8.35	26
Bogotá	7.80	27
Santiago de Chile	5.70	41
Belo Horizonte	5.45	43
Guadalajara	3.95	69
Porto Alegre	3.86	72
Recife	3.59	79
Monterey	3.58	80

Source: Largest Cities and Urban Areas in 2006 (City Mayors' Statistics) http://www.citymayors.com/

exceeded 2.5 per cent whereas in Latin America this rate was nearly doubled throughout the period 1940–60, peaking at 4.6 per cent in the 1950s. The breakdown of how urban growth occurred in Latin America is shown in Figure 6.2, which differentiates between big cities (metropolises), intermediate cities (more than 100 000 inhabitants) and towns (less than 100 000 inhabitants). What is most significant is the halving of the share of the population living in rural areas and the near doubling of the urban population. The massive growth and growth rates of the intermediate cities with over 100 000 inhabitants is also clear, although not as large as the 2-million-plus metropolises.

We have already mentioned the impact of rural–urban migrations in Latin America, but we now need to examine in more detail how people arrived in the cities. In the period of most intense urbanization, approximately 1950 to 1970, the number of rural–urban migrants was at its maximum. Around 70 per cent of Rio's growth during the first half of this period was accounted for by internal migration, but this proportion had dropped to around 40 per cent by the end of the period. Taking the Latin American metropolises as a whole, we find that while in 1950 around half of their growth was accounted for by internal migration, this proportion had declined to about a third in 1970 (Oliveira and Roberts 1994: 249). By the 1980s, the importance of rural–urban migration had declined significantly and there was now more of a tendency for urban–urban migration as people impacted by structural adjustment left the big cities in search of job opportunities or lower costs elsewhere.

Figure 6.2   Distribution of population, 1940–80*

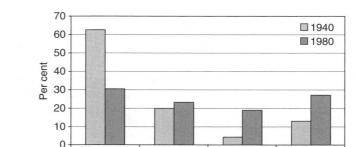

* Based on data for Argentina, Brazil, Chile, Colombia, Mexico and Peru.
Source: Oliveira and Roberts (1994: 245).

Clearly the main reasons for migration are economic, but these are not necessarily simple. As Laite writes in relation to Peru:

> As well as the poor peasant looking for work to make subsistence possible, these are subsistence peasants themselves, seeking savings to purchase tools, animals or even land, or looking for training possibilities either in trade or in further education. (Laite 1981: 124–5)

It is not simple desperation that drives people to migration; indeed it is often the younger and better-educated rural inhabitants who made the move to the city seeking to 'better themselves'. While men are most likely to predominate in moves to mining towns or the industrial complexes outside the big cities, it is women who clearly predominated in migration to the metropolises. As Gilbert sums up:

> It is not rural poverty as much as the difference between urban and rural living standards that is the essential cause of most cityward migration. While people living in areas of violence or in regions subject to natural disasters may move to save their lives, poverty rarely pushes people off the land. (Gilbert 1998: 44)

Once in the cities, the new arrivals and those already settled there faced a myriad of problems. Certainly the streets of the cities were not paved with gold. For a long time it was the theory of 'marginality' that was deployed to explain the role of the urban poor, a term used to describe those dwelling in precarious dwellings on the outskirts of the big cities, often without running water or electricity. Marginality was seen as a social problem and at times even as an individual one, to do with the attitudes of the 'marginals' themselves. They were seen as marginal to the socio-economic development of the cities and even dysfunctional. Others saw in this sector a potential revolutionary vanguard waiting to be mobilized or an explosive waiting to detonated. However, in reality the new migrants were totally functional to economic development in the cities, providing services at the margins of the system as well as labour for the factories and service industries. Nor can individual feelings of 'anomie' (normlessness, disorientation) or the much vaunted 'culture of poverty' theory substitute for a proper social analysis of living in the cities.

When the migrants first arrived in the cities their primary struggle was usually around housing. Whereas prior to the 1950s rented tenement-type accommodation prevailed, in the 1960s and 1970s there was a turn towards self-help housing, often involving cooperatives. At certain periods in some countries (such as Chile in the early 1970s) there were also serious movements of 'land invasions' as the poor sought out land on which to build their houses. The slogan of the Chilean *pobladores* (squatters) was 'our struggle is bigger than a house', meaning that housing was part of a broader struggle to establish a decent life in the city. Contrary to the marginality thesis, these *pobladores* were also centrally involved with the political process at all levels. They were not necessarily revolutionary and could often support populist or right-wing politicians who promised to 'deliver the goods' (as with Fujimori in Peru), but they were certainly not marginal to politics.

Establishing a precarious dwelling was and is the first stage, but then running water and electricity must be secured. Sometimes this is done illegally with supplies later 'regularized'. A basic road may be built and communications might become more fluid. As Gilbert puts it: 'The result of the settler's hard work is that whole settlements are gradually transformed into consolidated neighbourhoods' (Gilbert 1998: 88). This process is uneven, however, and not all acquire the resources to establish a secure footing in the city. Then the real problems begin as individual households and whole communities struggle to develop strategies for survival. Finding work has become increasingly more difficult, and precarious transport has become increasingly more expensive and overcrowded. The crisis of urban management was also exacerbated by the debt crisis of 1982, which made social spending a luxury. Since then the turn towards privatization of services, imposed by the new economic model, has made life in the cities even more difficult for the growing proportion of urban poor.

The future of the Latin American city will inevitably be conflictual but also exciting. São Paulo is now being seen clearly as a global city with Rio, Mexico City and Buenos Aires close behind. They are part of the worldwide system of production, finance and market expansion we call globalization, and integration into the world economy gives these cities a decisive role in the spatial dominance over the region. For the capitalist classes who live in the cities, and for those who service their needs economically and socially, the future looks dynamic. In a very real sense these social groups are becoming part of a world system and effectively becoming cut off from their own countries. In some instances this separation is physical, with the construction of gated communities where the rich live behind huge security to isolate themselves from the poor and their problems.

For the majority of the population, however, the Latin American city is a place of increasing violence, pollution and overcrowding. The sense of insecurity created can be gathered from Simon Strong's descriptive

Box 6.3   Mexico DF (Federal District) air pollution circa 1990

Or Mexico: will I be born here? You know where? Will I leave this country? Owing a thousand dollars, dead or alive! Will I be led to the DF? To breathe from birth eleven thousand tons of sulphur, lead, and carbon monoxide every day? To join a half million annual births – anal birds, antic words? To join a quarter of a million kinds who die of asphyxia and infection each year? To shit, to add my shit to that of millions of dogs, cats, mice, horses, bats, unicorns, eagles, serpents, plumed coyotes? To swallow thirty thousand tons of garbage per day? To join the vultures that devour the rot: blessed art thou, Our Lady Tlazoltéol, first star of the eternal night and of the invisible day, you who cleanse by devouring and then dirty it all in order to have something to clean; lady, can you compete with seven million automobiles, five million bureaucrats, thirty million pissers, shitters, eaters, fuckers, sneezers? Am I going out into that country? So that they can tell me that thanks to oil we're in good shape? That from now on we'll have nothing to worry about, just to administer our wealth? That I'll have my refrigerator even though I may not have electricity, and my Walkman so that people can be jealous when I walk the streets that are buried in garbage and fires? (Fuentes 1990: 525)

Shortly after Carlos Fuentes wrote these lines, the Mexican government announced a US$4.6 billion programme to clean up the air of Mexico City. This was partly aimed at the forthcoming NAFTA negotiations and to forestall the accusation of environmental 'dumping' by companies relocating where environmental controls were lax. Controls over private car use in the city were introduced; the giant PEMEX oil refinery was closed down; companies were told to control emissions or face closure. Trees were planted along with other restorative measures to regain environmental quality. However, in the early twenty-first century there would be many who would argue that the surreal description of Fuentes still holds true.

account of Lima:

> Around the packed streets in downtown Lima ... the nauseating smell of urine, rotting fruit and burning rubbish cloyed the air ... Sewage seeped into the water. Traffic grew ever more congested not because there were more cars or even buses to relieve the chronic pressure on Lima's battered public transport, but because the street sellers have moved from the pavements into the inside lanes. (Cited in Gilbert 1998: 165)

This picture could be replicated in Buenos Aires, Mexico City or São Paulo, (Box 6.3). But not all is gloom and doom across the continent, and the movement for good governance in the cities has taken off. A city needs to have a sustainable environment, and adequate provision of public goods and a policy to create stronger and more equitable development if good governance is to be ensured.

Poverty and Welfare

As the Inter-American Development Bank noted in the late 1990s: 'Latin America is the area of the world where income distribution is worst, and that situation has not improved in the nineties' (IDB 1997: 1). By the year 2000 it was estimated that 35 per cent of Latin America's households were officially 'poor' and a further 15 per cent were 'extremely poor' or indigent. Measured in absolute numbers, these mean that at the turn of the century there were 211 million poor people living in Latin America. Why was this the case in a continent which remains rich in natural and human resources? Where does it leave the modernization theory which promised development in the 1960s? Where does it leave the neo-liberal 'revolution' of the 1980s which also promised development if free-market recipes were followed? Why did Argentina virtually collapse as a coherent social entity in 2001 when at the start of the last century it was considered among the 10 richest countries in the world?

The economic restructuring of Latin America in the 1980s had a severe impact on individuals, households and enterprises. A sharp decline in per capita income in most countries had the effect of exacerbating already unequal levels of income and wealth. The social impact of the structural-adjustment policies implemented after the 1982 debt crisis was inevitably greatest on the poorest section of the population. However, it should also be noted that the new economic model produced winners as well as losers, for example the beneficiaries of the great sale of state enterprises. What the great drive towards competitiveness, unleashed by the new economics, has thus produced is a much greater degree of differentiation between individuals, households and enterprises. This differentiation in turn can be disaggregated in terms of the differential impact by gender, by race/ethnicity and by generation, with the elderly and the youngest suffering disproportionately from the social impact of neo-liberalism.

Poverty levels in the households of Latin America can be gleaned from Figure 6.3. We see a steady upwards trend in the number of households suffering from poverty and extreme poverty, with the poverty rates continuing to be much higher in rural areas (54 per cent

Figure 6.3   Poor and extremely poor households, 1980–2000 (percentage)

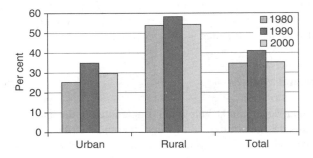

Source: ECLAC (2001: 38).

of households) than in urban ones (30 per cent of households). Also, while the actual number of poor people is much greater in urban areas given the much greater population, the numbers of extremely poor people are about equal – which demonstrates the intractability of rural poverty.

Income distribution levels are also very important as they help us to see how some have benefited while others have lost. At the start of the new century, the richest 10 per cent of households in Latin America take about a third of the national income, while by contrast the share of income of the poorest 40 per cent of households barely surpasses 10 per cent of the total (ECLAC 2000: 6). Only Costa Rica and Uruguay stand out from this bleakly unequal picture with all the social tension it inevitably generates. Brazil has the dubious honour of being the most unequal among Latin America's already unequal societies. In Brazil the income of the top 10 per cent is 32 times greater than that of the bottom 40 per cent of the population (the ratio for Latin America as a whole is 20 per cent). It is hardly surprising that in the interests of economic efficiency, not to mention good governance, the World Bank is seeking to redress this balance to produce sustainable development.

The third element to consider after poverty and income inequality is employment and unemployment. With the demographic context set by a 2.5 per cent annual increase in the working-age population and expanding female population rates, job-creation is an urgent necessity. The Inter-American Development Bank recognizes that the new economic reforms may have led to a certain recovery of growth and productivity, but 'they have slowed the pace of employment growth and may have been one cause of the rise in unemployment rates' (IDB 1997: 58). The restructuring of production leading to a decline of the industrial sector and the dramatic shrinking of the state sector have only worsened an already critical situation. Unemployment rates are notoriously difficult to calculate, but it is estimated that around a fifth of those living in poor households are unemployed. The only source of job-creation is the informal sector and, increasingly, the illegal economy. The volatility of the jobs that do exist is seen from the dramatic impact of the economic crisis that hit Argentina at the end of 2001.

Before we turn to the welfare state's responses to the social situation described above, which Guillermo O'Donnell (1997: 49) has rightly termed a scandal, we need to consider the broader social agenda. While the environmental sustainability of the new economic model is certainly an important issue, its social sustainability is equally so. To tackle the great levels of poverty and inequality that exist in Latin America will not be an easy task, but it is necessary if the political economy of the region is to be stabilized. The quality of democracy is also completely dependent on providing a decent life for all instead of the prospect of increased and widening destitution. While some social sectors may feel that their prospects are more tied to the global economy than the local one, in the long run if they wish to continue living in Latin America they will necessarily need to attend to the damage done to the social fabric of each country by the global ideology of neo-liberalism.

Traditionally the role of the state has been to alleviate poverty through various welfare measures. Today, as Evelyn Huber puts it:

> Social policy in Latin America ... stands at the crossroads between market-determined, private, individualistic and inegalitarian models on the one hand, and market-correcting, public, solidaristic, and egalitarian models on the other hand. (Huber 1996: 141)

While most countries in Latin America have not enjoyed a welfare state such as the postwar British model, they did develop welfare measures that are now being undermined by the effects of the new economic model (see Chapter 4). During the period of state-led industrialization a sizeable industrial working class was formed which created a constituency for social insurance measures. This involved in particular state protection against loss of earnings caused by illness or accident. In Argentina it was the Perón regime (1945–55) that created a Latin-American-style welfare state with strong support from the trade unions which themselves played a key role in administering welfare measures.

However, the debt crisis of 1982 brought to a head a set of long-running problems in Latin American welfare states. The rising cost of healthcare along with increasing life expectancies was more than matched by declining contributions from members of insurance schemes and poor investment returns. With the end of state-led industrialization and production for the internal market behind tariff barriers the problems were bound to get worse. Employers could no longer pass on to the consumer the cost of their welfare contributions as free-market mechanisms began to take grip. The fiscal crisis of the state due to the international debt crisis meant it could not take up the slack, and what began to emerge was a new free-market welfare model along the lines of Margaret Thatcher's 'reform' of the welfare state in Britain. The new model welfarism was based around privatization of most welfare functions, public–private partnerships elsewhere and a generalized commitment to decentralization and flexibility in dealing with poverty. Overall, market mechanisms would have to prevail.

It was Chile under Pinochet that went furthest in promoting a new 'market-friendly' welfare model. Immediately after the 1973 military coup, employers' contributions were slashed and pensions were allowed to deteriorate in not being adjusted to inflation rates. In 1980 a new pension scheme was established in Chile that became an international model for other free-market reformers (see Box 6.4). Employers were now not required to make any contribution at all and pension levels were tied directly to the economic performance of the country. For the middle classes a private health insurance scheme was created which effectively led to a two-tier system. Not only did state-provided welfare decline in quality, but its coverage also became more limited as the labour reforms created a much bigger informal work sector beyond the protection of the law. Significantly, the post-1990 democratic regimes in Chile have increased social spending but have not even sought to open a debate on the desirability of a two-tier welfare system.

The retreat from universal and democratic welfare models was not inevitable, however. As Huber (1996: 175) notes, there is the case of Costa Rica which not only has maintained a social-democratic welfare state but 'is a rare case of a small country that could resist pressures for a move to a neo-liberal model and instead could protect that pattern'. Universal healthcare and the decisive use of state resources helped to mitigate the worse effects of the 'lost decade' of the 1980s. Likewise,

Box 6.4   Pensions: the Chilean model

Margaret Thatcher's admiration for General Pinochet predated his assistance to Britain during the 1982 war with Argentina in the South Atlantic. It was in fact Pinochet's 1980 pension reform law which sparked off that particular relationship. At first the economic managers of the Pinochet dictatorship were content to simply adjust some anomalies in the pension system. Retirement ages were made uniform as was the system of pension adjustment that was tied to the consumer price index. Eliminating some of the most glaring pension privileges and establishing a uniform minimum pension did not seen to be terribly 'revolutionary' neo-liberal measures, but the 1980 law established a new pension scheme which has become a global model for neo-liberal reformers.

In keeping with the general new-economic-model philosophy of reducing the state role and increasing that of the market, the new pension law was market-based. Neither employers nor the government would make a contribution to the individual's pension scheme, and the onus was totally on him or her. The individual would, henceforth, contribute to a private profit-making pension fund administrator who would invest these contributions. The returns on one's pension fund would thus hinge totally on the overall performance of the economy, and the individual's fortunes were tied directly to those of the national economy through the market. New entrants to the labour force were obliged to enter the new scheme but an effective advertising campaign managed to secure compliance from most of those in the old pension schemes.

Within a decade of the new pension law being approved, its impact was quite clear. Only slightly over half of the labour force was contributing to the new scheme, as many were either self-employed, unemployed or unable to contribute. The private pension companies were not regulated in terms of the commission they charged, on the grounds that market mechanisms would prevail. Typically they charged not only a flat fee but also a percentage of the individual's contribution and this had a highly regressive impact. The new system also proved more expensive to administer than the old, allegedly inefficient system did. Most importantly, the allegedly superior market system led to a strong concentration of the private pension companies: by 1990 nearly three-quarters of all pension funds were controlled by just three private companies.

Source: Based on Huber (1996).

Uruguay was one country where inequality levels were actually reduced in the 1980s through decisive state action. And it is not only small social-democratic countries which have continued a welfare orientation; even the giant Brazil with all its social problems has continued with a much more state-driven welfare policy and has rejected the Chilean model. Whatever the shortcomings of Brazilian welfare the fact is that over 90 per cent of the population is covered by social security and there is universal access to healthcare. There is always an alternative to market fundamentalism.

7
Social Movements

Latin America is in many ways the continent of social movements. From Zapata to the Zapatistas, from Ché Guevara to the Sandinistas, revolutionary social movements seem synonymous with Latin America. This chapter takes a broad historical view of social movements to place these evocative names in their rightful context. Firstly we examine the impact of nationalist movements from Peronism onwards, conscious of their continued importance given the condition of dependency analysed above. We then turn to the urban labour movements and their rural counterparts that have had a huge impact in a number of Latin American countries. Only then will we turn to the 'new' social movements with which readers will perhaps be more familiar, such as the women's movement, the environmental movement, various 'ethnic' movements and the human-rights movement which assumed a critical role during the period of the dictatorships.

Nationalist Movements

In the post-Second-World-War period nationalist regimes came to power in a number of countries and nationalism generated powerful social movements. There was a certain synchronization with the economic policy of state-led industrialization analysed in Chapter 3. During the pre-1930 'golden era' of agrarian-based exports, integration with the world system was taken for granted. Now, with an inward-oriented industrial development policy in place in the largest countries, nationalism came to the fore. In some cases it was fostered from above, and nationalism certainly became the official state ideology in most countries. Nationalism, with its vague populist socialism, was the way the working people were incorporated into the political system. Yet nationalist movements could also develop a strong radical edge, and the fight against imperialism or foreign domination of the economy was often a strong mobilizing influence.

General Juan Perón in Argentina and the Peronist movement that followed him are probably the epitome of the nationalist political and

Box 7.1   The world of Peronism

Peronism did not create a culture of its own in the orthodox sense: indeed, Peronist realism was not a memorable cultural revolution. Yet it did create a popular culture where nationalism was never totally able to drown out the rebellious contestatory elements. A mediocre piece of theatre, *Camino Bueno* (Good Road) played in 1947 illustrates this quite well. Set in Santa Fé province on the eve of the 1946 elections, a group of *peones* (labourers) discuss the prospects in the *almacén* (local store):

> Romero: Yo no sé nada de política, Lindoro (I don't know anything about politics, Lindoro).
> Sergeant: Pero usté é' peronista? (But you are a Peronist?)
> Romero: Todos somos. (We all are.)

They then hear Colonel Perón speaking on the radio (a vital organ in the diffusion of popular culture, then and still now), and Lindoro, another *peon*, expresses their views:

> Al fin y al cabo el hombre lo único que quiere e' que no haiga más unos muchos todos pobres y unos pocos todos ricos ... Lo unico que quiere e' que haiga una nivelada.
>
> (At the end of the day, all the man wants is that there should not be many who are all poor and a few who are all rich ... He only wants to have a levelling.)
>
> →

social movement in Latin America. Perón came to power in 1945 on the back of a massive popular demonstration of support, a support partly based on the trade unions but even more so on recent rural migrants who had arrived in the capital Buenos Aires and were not organized politically. In one word, Perón gave them 'dignity' in a social world where they were treated with ill-disguised contempt by the middle class who deemed them 'blackheads' (*cabecitas negras*) after their skin colour which was darker than that of the *porteño* (Buenos Aires) inhabitants. Until he was overthrown by a military coup in 1955, Perón set about a vigorous industrialization programme, facilitated trade union industrialization and helped to create a powerful nationalist (though also personalist) social movement. Peronism has remained an enigma for social analysts ever since, but Box 7.1 may give some idea of what made the movement so popular.

> →
>
> They swear that if Perón is cheated of victory they will burn the factories, destroy the *estancias* (estates) and string up the bosses.
>
> Peronism burst on the scene on 17 October 1945. That popular demonstration was also a cultural event, at least in a negative sense, for the dominant class. Jorge Abelardo Ramos, a pro-Peronist Marxist, describes those fateful events:
>
>> Buenos Aires was occupied by hundreds of thousands of furious workers. Their slogans are primitive but unequivocal: 'Death to the oligarchs' or 'No top hats and walking sticks!' (*Sin galera y sin bastón!*) 'We want Perón!' The columns of workers flowed into the Plaza de Mayo ... Tired by the march, many demonstrators washed in the Congress fountains; their modest dress, their provocative attitude, their distempered shouts, caused horror for the spectators from the 'democratic' parties who witnessed in stupefaction the conquest of Buenos Aires.
>
> The marchers walked along in their shirtsleeves, or rode on horseback, or on the backs of lorries or in hijacked buses. The well-dressed city gents of Buenos Aires – who could compare with the best of Rome, Paris or London – stared in horror. Beyond its political significance this was a cultural event, with the culture of the elite being swamped by the masses. The left-wing parties and especially the communists, joined the chorus of 'civilized' protest at this invasion of their city by the unwashed hordes. Many recalled President Sarmiento (1868–74) warning that Argentina faced a choice between 'civilization or barbarism' ...
>
> (Munck 1987: 234–8).

For a long time European and US authors found in Peronism a peculiar Latin American brand of fascism. Indeed, Perón admired Italy's Mussolini and refused to support the allies during the Second World War. His methods were quite authoritarian and his brand of 'real' democracy sometimes rode roughshod over the conventions of real democracy. In contrast to this view, left-wing supporters of Peronism in Argentina argued that this was quite simply the local 'road to socialism' in so far as nationalism was necessary to overcome foreign domination. In reality neither the fascist nor the socialist label is adequate. Peronism was, and still is though much diminished, a nationalist social and political movement. It dominated the history of contemporary Argentina, with Perón coming back as president in 1973 before dying in 1974, and has been the model for mainstream nationalist movements across Latin America, in Brazil and the Andean countries, and even in Central America (where it took a much more right-wing form).

Today, Hugo Chávez in Venezuela seems possibly to be recreating the Peronist model, and to some extent that would indicate that this type of nationalism is far from dead. Following an aborted military–civilian coup attempt in 1992, Chávez was finally elected president in 1998. Immediate parallels were drawn with General Perón's meteoric rise in the 1940s on the back of a military–populist uprising. A radical populist, much like Perón and other Latin American leaders in the 1940s, Chávez soon began to make his mark. His foreign policy was decidedly independent, calling for Cuba's readmission to the organization of American states, giving shelter to Colombian guerrillas on the run and seeking to radicalize OPEC (Organization of Petroleum Exporting Countries). His economic policy was decidedly against the new economic model promoted by Washington. Chávez received his support from among the poor and social excluded of Venezuela, while he has been vilified by the country's sizeable and once very well-off middle classes.

If Peronism and Chávismo are nationalisms 'from above', to some extent, there is another more revolutionary form of nationalism associated with the Cuban Revolution in 1959 and, later, with the Nicaraguan Revolution of 1979. It is often forgotten that the main slogan of the Cuban Revolution, and its followers across the continent in the 1960s and 1970s, was quite simply *Patria o Muerte* (Country or Death). The Cuban Revolution was led by a radical nationalist movement, the 26th July Movement, and not by the Communist Party. Fidel Castro, its leader, later declared for socialism in 1961 but he is, above all else, a nationalist leader. We cannot understand the longevity of the Castro regime in Cuba, and its considerable legitimacy at home in spite of all its glaring problems, without starting from the standpoint that it represents a nationalist movement. The continued and implacable opposition of the USA – through the economic blockade and political demonization – more or less ensures that the nationalist instinct to defend the regime will persist.

Throughout the 1960s and the early 1970s, the Cuban Revolution spawned many supporters across Latin America. The death of Ché Guevara in Bolivia in 1967 symbolized the end of the attempt to generalize or 'internationalize' the Cuban Revolution. In the Southern Cone countries in particular, but also in Central America and elsewhere, 'Guevarism' became the new radical ideology. While its main visibility to the outside world was in terms of its espousal of armed-struggle methods, we should not forget these movements usually defined themselves as national-liberation movements. The theory was that the leaders of these countries had sold out to imperialism and a new 'second liberation' (following that from Spain and Portugal in the colonial era) was necessary. What is most clear in retrospect is that these movements had most impact when, as in Argentina and also in Colombia, they could successfully merge with larger nationalist social movements or ideologies.

In 1979 just as the Cuban Revolution seemed to have definitively waned as an influence in Latin America, the Sandinistas seized power in Nicaragua. The Sandinistas were, significantly, named after a General Sandino who forged a powerful peasant-based guerrilla army to fight against the US military occupation of Nicaragua between 1927 and 1932. The new Sandinistas built on his legacy of national unity and resistance in forging a cross-class alliance against the dictator Somoza in the mid 1970s. Though the Sandinistas contained socialist, even Marxist, currents, their dominant strand led by the Ortega brothers was quite clearly nationalist in orientation. With the support of nationalist governments in Mexico, Venezuela, Costa Rica and Panama, the Sandinistas defeated Somoza's already discredited regime in 1979 amidst a widespread and popular uprising. In seeking to rebuild a devastated country the Sandinistas appealed to socialism, but nationalism would remain a dominant factor.

The Sandinistas faced a regrouped National Guard (Somoza's army) from across the border in Honduras, given powerful backing by the Reagan administration in the USA. As Nicaragua slipped into civil war the Sandinistas appealed more and more to nationalism in a vain attempt to drive back the US-sponsored terrorist attacks on the country. Eventually they were forced to call elections in 1990, which they lost even though they then returned to power in 2006.

While the Sandinistas are often seen as part of the 'old' nationalist-socialist social movement tradition, the Zapatistas in Mexico, who came to prominence early in 1994 with a dramatic uprising in the Lacandón region, are seen as exemplars of the 'new' guerrillas of the internet era. In fact, for all their original methods of struggle and support internationally, the Zapatistas are inseparable from the history of Mexico's national revolution. After all, Zapata was the leader of one of the peasant armies during the Mexican Revolution of 1910. The point is that nationalism is almost always a component part of major social movements in Latin America, certainly in all those that are oriented towards macrolevel political change.

Labour Movements

Workers have formed social movements ever since the Industrial Revolution, and even before then. The first stable trade union movements in Latin America were formed in relation to the export-sector economy. Thus dockers in Brazil and Argentina were among the first workers to organize, as were (later) the miners of Chile and the oil workers of Venezuela. Especially in the Southern Cone countries, immigrant workers, particularly from Italy and Spain, brought with them the organizing traditions and the political ideologies of anarchism, syndicalism and socialism. In the outward-oriented economy of the pre-1930 period, key sectors of workers such as the dockers and miners, but also the railway workers, had considerable bargaining power in that they could paralyse a major economic activity. However, this was also a period when the state was prepared to use intense repression to thwart labour in organizing, and not everywhere was it able to consolidate as a viable social movement.

With industrialization after 1930, and particularly following the Second World War, the urban labour movement tended to become 'nationalized'. That is, it began to turn away from its internationalist origins (which fitted with the largely immigrant nature of the working class) to become a national social force. Trade unions became a key social component in many nationalist movements even though they often had their own 'social' agenda on behalf of their members. Nationalism tended to coopt the labour movement as in Argentina, Brazil and Mexico in particular, but it also granted it a degree of legitimacy. The urban labour movements thus developed in the 1950s and 1960s into quite influential organizations, able to articulate labour interests perhaps more effectively than the anarchist and communist movements which had prevailed pre-1930. However, communist and socialist ideologies did operate in some countries on the one hand, and nationalist unions could become very conservative on the other hand, as we shall see.

Chile is probably the country in Latin America where labour politics most closely resembled the European model with socialist and communists vying for influence. In 1970 a coalition of these political parties led to a remarkable electoral victory for Latin America's first Marxist president, Salvador Allende. Under Allende, until he was overthrown by a military coup led by General Pinochet, there was a remarkable flourishing of labour as a social movement. There were important experiments in self-management in many enterprises, and communal food distribution methods emerged to counter the black market encouraged by the right wing. In the shanty towns (*poblaciones*) there was much political activity, and in the countryside peasant councils emerged in many areas. The Chilean experiment in democratic socialism, although brief, had considerable impact in the region and, especially, internationally. It forms part of the legacy of the contemporary labour movement and its debates are still cropping up in new contexts today.

In Colombia and Peru the classic socialist/communist labour politics prevailed if not quite as clearly as in Chile. In Colombia the communist-influenced trade unions pioneered a new form of social mobilization in the 1970s known as the *paros cívicos* (civilian stoppages). These centred less around traditional trade union issues (like wages and conditions) but also on the provision of public services such as water, electricity and waste disposal. A very wide range of social sectors were usually involved, including professional associations, in completely paralysing the major cities. In Peru, following the 1968 'progressive' military coup there were a whole series of experiments in industrial democracy. More recently both Colombia and Peru have been dominated by agrarian insurgent movements, namely the communist-led FARC (Revolutionary Armed Forces of Colombia) and the more 'Maoist' Sendero Luminoso respectively. They have tended to put the urban social movements somewhat in the shade, not least because of the intense repression that has been unleashed by the state since their emergence.

In Argentina, the Peronist social movement probably shows most clearly the weaknesses and strengths of the more typically Latin American nationalist/populist labour tradition. From when Perón was driven into exile in 1955 until his triumphant return in 1973, the social movement that bore his name gained considerable strength. On the one hand this comprised a political class of union bosses and career politicians who pinned their colours to Perón's mast. There was also, however, an informal rank-and-file social movement based in the factories and working-class neighbourhoods. An extraordinary level of organization and social solidarity emerged, based on dense networks both within the workplace and in the wider community. Characteristically, this Peronist movement survived the death of its supposedly irreplaceable leader in 1974 and has gone on to become a vital part of the mechanisms for survival deployed by the nearly half of the population in Argentina deemed officially to be living in poverty.

In Mexico, the 1910 Revolution is often seen as a peasant revolution but it also led to a great empowerment of the urban working class. After being involved in fighting against the peasant armies, the trade unions went on to become a key pillar of the post-revolutionary regimes. At first

Box 7.2   Brazil's industrial vanguard

Contemporary Brazilian politics and the role of the Workers' Party (PT) in particular cannot be understood without reference to the formation of a conscious industrial working class in São Paulo's industrial belt in the mid 1970s. This focused around the Brazilian auto workers and other metal workers in relatively well-paid employment. In terms of trade union organization there was a slow recovery from the repression unleashed by the 1964 military coup. But by 1978 there were a number of strikes in the car plants led by radical organizations. By 1979 these strikes had grown in importance and spread from São Paulo's industrial belt to include professionals and remote provinces alike. A new wave of trade unionism had begun based on a classic proletariat (in Marx's sense) working in large factories under tight managerial supervision.

An important feature of the *novo sindicalismo* (new unionism) was the advanced and democratic level of organization it displayed. There were elections for shop-floor representatives and general strike committees, frequent struggles cutting across occupational categories and massive street demonstrations. The strikes were also crucial in developing and articulating resistance in the neighbourhoods. There was, indeed, a fusion between the day-to-day struggle of the *bairro* (neighbourhood) over issues such as health and housing, and the new factory organizations. To take this remarkable social upheaval to a higher plane, the São Paulo metalworkers' union voted in 1979 to struggle for a 'workers' party' to advance their interests in the political arena. Its founder, metalworkers' union leader Luís Inácio da Silva, declared that this would be a party 'without bosses, without foremen and without sell-outs, a party that would fight to defend the economic and democratic rights of the workers and for socialism' (cited in Munck 1988: 121).

the communist influence was considerable but gradually nationalism came to the fore. By the 1950s the union watchword had changed from 'For a society without classes', to 'For the independence of Mexico'. Corporatism – state control over the trade unions – has tended to make the trade unions into government supporters but it has also given them considerable resources. There are now radical union currents vying for influence within the broader labour movement. This is particularly the case since 1994 when Mexico joined NAFTA (North American Free Trade Association) and its trade unions began to cooperate with their US and Canadian counterparts in an effort to create a common North American trade-union strategy.

It was in Brazil that the break with the old trade unionism was most dramatic in the 1980s and led to a 'new' unionism that was hugely influential both in the country and internationally. Since the 1940s the

Brazilian trade unions had been closely tied to the state in a corporatist model. The 1964 military coup had further repressed them but by the late 1970s vigorous industrialization and the first glimmers of democratization created the conditions for the emergence of Latin America's most powerful contemporary labour movement. Major strikes occurred in 1978 and 1979 in São Paulo's industrial belt, where the car industry was the main employer. In conditions reminiscent of Britain's Industrial Revolution, thousands of car workers began to organize, usually outside the channels of the largely moribund trade unions. They involved the whole community in this mobilization and received much support from the more radical sections of the Catholic church, with the first union assemblies taking place in church halls.

While some sectors continued to organize along traditional trade-union lines, the 1979 metalworkers' strike of São Paulo led to the emergence of a 'new' social movement unionism which rejected state control over the trade unions and association/subordination in relation to the established political parties. Instead it moved to set up the Workers' Party that became a major national political force. The Workers' Party gave workers a clear independent political voice for the first time and had great international influence, especially in South Africa. The union movement itself oriented in a more social direction, taking up the issues workers were engaged with outside the workplace such as housing, healthcare and transport. A broad supportive network was thus formed as factory and community began to merge. The democratic way in which this new (but also old) social movement organized was also quite distinctive and helped it to gain a dominant role in Brazil and indeed across Latin America by the 1990s.

Rural Movements

There is a long-standing tradition of analysing revolutions as peasant revolts, from China to Russia and from Mexico to Cuba. However, it is not some abstract desire for land that motivates the rural population as a whole. Rural social movements emerge among different sectors of the rural population – smallholders, tenant-farmers, sharecroppers or landless workers – with quite distinct dynamics. As Barrington Moore writes:

> [W]here the peasants have revolted, there are indications that new and capitalist methods of pumping the economic-surplus out of the peasants had been added while the traditional ones lingered on or were even intensified. (Moore 1969: 473)

This was certainly the pattern in Mexico where old and new forms of exploitation were combined. However, neither the Mexican Revolution nor certainly the Cuban Revolution can be considered simply 'peasant revolutions'. Different sectors of the rural population were certainly involved (more so in Mexico), but so were sectors of the middle class and the political aspects of struggling for democracy over authoritarian systems of rule were dominant.

Short of involvement in massive national upheavals, the rural population has formed social movements in a number of countries. In Brazil, rural organization goes back to the 1960s when the famous Peasant Leagues were formed in the north-east under the leadership of Francisco Julião. The Leagues not only organized smallholders, however; they were most active in taking up the cause of the sugar plantation workers. By the mid 1960s a national confederation of rural workers (CONTAG – Confederação dos Trabalhadores na Agricultura) was also formed which had considerable success in organizing the rural poor. By the 1980s CONTAG had 2750 individual unions affiliated to it, and covered some 90 million rural workers. It was the agricultural modernization of the 1970s which explains the different appeals of the Peasant Leagues and CONTAG, and the success of the latter. While the Peasant Leagues had appealed to sharecroppers and tenants with insecure access to land, CONTAG took up the cause of rural workers (and small farmers) which became more important as capitalism transformed agriculture.

The most visible Latin American rural movement is undoubtedly the Brazilian MST (Movimento Sem Terra – Landless Movement). Formed by Catholic and Marxist activists, the MST calls for the immediate distribution of land to the landless under the slogan 'occupy, resist and produce'. The Brazilian constitution allows for the redistribution of under-utilized land so, in principle, the demands of the MST can be met. However, the big landowners are extremely concerned about the precedent that any distribution of land may set and have responded with repression. The Cardoso and later Lula governments tried to reconcile the two sets of interests but without much success. The MST have been very active indeed in recent years, spearheading over 1000 land invasions or takeovers of big estates, demanding their expropriation and government support to settle landless rural families there. For some critics the MST is a nineteenth-century movement responding to a nineteenth-century problem: the lack of land. However, it can also be seen as an active ingredient in the growing counter-globalization movement practising the slogan of 'Another World is Possible' and carrying out an intelligent strategy of creating transnational alliances through Vía Campesina (www.viacampesina.org).

In Colombia there has also been a long tradition of rural organization and revolt. During the period known as *La Violencia* (The Violence) from 1948 to 1958, peasant farmers fought a civil war on behalf of two mainstream parties. Under the leadership of the Communist Party, though, they had also consolidated what were known as independent 'republics' (later these would be understood as 'liberated territory') in remote rural areas. In the 1960s the peasant republics were consolidated and formed the base for an assault by the FARC (Revolutionary Armed Forces of Colombia) and other guerrilla groups on state power in the 1970s and 1980s. Since then the country has slipped into a civil war even more bloody than the original *La Violencia*. At one point the government had allowed the FARC to retain open control of certain parts of the rural territory. The rural population are involved on all sides of the current conflict – guerrillas, government-backed paramilitaries, drug barons and so on – and will not necessarily gain from its outcome. The point is that rural social movements are not a thing of the past and they are constantly recreated in new situations.

In Peru the countryside has also been a ferment of organization and agitation since the 1960s at least. In the early 1960s there was an active peasant movement in the La Convención area that turned to armed actions under the leadership of the Trotskyist Hugo Blanco. Violence emerged largely because of landowners' resistance to peasant organizing and demands. This movement was largely defused by the reformist military government that came to power in 1969, but later in the 1980s a new peasant revolt began in the remote province of Ayacucho under the leadership of the Maoist Sendero Luminoso (Shining Path) guerrilla organization. In the early 1990s, the Sendero Luminoso appeared to be a serious threat to the state but their main leader was captured in 1992 and the movement has since declined. The rural population had often supported Sendero in spite of (or because of) its brutal methods, but they have also turned in increasing number to the self-defence *rondas campesinas* (peasant circles) sponsored by the government to confront Sendero.

In Ecuador the indigenous Quichua predominate in the rural highlands and were the main promoters of a monumental indigenous uprising in 1990. Struggles over ethnic rights and recognition prevailed, but the question of land was never far behind. As one analysis shows, 'The indigenous movement in Ecuador can be said to have shifted from class-based to identity-based, but it was never divorced from the struggle

Box 7.3   Ecuador 2000: chronology of an indigenous uprising

Early in 2000 an unprecedented uprising of indigenous peoples in Ecuador overthrew that country's government in a massive and peaceful mobiliza-tion. Seen through the eyes of some participants this was a remarkable event in Latin American, and world, history:

> From the night of Sunday 16th of January [2000] hundreds of men and women advanced on the Ecuadorian capital Quito, delegates of their indigenous communities and organized by CONAIE (Confederation of Indigenous Nationalities of Ecuador). Their objective: to recover their voice after 500 years of being silenced, to recover for all the dignity of the peoples and the country, and to construct a different society, one which was more democratic, more just, more tolerant ...

> On Monday 17th, utilizing the knowledge and skills learned in many years of resistance, the indigenous delegates were able to break the mil-itary and police fence around the capital ... The 'mestizos' of the capital viewed with indifference as small groups of indigenous people entered the city surreptitiously ...

> On Tuesday 18th, various strong mobilizations began within Quito which gained the sympathy and support of numerous urban social sectors – students, women, trade unions, ecologists and human-rights activists – for the proposal of CONAIE to have a People's Parliament.

> On Wednesday 19th, over 20 000 people joined a demonstration – women and men, young and old – which peacefully marched through the city centre, accompanied by Andean music groups, dance troops, religious hymns and alternative rock music. Their demand: to all build a new country. That night the indigenous people built an impenetrable human barrier around Parliament and the Supreme Court.

$\rightarrow$

for land' (Selverston 1999: 176). Already in the 1970s an agrarian reform had transformed the rural indigenous population from no better than indentured servants into rural labourers. Now things were going the way of the mechanized sugar-cane and banana production sectors on the coast. Thus the struggle over land was becoming not only an economic necessity, but a matter of cultural survival as well as traditional society disintegrated. This movement culminated in the massive indigenous uprising of 2000 which actually led to the unprecedented collapse of the government as the country virtually rose up in solidarity and protest (see Box 7.3).

It is the Zapatistas of Mexico, however, who have captured the popu-lar imagination at an international level. In the remote southern province

→

On Thursday 20th, the army and police made a great show of strength but the indigenous barrier around Parliament remained intact. The government underestimated the march and its impact and, in a fit of incomprehension the 'Minister of the Interior' declared that it was 'just a small group of drunken Indians'.

On Friday 21st, the Parliament buildings were seized by the demonstrators. Armed with small sticks, machetes and hopeful grins, they decorated the cold scenery with their rainbow colours ... A government 'for the people, by the people' was set up against corruption and neo-liberalism, for economic equity and human development. By midday, for the first time in Ecuador's history, the indigenous *'wipala'* flag decorated the National Congress building.

Throughout Friday afternoon representatives of all the different peoples of Ecuador came to the National Congress: the Quechua people – Otavalos, Caronquis, Cayambia, Kitus, Panzaleos, Puruhaes, Chibullos, Salascas, Guaranjas ... migrants from the big cities, Quichuas from the Amazon, members of the Epera, Chachi, Tsáchila, Shuar and Achuar nationalities, poor peasants, committed Christians, intellectuals, all the committed people of Ecuador.

By Friday afternoon, in view of the political situation, the Army High Command called on President Mahuad to resign. At 1700 hours he left the Presidential Palace under armed guard. By 1830 hours Quito's people, indigenous, youth, soldiers, advanced on the Presidential Palace to consummate the overthrow of President Mahuad. Cheered by thousands, a march of some 50 000 people advanced to seize the Presidential Palace and declare a 'Popular Government'.

(Translated and adapted from: http://icci.nativeweb.org/levantamiento2000/cronica.html)

of Chiapas the mainly Mayan peasants had been feeling the squeeze from agricultural modernization which rewarded the capitalist sector to their detriment. Things would only get worse when Mexico became integrated with NAFTA in 1994 and agrobusiness came into its own. On the other hand, Chiapas was the organizing site of a small Marxist group, the EZLN (Ejército Zapatista de Liberación Nacional – Zapatista National Liberation Army), which had failed to establish a base in the cities. These two elements came together in a remarkable uprising in Chiapas (henceforth known as the Zapatista rebellion) in early 1994. In the years since then the Zapatista movement has gained strength both nationally and internationally. In its confluence of peasant uprising, 'ethnic' revival, anti-globalization protest, guerrilla movement and nationalist revolution,

Chiapas is probably unique but it may also point to the complexity of rebellion in the future.

Rural social movements in Latin America thus span from the early 1900s to the early 2000s, reflecting old social problems and new ones in differing combinations. While the rural population declined decisively in the postwar period (see Chapter 6), rural social movements continue to emerge. As Cristóbal Kay argues, 'The peasantry is striking back and it would be a serious mistake to dismiss these new peasant and indigenous movements in Latin America as the last gasp of rebellion' (Kay 1999: 298). Indeed, not only is the access to land still a burning issue, but new issues around ethnicity and environment (see the next section) are now coming to the fore in motivating rural social movements. The Chiapas rebellion, for example, is at one and the same time an 'old' rural revolt over land, an affirmation of indigenous identity and a reassured revolt against the impact of neo-liberal globalization on a rural community. It is also, of course, inseparable from the history of Mexico and cannot be understood fully outside this context.

New Movements

In examining nationalist, labour and rural social movements we have seen that a distinction is often drawn between these and those deemed 'new' social movements. The latter are considered to be more concerned with identity than class or state-related issues and may include gender, 'ethnic', human-rights and environmental movements, all of which we will now consider briefly. A nationalist movement or a traditional labour movement invariably oriented its action towards the state, either to 'capture' it or to make it take some measure it wished to see implemented. A human-rights movement, by contrast, may appeal to an 'international community' and not the national state. Gender- or 'ethnic'-based social movements may often be more about the construction of a national identity than placing demands on the state. However, as we have already seen above, for example, in the interface between rural and indigenous social movements it would be wrong to draw a hard and fast line between 'old' and 'new' social movements, let alone to consider one set better or more radical than the other.

The women's movement is often seen as an exemplar of the new social movements. Organizing autonomously, not tied to political parties and stressing the affirmation of identity, they challenged the very basis of patriarchal society and traditional male-oriented ways of changing it.

Most Latin American countries, but particularly those in the Southern Cone, had seen the emergence of classical 'liberal' feminism pursuing the emancipation of women in the early twentieth century. Oriented towards suffrage issues, this was the beginning of feminism's bid to 'engender' citizenship, clearly essential if it is to be meaningful to the whole population. This early feminism could probably be classified as an 'old' social movement in so far as it made demands on the state and was clearly political in its orientation. The 'new' feminism of the 1970s was to be quite distinctive, even though there were obvious continuities with the first wave.

Feminism in Latin America since the mid 1970s was inseparable from the struggle against the military dictatorships. While male analysts saw only the class and political factors at work in this process, feminists realized that the military regime and its actions were related intimately to the patriarchal state. Feminist issues inevitably took on a different complexion in this situation. Male violence was tied to the state more specifically than elsewhere, and campaigns on women's reproductive choice could not be separated from the forced sterilization engaged in by some international agencies. Furthermore, many Latin American feminists 'see their movement as part of the continent's struggle against imperialism' (Sternbach *et al.* 1992: 213). By the 1990s Latin American feminisms had proliferated and become more diverse in the new democratic context. For some feminists 'the heroic days of barricades and demonstrations seem to be over, at least for the time being', and some even argue that 'there is no longer a women's movement ... democracy co-opted the feminist discourse and demobilized the movement' (cited in Alvarez 1998: 305).

Of course not all women engaged in social movements are feminists, and from the 1980s onwards there was a flourishing of activity by *mujeres populares* (working-class women) in a myriad of social and political movements. Women have been the mainstay of community organization both under the dictatorships and in the era of structural adjustment since then. Women had come to the fore of the struggle for human rights (see below) and the empowerment this created was generalized to some extent. As repression and poverty ground down poor communities, so women began organizing alternative communal methods of food provision and preparation. The *ollas populares* (communal pots), for example, were large outdoor dining-halls which effectively subverted the private/public divide as well as filling a very real social need. In a whole range of social and economic activities women began to take a leading role under the dictatorships and continued and expanded their roles later.

In 30 years of activity, Latin American feminism has made considerable gains in spite of the diversity of its component parts today. Gender
issues have become politicized in Latin America as never before, and the
days of unchallenged 'machismo' are over in most countries. For
Lievesley, it is clear that, while the state and political parties must now
take account of the 'gender agenda', on the whole 'the aim has been to
manage women by appropriating the language of the women's agenda'
(Lievesley 1999: 142) with the objective of 'sanitizing' them. That is
certainly the case and we should not read too much into the emeregence
of the few female presidents who have come to office (Violeta Chamorro
in Nicaragua after the Sandinistas, for example), or the smattering of
women in the upper echelons of political parties. However, if we take a
broad social view of gender relations as a whole we do see the permanent and prominent role of women in community politics and in all the
radical movements for social change such as, notably, the Workers' Party
in Brazil.

 'Race' and 'ethnicity' are other axes along which autonomous new
social movements have formed in Latin America. Some of these go back
to the 1920s but they really began to flourish from the mid 1960s
onwards. They worked on the basis that modernity and development had
signally failed for blacks and the indigenous peoples. Citizenship certainly was seen as an empty word in societies cut across by all forms of
racism, discrimination and oppression. Official state pledges towards
multiculturalism – even pious affirmations of our 'indigenous cultures' –
meant little to poor, marginalized and socially excluded populations.
Even ostensibly revolutionary states, such as the Sandinistas in
Nicaragua, found it hard to deal with the demands of their indigenous
populations. In the development of social movements based on race and
ethnicity we see a very strong role for culture and the construction of
identity, but that does not mean that material conditions – land and
poverty – are not also an integral element of this resistance.

There are major black social movements in Brazil and Colombia. In
Brazil the 'new' black movements emerged in the late 1970s with the
'decompression' of the military dictatorship, and alongside the new
labour, environmental and women's movements. International influences,
particularly from African-Americans, were considerable and the cultural
identity element predominated. The history of resistance by black
Brazilians was recovered and there was active participation by black
activists in the emerging Workers' Party. There was also a flourishing of
Afro-Brazilian culture and music in particular, not to mention the influential hybrid religious practices of *candomblé* and *macumba* in which

African deities merged with Christian saints. What is probably most akin to the 'new' social movements is the diversity of this movement. As Wade writes:

> Within all these organisations and groups, there is great debate about what weight to give class, race, gender and so on as organising, mobilising principles – should blacks seek to participate in national political structures along class lines, or work against these through socialism, or focus on reaffirming black identity above all else. (Wade 1997: 97)

The indigenous social movements are most active in Central America and in the Andean countries. In Guatemala in particular there has been a strong pan-Mayan movement since the mid 1980s committed to indigenous cultural revitalization. In Ecuador the 'new' indigenous movement of the 1990s has been probably the most important national social movement in that country. It is particularly interesting because it highlights the tension between class and ethnicity in the generation of social movements. According to the leaders of this movement in Ecuador:

> There were two visions: the indigenist cultural vision, focused on bilingual education, and the class vision, focused on land conflicts. The two merged when we realized we could not have our culture without land. (Cited in Selverston 1999: 176)

While there is a line of continuity between this type of movement and the great indigenous revolts against the Spanish conquest, we undoubtedly have a new situation today. The modern indigenous movement is fighting against social exclusion and for a model of development which is sustainable both socially and ecologically.

We turn now to the human-rights movement that became a new feature of political life in Latin America under the dictatorships. A new ideological dimension entered Latin American politics, namely the ethical element and the need to respect certain fundamental social values. As regimes tortured, imprisoned and 'disappeared' their own citizens, so the demand for life became paramount and non-negotiable as other political demands might be. What seemed a rather naïve humanist assertion went to the very core of the military ideology and its attempt to cow civil society into silence. This was a movement quite distinct from that of Western liberal defence of established human rights. As Marta Sondereguer put it: 'Human rights are no longer what we had before, and must respect, but that which comes later and must be constructed. They become a horizon, a utopia' (Sondereguer 1985: 11). Appealing to old, even traditional or conservative values, the human-rights movement introduced a very new, effective and ethical dimension into Latin American politics.

Apart from the Co-Madres in El Salvador, which was inspired by the liberation theology of the murdered Archbishop Romero, it was the Mothers of the Plaza de Mayo in Argentina who most clearly symbolized the new human-rights movement in Latin America. In 1977 these mothers and grandmothers of the 'disappeared' began a silent weekly protest outside government house in the Plaza de Mayo. Wearing white handkerchiefs on their heads they were at first dubbed 'crazy' (*Las Locas*), but they gradually gained influence both at home and internationally, so much so that the regime took the extreme measure of 'disappearing' some of them. Interestingly, in terms of what makes up a new social movement, the Madres argued that they were not making a political point but a moral one. Rather than seeing politics as 'the art of the possible', as it usually is, the Mothers argued that 'For us nothing is possible if there are no ethics in political decisions.' This was certainly new in Latin American politics, and for social movements generally.

The Madres were, understandably, disenchanted with politics and politicians. In the early days of the military dictatorship, fear gripped the political class and much of society as many turned a blind eye to the repression. The Madres made a clear ethical point about the right to life; they effectively held to account not only the regime but also the opposition parties who, more or less, held up their hands in despair. What is also clear is that it showed up the limitations of a patriarchal logic in politics. Marching alone in small groups around a square seemed ineffective and futile, but as the Madres argued:

> What happened was that the men applied masculine logic – this won't lead to anything, this won't lead anywhere, such a thing is impossible. This strange phenomenon of mothers meeting to create a kind of group awareness, which gradually put pressure on the power structure did not fit into their logic. (Cited in Carmen Feijoo and Gogna 1990: 91)

But it did fit into the logic of democratization and human rights and henceforth it was a major part of the international agenda when dealing with Latin America.

Another major landmark in the development of a human-rights regime in Latin America was the arrest of General Pinochet in London in 1998 (see Box 7.4). Prompted by an extradition warrant from a Spanish judge who was seeking to prosecute Pinochet for the murder of Spanish citizens, the English Law Lords were given a difficult problem. Henceforth

Box 7.4   General Pinochet visits London

In October 1998 General Pinochet the former military dictator of Chile was arrested in London on account of an extradition warrant from a Spanish judge investigating human-rights crimes in relation to Spanish nationals during the dictatorship. The first judicial ruling in the English courts was that Pinochet enjoyed sovereign immunity for any actions committed while exercising the duties of office. A while later, on appeal, the House of Lords issued a landmark ruling which in essence determined that murder and torture are not the functions of a head of state and thus did not enjoy immunity from prosecution. A third panel of Law Lords in March 1999 ruled quite categorically that crimes against humanity cancelled out the traditional immunity enjoyed by heads of state. From now on sovereign immunity would not mean sovereign impunity (Burbach 2005).

Pinochet was to be handed over to the Spanish courts but the British home secretary intervened and allowed him to return to Chile on humanitarian rather than legal grounds. What happened subsequently in Chile was extremely significant in terms of the evolution of a human-rights culture in the whole of Latin America. Gradually the fear of Pinochet, his generals and the long night of the dictatorship subsided. The government did not move decisively on the human-rights front but it did begin to support human-rights actions in the courts whereas before it took a 'hands off' stance. The armed forces themselves began to accept that Pinochet would have to stand trial for his crimes against human rights. Pinochet was stripped of his immunity by the Supreme Court in 2000 and was forced to face charges relating to his repressive rule. In 2002 the socialist politician Michelle Bachelet was made minister of defence, which brought back the past and her father's death at Pinochet's hands. In 2006 Pinochet died with few friends left and the democratic government of now President Bachelet dispensed with the customary state burial for him and thus also truly buried the dictatorship and its legacy.

the notion of national sovereignty and political immunity for ex-presidents (even illegal ones) had prevailed. Reflecting the changing international climate it was ruled that Pinochet's crimes against humanity committed in Chile were something he would be held accountable for abroad. The fact that the ex-dictator was eventually allowed to return to Chile on the grounds of ill-health could not alter the fact that, henceforth, human rights were inalienable, international and legally binding. Within Chile and Latin America generally, Pinochet's enforced stay in London had a hugely encouraging effect. Human rights were not only a 'new' social movement; they were now part of a global movement to counter their abuse.

Finally, we turn to the environmental movements which, to the international observer, are probably most prominent given the Amazon rainforest issue and the famous Rio Conference of 1992. The environment is seen to transcend politics, certainly class politics, and is even seen as 'above' politics. In that sense it is seen as a new issue which takes social movements beyond left and right in political terms. However, there is also a Third-World ecologism which stresses much more the Western and capitalist nature of development. Thus the ecological movement is driven in an anti-imperialist direction. In one variant, environmentalism stresses indigenous culture and the harm done to or by contact with the West. Environmentalism in the Third World – and for example in the Andean countries – thus links with indigenous peoples in promoting an alternative development model. Elsewhere in Latin America there have been environmental movements which like some of the feminist movements have mirrored the new movements of the West in the way they are oriented.

In Venezuela there is a long-standing concern with the environment, probably not unrelated to it being an oil-producing country and, in its heyday, quite prosperous. When oil prices collapsed in the 1980s the economic crisis was also an environmental one as ways 'beyond oil' were sought. In a similar way, when the tin market collapsed Bolivia was also hit by a drought which drastically reduced food production. The response of the largely urban environmental movement in Venezuela was to promote the notion that 'small is beautiful', very much along the lines of the international new environmental movement. There was no attempt to set up a political party and there was a rejection of an idea that political power was necessary to change things. Instead, the alternative environmental movement sought a general greening of public opinion and the political culture. Though legislation has been passed to protect the environment in Venezuela, the environmental movement has not made significant links with other sectors.

The environmental movement in Brazil inevitably has a distinct focus compared with the international movement to protect the environment. Much of the agenda of Western environmentalism seems irrelevant to an Amazonian rubber-tapper or the indigenous peoples of the area. The founder of the Brazilian Green Party, Fernando Gabeira, has recognized that in Brazil it is necessary to struggle against pollution and misery at the same time, even coining a new word '*poliséria*' (pollution/misery) to encapsulate that orientation. A case for 'no growth' or even 'conservation' cuts little ice in a country where development (economic and social) is so pressing. Of course, desertification is itself detrimental to social development and hence environmentalism can be made relevant. Here it is a case of a new social movement transforming itself and reaching out to make alliances with the poor and dispossessed of Brazil to create a genuinely socially sustainable growth model.

In conclusion, we can say that social movements (old, new and old/new) in Latin America can potentially deepen and enrich democracy. What this myriad of diverse voices might have in common is a radical democratic impetus. The days when it was thought that 'seizing the state' could resolve all social problems are well and truly over. However, there is no hard-and-fast distinction between social movements pursuing 'identity' questions and those pursuing material improvements. Clearly one needs to have some identity to form a social movement, and pursuing collective material objectives is an excellent way to forge identity. It might be said that the long era of military dictatorships and the social disaster of the new economic model had one good effect in so far as they helped unleash a series of transformative and liberatory social and political projects. These are now embattled and often fighting for survival but they will almost certainly play an active role in ensuring democratic governance in Latin America in the decades to come. The rich tapestry of Latin America's social movements also serves as inspiration for others across the globe concerned with developing a sustainable and more democratic alternative to neo-liberal globalization.

8
Culture

In Latin America, perhaps more than elsewhere, culture is political and politics are cultural. This chapter takes culture to mean more than the arts and the theatre, and to embrace the whole process whereby we make sense of our lives and produce the meanings that configure our social worlds. Cultural politics thus refers to the struggles individuals and social groups engage in over meanings and representations. Cultural politics is, above all, about identity, the ways in which we constitute our sense of ourselves. This chapter begins with a broad overview of the ideologies for change and transformation which have influenced postwar Latin America. It then turns to the role of religion in society, focusing particularly on the influential 'Theology of Liberation' and recent religious trends. Next we turn our attention to the so-called literary boom of the 1970s (Gabriel García Marquez, among others), which helped put Latin America on the world cultural map. Finally we examine various facets of contemporary popular culture, from the famous *telenovelas* (TV soaps) to the carnival.

Ideologies of Change

After what we now know as Latin America was conquered by Spanish and Portuguese colonialists, the main driver for social change was their particular conception of civilization. This ideology is perhaps best encapsulated in the works of Argentina's famous president/writer Domingo Faustino Sarmiento's (1811–88), especially his *Facundo* (sometimes known as *Civilisation or Barbarism?*) of 1845. Sarmiento epitomized the European ethic of progress as he saw it, against the practically illiterate gaucho of the pampas. The European nation would prevail over the American one through universal education on the one hand, and a ruthless extermination of the indigenous peoples on the other (the infamous *Conquest of the Desert*). For Sarmiento the civilization/barbarism divide was absolute (see Box 8.1).

In Brazil, Euclides da Cunha (1866–1909) wrote the epic *Os Sertões* (Revolt in the Backlands) in 1902 with a similar theme of civilization

Box 8.1 *Civilization or Barbarism?* (Domingo Faustino Sarmiento, 1845)

The city man dresses in European clothes, lives a civilized life ... [in the city] are the laws, the ideas of progress, the means of instruction, municipal organization, regular government, etc. When one leaves the city area everything changes. The country-man wears different clothes which I will call American ... his needs are limited. They seem to be two different societies, two nations foreign to one another.

The Argentine cities, like almost all the cities of South America, have an appearance of regularity. Their streets are laid out at right angles, and their population scattered over a wide surface, except in Cordoba, which occupies a narrow and confined position, and presents all the appearance of a European city, the resemblance being increased by the multitude of towers and domes attached to its numerous and magnificent churches. All civilization, whether native, Spanish or European, centres in the cities, where are to be found the manufactures, the shops, the schools and colleges, and other characteristics of civilized nations.

The whole remaining population inhabits the open country, which, whether wooded or destitute of the larger plants, is generally level, and almost everywhere occupied by pastures, in some places of such abundance and excellence, that the grass of an artificial meadow would not surpass them ...

Moral progress, and the cultivation of the intellect, are here not only neglected, as in the Arab or Tartar tribe, but impossible. Where can a school be placed for the instruction of children living ten leagues apart in all directions? Thus, consequently, civilization can in no way be brought about. Barbarism is the normal condition ...

Country life, then, has developed all the physical but none of the intellectual powers of the gaucho. His moral character is of the quality to be expected from his habit of triumphing over the obstacles and forces of nature; it is strong, haughty, and energetic. Without instruction, and indeed without need of any, without means of support as without wants, he is happy in the midst of his poverty and privations, which are not such to one who never knew nor wished for greater pleasure than are his already.

Source: Sarmiento (1961: 29–32; my translation).

versus barbarism. In this work the republic's army under its positivist banners of 'Order and Progress' faces the peasant revolt of Canudos in the impoverished north-east of Brazil. The modern bureaucratic army eventually defeats the guerrilla army of the peasants with its local knowledge and messianic faith, but only after suffering severely at its hands.

Imbued with the notion of the white man's civilizing mission, da Cunha cannot stop himself from empathizing with their *mestizo* (mixed-race) opponents. Modernization, even the civilization of the European, is shown to be cruel and their notion of 'progress' somewhat empty. Likewise Sarmiento could not avoid a sneaking admiration for the freedom of gaucho life in the pampas. The fine poem of gaucho life *Martín Fierro* (by José Hernandez in 1872) was not only about social justice but firmly rebutted the assumed cultural superiority of Sarmiento's civilizing mission, albeit after the defeats in the battlefield were completed.

In the early twentieth century a reaction to the Eurocentric notions of civilization occurred with a celebration of Latin American 'otherness'. The Uruguayan writer José Rodo (1871–1917) published his influential essay *Ariel* in 1900. Its symbolism, based on Shakespeare's *Tempest*, posed Latin America as Ariel, the noble winged spirit, against the North American, gross Caliban, standing for cultural barbarism. Ariel's spiritual anti-imperialism, to call it that, had considerable influence in the rest of the century in spite of its elitist vision of materialism as mediocrity. The heritage of Ariel is taken up in the contemporary era by the idealized magical realism of *macondismo* (based on Gabriel García Marquez's mythical village of Macondo, on which see 'The Literary Boom', below). European and North American instrumental rationality is rejected by *macondismo* in favour of a specifically Latin American form of rationality based on magical realism, but somewhat undefined. In terms of cultural politics we see here a form of 'nativism' contesting the imported Euro-US ideologies of change based on order and progress.

In the postwar period, cultural politics continued to resonate in the literary domain but for many the epicentre lay in the social and political sciences which grappled with the question of Latin America's 'difference' or, more bluntly, underdevelopment. Where the US-sponsored modernization theory saw integration with the world economy as the *sine qua non* of development, the dependency approach argued for disengagement and the formulation of a national 'non-dependent' development path. In terms of cultural politics, the dependency school denounced what it called 'cultural dependency' on the USA that led Latin American countries to constantly chase after a consumerist mirage. The dominance by transnational corporations was seen to lead to national disintegration in Latin America, in economic, social and cultural terms. The model for breaking with dependency was seen as Cuba, which in the 1960s set about economic diversification, political radicalization and the export of its revolution to the rest of Latin America through its support for various guerrilla movements.

By the late 1970s and definitively in the 1980s, the dependency approach in economic strategy and cultural politics began to lose purchase on reality. Many factors led to the effective demise of the 'strong' version of dependency theory: Cuba was no longer so attractive given the clearly evident traits of political authoritarianism, nor was it a credible alternative for large industrialized countries such as Mexico, Brazil or Argentina; and further afield the success of the East Asian 'tiger' economies showed in clear empirical fashion that integration with the world economy was not inimical to economic development on the periphery. There were also internal flaws with the dependency approach that tended to neglect internal social and political factors given its emphasis on the external dimension. Ultimately, though, the dependency approach failed politically as the various military interventions (see Chapter 2) and most notably the Chilean coup of 1973 put paid to the idea of a democratic space where the cultural politics of dependency theory could flourish and be put into practice.

Dependency was not just a mode of socio-economic analysis; it also motivated and legitimized a hugely influential political ideology of change based on the Cuban Revolution of 1959. Guerrilla movements inspired by the Cuban example, and more specifically its charismatic supporter from Argentina, Ché Guevara, sprung up across the continent in the 1960s and early 1970s. The choice was clear: 'Liberation or Dependency'. This was clearly a cultural politics as much as (or more than) a military move to seize power. The example of the heroic guerrilla would ignite a popular insurgency according to the 'Guevarist' ideology for change that dominated radical thinking for a decade or more. Yet, except for Central America, these movements not only did not come close to power; they also failed to significantly alter the political process. The military regimes of the late 1970s and early 1980s eventually buried all hopes for revolutionary transformation along the lines of the 'all or nothing' of the Cuban-inspired revolutionary generation.

The general mood changed in the 1980s: 'If revolution was the articulating axis of the Latin American debate in the 1960s, in the 1980s the central theme is *democracy*' (Lechner 1986: 33). The quasi-religious conceptions of politics on the left was replaced by a new, more democratic pluralism as politics was, in cultural terms, desacralized, that is shorn of its religious fervour. The megalomaniac vision of the military rulers like Pinochet and Videla made the left more sceptical of its own previous confidence in a future of its own making. Now the future seemed more uncertain. The concept of difference became more widely accepted and cultural politics were less dominated by the notion that adversaries should be liquidated. Civil society was rediscovered in all its diversity and political divisions were no longer quite so categorical. The failure of the dependency-inspired absolutist vision gave way to a more open-ended radical democratic approach and a less restrictive cultural politics.

The unitary focus of the dependency approach shattered, other ideologies of change emerged, often based on what is called 'identity politics'. These new collective identities of the ecological, gender, sexual politics, ethnic, human-rights and other social groups inevitably took a cultural form. Because, as Alvarez *et al.* explain, 'In their continuous struggles against the dominant projects of nation building, development and repression, popular actors mobilize collectively on the basis of very different sets of meanings and stakes' (Alvarez *et al.* 1998: 6). The various social groups establish meaning for their position in society through a cultural politics; that is how their identities are built and their ideologies for change are developed and mobilized. Once the unified terms of 'Liberation or Dependency' were left behind, a whole series of social struggles emerged based on a discursive construction of identity where many alternative, minority or oppositional voices could be heard.

One of the most interesting ideologies of change to emerge in the 1980s and 1990s was that known as *neo-Indigenismo*. Reaffirming a specific sense of Meso-American identity, this tendency had a significant effect on the cultural politics of the region. Against all efforts at European 'civilization' (for which read assimilation), the various indigenous cultures of the Andean countries and Central America (including Mexico of course) seemed not only to be intact but even flourishing. Pre-Conquest identities were being posed as the basis for a future Latin American identity that was more attuned to the region's otherness. A linear notion of time, in which 'modernization' and other ideologies of change were based, was firmly rejected. Social reality and change were viewed less in anthropocentric (human-centred) terms and much more through a broader 'cosmocentric' vision. What *neo-Indigenismo* was providing was also a more genuinely alternative development approach than that articulated by dependency that, ultimately, was a mirror image of the Eurocentric modernization approach.

The ideologies of change we have very briefly surveyed here all inevitably address the question of 'what' Latin America is. As Vivian Schelling writes:

> Emerging out of the violence of conquest as a half-breed, mestizo culture, full of ambiguity, split between a dominant Europe and a

subordinate African and indigenous world, Latin America belongs not quite anywhere, its search for identity necessarily following a labyrinthine path. (Schelling 2000: 9)

From Sarmiento through to *neo-Indigenismo*, the various ideologies of change come back to the question of what sort of society Latin America is and should be. There is no doubt about the continent's 'hybridity' – partly American (with an African element), partly European – and resistant to easy categorization. In directly political terms the final ebbing of the revolutionary wave that began in the 1960s has given way to a generalized but rather disenchanted democracy (see Chapter 2). In the wake of neoliberalism's apparent collapse as an economic model (see Chapter 3), we can confidently expect new ideologies of change to emerge in the period to come (see Chapter 5).

Religion and Society

The 'conquest' of Latin America and the subjugation of indigenous peoples were carried out in the name of religion, specifically Catholicism. Economic plunder was complemented by a drive for cultural supremacy in which religion played a key role. Many years later in the early 1980s the military dictators of Argentina would claim they were operating on behalf of 'Christian' values against the atheistic 'communist' threat. Yet in Latin America priests have died in guerrilla uprisings, most notably Camilo Torres in Colombia in 1966, and movements for social change have been inspired by radical versions of Christianity. The oppressed indigenous peoples in the end accepted Christianity but through a process of 'syncretism' (the unification or reconciliation of different schools of thought), which incorporated it within their own traditional cosmovisions. The dominance of Catholicism has also been more openly confronted in recent years by the remarkable rise of Pentecostalism on the one hand and the revival of the African-inspired faiths and rituals of Umbanda and Candomblé on the other (see below).

The 1960s were a period of great turmoil in the Catholic churches of Latin America. The Second Vatican Council announced a new policy of renewal and openness (within limits) of the Catholic church, and in Latin America the 'option for the poor' was expressed most clearly in the Medellín document of 1968. While the Vatican had carried out its own 'perestroika', it had not really addressed the question of poverty and social inequality centrally. Medellín, however, was the starting point of a new 'Theology of Liberation', which viewed inequality as a 'rejection of God's peace'. Real, or social, liberation was now to be as central for the radical Christian as the theological concept of salvation through God. To overcome or redeem the original sin and to be able to live fully in the 'Kingdom of God' political liberation was essential. The distance from a church that had nearly always sided with the state was clearest in the oft-repeated phrase of this period that 'the struggle for liberation is a holy one'. This was a crucial Latin American contribution to global theological discourse.

The term 'Theology of Liberation' may be a vague one but it did signal a veritable cultural revolution in the Catholic church. To even join the terms theology and liberation together was shocking to a complacent Christian world view. Religion was being viewed quite sensibly as a form of cultural politics and not as a separate or private domain. Its socioeconomic framework was unambiguously based on dependency theory, then in its heyday. While being modernizers in the Catholic church, the Liberation Theology thinkers were opponents of modernization 'made in USA' in the economic, political and cultural variants. The Christian duty was henceforth defined as struggling for a 'just society' and for the creation of a 'new man'. The influence of this radical church has been mainly seen in Brazil, but it was also extremely influential in the revolutionary uprisings of Central America in the 1980s. In Chile a more muted (or reformist) version of this radical thinking made the Catholic church into one of the most solid and consistent opponents of the Pinochet dictatorship (see Box 8.2).

What the radical Catholic church meant in practice varied from country to country. Where it probably had most impact on social movements for change was in Brazil, especially through the CEB (Communidades Eclesiais de Base, or 'base communities'). Designed to provide an active role for the laity, the CEBs at their height involved over 2 million people in Brazil compared with around only 10 000 in Chile. They had local leaders and built up a genuine sense of community in pursuit of a church committed to social justice. As David Lehman writes: 'The informal church [as he calls the CEB and associated strands] has provided an institutional and ideological framework for popular movements after the decline or repression of Marxism' (1990: 147). Indeed, it is impossible to conceive of the movements for social change in Brazil, such as the Workers' Party and the Landless Movement, without understanding the critical cultural and political role of its radical Catholic church. Much the same could be said for Central America.

The shift in the cultural politics of the Catholic church can be seen most clearly in a comparison of the 'religious question' in Cuba and Nicaragua. Until quite recently, as with the Pope's visit in 1998, the Cuban Revolution had a standoff, if not hostile, relationship with the Catholic church. There was a general belief in the Marxist view that religion was a compensation for the self-alienation of capitalism, the need for which would simply disappear under communism. In Nicaragua, on the other hand, throughout the revolutionary period the Sandinistas were deeply imbued with Liberation Theology ideas and religious participation in the revolution was extremely visible. While in Cuba religious beliefs (particularly Afro-American ones) were viewed as superstition, in Nicaragua there was a genuine symbiosis between Sandinismo and the radical strand of Catholicism. Then, of course, in the Cuba of the early 1960s there was no cleric of the stature and radicalism of Archbishop Romero (murdered by the regime in El Salvador in 1980) who was symbolic of a committed and engaged church.

While, overall, Catholicism remains the dominant faith in Latin America, there was, in the last decade of the twentieth century, a remarkable flourishing of evangelical Protestantism, particularly of Pentecostalism. It is estimated that by the turn of the century some 15 per cent of the population were Pentecostals in many countries, which would mean 20 million faithful in Brazil alone. Though politically conservative, Pentecostalism is, in social terms, a church of the poor. For some writers, like David Martin (1990), Pentecostalism represents a penetration of Anglo-Saxon modernity into the Iberian-Catholic culture of Latin America. Many on the left see Pentecostalism, or at least similar sects, as just the latest variant of cultural imperialism. Such a broad-brush view, whether in support or opposition, hardly recognises the complexity of the Pentecostalist 'revolution'. It is necessary to recognize at the start that this is a quite particular form of Protestantism and one which has found roots in the local popular culture, in particular through its powerful oral tradition.

Pentecostalism, at its strongest in Mexico and Brazil, is a religion of the urban poor and of women in particular. A charismatic branch of Protestantism, it focuses hugely on faith-healing, which at least in part explains its appeal given the incidence of poverty-related illness in the shanty towns of Latin America. For Andrew Chestnut, Pentecostalism has become Latin America's most dynamic popular religion because 'Pentecostal proselytization methods and liturgy evolved through the different eras of growth, but the core of the message remained unchanged: "Accept Jesus as your saviour and you will be healed"'

Box 8.2   Liberation theology

Liberation theology was a term originating from Latin America in the early 1970s to signify that the Catholic church should focus on liberating the people from poverty and oppression. The Second Vatican Council and the 1967 papal encyclical *Popularum Progressio* encouraged these moves but its roots were firmly Latin American. Given the social and political turmoil of the era even the Catholic hierarchy of Latin America felt compelled to go along with the new radical theology. A landmark event was the 1968 conference of bishops in Medellín, Colombia, which declared among other things that:

> We wish to affirm that it is indispensable to form a social conscience and a realistic perception of the problems of the community and of social structures. We must awaken the social conscience and communal customs in all strata of society and professional groups regarding such values as dialogue and community living within the same group and relations with wider social groups (workers, peasants, professionals, clergy, religious, administrators, etc.).
>   This task of '*concientización*' and social education ought to be integrated into joint pastoral action at various levels. (Medellín Conference Documents: Justice and Peace)

For liberation theology, religion was not a system of timeless truths that simply required repetition and systematization. Theology needed to be dynamic and to engage with 'praxis' with regard to the social context. Theological truth was not a pre-given but could only be discovered in a particular historical context and through personal participation in the struggles of the people. In practice the liberation theologians in Latin America 'bought into' the then emerging dependency analysis. Thus they saw Latin America as having been victimized by imperialism, colonialism and the multinational corporations. They made a conscious option for socialism as the only path out of dependence, exploitation and misery.

→

(Chestnut 1997: 48). The new economic model (Chapter 3) has provided a surplus of the pathogens of poverty which Pentecostalism responds to. A neo-Pentecostalism (the transnational Universal Church of the Kingdom of God) has since emerged based (paradoxically or not) on a syncretizing or merger with Umbanda on the one hand, and a television-driven hype redolent of the US evangelist tradition.

Another competitor of the Roman Catholic church is represented by the various Afro-American cults such as Santería in the Caribbean and Umbanda in Brazil. Umbanda has a similar conception of good and evil to that of Catholicism, but this is fused with African religious elements

→

Where they parted company with orthodox Marxists was in arguing that human liberation had a spiritual dimension going beyond economic freedom.

From one example among many we can take the 1980 statement of the Brazilian Catholic church in relation to the land question. We need to recall that hundreds of priests have been murdered by rapacious landowners for having assisted rural families in their struggle for justice. The statement explains in part the doctrinal foundation for the belief that 'The Land is God's Gift for all People' and then goes onto argue that:

> God continues to watch over the people ... And God challenges us: How can we bring it about that the earth may belong to all? How can we assure that the dignity of the human person be respected? How can we bring it about that Brazilian society overcome institutionalized injustice and reject political options opposed to the gospel? We believe the challenges here formulated are positive. However, we are aware that without concrete actions to respond to these challenges, the Church will not be a sign of God's love for human beings. Hence: (1)As a first gesture, we want to place the problem of the possession and use of the Church's property under scrutiny and re-examine constantly its pastoral and social purpose, avoiding speculation in real estate and respecting the rights of those who work on the land. (2)We commit ourselves to denounce patently unjust situations and the violence perpetrated in the areas of our dioceses and prelatures and to combat the causes that produce such injustices and violence, in fidelity to the Puebla commitments. (3)We reaffirm our support for the just initiatives and organizations of workers, placing our energies and our means at the service of their cause, in conformity with those same commitments. Without replacing the people's initiatives, our pastoral activity will stimulate conscious and critical participation by workers in unions, associations, and commissions, as well as other kinds of cooperation, so that their organizations may be really independent and free, defending the interests and coordinating the demands of their members and their whole class. (*The Church and the Problem of Land*, 1980)

and some Amerindian ones in a spiritist discourse practising homoeopathy and faith-healing. Unlike the Pentecostals, Umbanda spiritual leaders do not frown on alcohol – in fact one spirit, Cabocla Mariana, seems to personify its virtues. Another influential cult of possession is Candomblé, which does not draw a hard-and-fast distinction between good and evil and has a much less diluted African heritage than Umbanda. In Candomblé, the followers are active participants through the lives of the male and female deities they follow. Through possession, the body of the follower expresses the character of the divinity and also leaves the profane world for a sacred one. For the urban poor, as for the slaves before, these cults offer some refuge from a hostile environment. A plurality of religious faiths has not necessarily led to peaceful coexistence and mutual tolerance. On the contrary, most faiths accuse each other of being false paths to spirituality and advance their own version as the 'one true path'. We have noted theological and social points in common, but ultimately competition (as befits the neo-liberal era) seems to prevail. José Jorge de Carvalho notes that religious 'interfaces are increasingly frequent, and because of this the language of fraud, deceit, the false and the inauthentic becomes the shadow of contemporary religious cosmopolitanism' (Carvalho 2001: 286). The repression and intolerance of old is replaced by an unbridled cultural political competition. The Universal Church of the Kingdom of God, for example, has made intensive and fervent use of TV and open-air rallies to denounce what its adherents consider to be the exorcism rituals of Umbanda and Candomblé. Of course, among the poor these social communities of faith are the most active competitors of the neo-Pentecostals, so this fundamentalist attack is not surprising.

Religion, in various forms, undoubtedly plays a major role in the cultural politics of Latin America and will continue to do so, trends towards secularization notwithstanding. The Catholic faith, in its Amerindian as much as its Iberian idioms, continues to hold huge cultural significance. The rise of Pentecostalism is not a simple expression of 'modernization' (as in a crude application of Max Weber's Protestant ethic theory), but it does reflect the massive social and economic changes of recent decades. The Afro-American faiths can be expected to flourish and there is a revival of traditional indigenous cosmovisions as well to consider. Poverty and oppression create the need for a cultural framework to understand and 'live' them, and religion as a form of cultural politics provides this in varying ways. If Marx is often quoted as dismissing religion as the 'opium of the people', it is well to remember that he also considered it to be a 'sigh of the oppressed'.

The Literary Boom

In the 1960s, Latin America's literary boom, or the 'New Novel', placed the continent's literature firmly on the world map. There are very few literary people in the North who have not at least heard of Gabriel García Marquez, Mario Vargas Llosa or maybe Isabel Allende. The literary, political and cultural significance of this literary boom is disputed but its impact has undoubtedly been a major one.

Box 8.3   Julio Cortázar (1914–84)

Cortázar was born in Brussels but returned to Buenos Aires (Argentina) with his diplomat family when he was 4 years old. In 1944 he became professor of French literature at the national University of Cuyo (Mendoza) but in 1951 he emigrated to Paris in opposition to the government of Juán Domingo Perón which he found inimical as did his compatriot Jorge Luis Borges. From 1952 onwards he worked as a translator for UNESCO, with Edgar Allan Poe, a strong influence on his own work, among his projects. Among his most notable works are *Los Premios* (The Prizes; 1965), *Rayuela* (Hopscotch; 1966), *El libro de Manuel* (A Manual for Manuel; 1978) and *Nicaragua tan violentamente dulce* (Nicaragua So Violently Sweet; 1983). Carlos Fuentes called him 'the Simón Bolívar' of the novel.

Rayuela is a dazzling literary experiment that influenced Gabriel García Marquez and Mario Vargas Llosa among other leading lights of the 1960s literary boom in Latin America. Its open-ended structure asks the reader to choose between a linear and a non-linear structure. Its striking stream-of-consciousness idiom is reminiscent of the improvized jazz aesthetic. His innovative and poetic use of language is balanced by a fine sense of humour and of the absurd. Of the book's 155 chapters, the last 99 are deemed expendable by Cortázar and he allows us to progress from chapter 1 to chapter 56 or by 'hopscotching' across the book following a table he provides. All this profoundly alters the experience of reading in ways that 'metafiction' (not yet then named) wants us to do in literary studies. Cortázar greatly expanded what it means to write and tell a story at a very early stage.

Reading: Cortázar (1966).

As Gerald Martin explains:

> Each of the great 'boom' novels of the 1960s was about some kind of quest and about the nature of Latin American identity; each also provided a metaphor for the course of Latin American history; they were also linguistically exploratory and structurally mythological. (1998: 191)

To put flesh on this bold and complex diagnosis we shall turn to some of the major exponents of the literary boom, namely Julio Cortazar (Argentina/Paris), Carlos Fuentes (Mexico), Mario Vargas Llosa (Peru) and the undisputed leader of the pack, Gabriel García Marquez from Colombia.

Julio Cortazar (1914–83) was born in Argentina but spent much of his adult life in Paris. His literary mission was the exploration of Latin American identity and his inspiration was undoubtedly James Joyce and his revolutionary literary techniques. His most famous novel *Rayuela* (Hopscotch) appeared in 1963 and immediately achieved a huge impact. Based on a comparison of two cities over here and over there, *Rayuela* is a bold rejection of Eurocentric rationality and rediscovery of America. It is no simple nativist text, however, and it is suffused with surrealist themes. Cortazar refuses a linear logic and revels in the revolt against convention. He seeks not to impart truths but to make the reader explore and discover new cultural political horizons. A firm supporter of the Cuban Revolution, Cortazar was an engaged writer but he refused the role of 'political' writer. He is clearly the author most admired by the big-three writers of the boom – Fuentes, Varga Llosa and García Marquez.

The work of Carlos Fuentes (born 1928) is inseparable from the history of the Mexican Revolution and the travails of Mexican identity. Perhaps his major work, *La Muerte de Artemio Cruz* (The Death of Artemio Cruz) appeared in 1962 and focused on the conscience of a 'new man' of the post-revolutionary era. His idealism has foundered in the swamp of the contemporary political system, and cynicism rules his life. The Mexican Revolution is seemingly being observed from the perspective of the then young Cuban Revolution, literally as Fuentes wrote *Artemio Cruz* partly in La Habaña. It was an early announcement of the death of the Mexican Revolution that finally occurred with the Tlatelolco massacre of 1968 when the government ordered the slaughter of protesting students on the eve of the Olympic Games. There is realism aplenty in this novel as a rendering of Mexico's long post-revolutionary democratic decline, but it is also brilliant and audacious, prefiguring the term 'magical' which would come to describe the boom novel in Latin America.

A later novel, *Christopher Unborn*, achieved little of the notoriety of *Artemio Cruz*, but is significant as a turn beyond modernism towards postmodernism. In it the author deconstructs the notion of totality that predominates in the modernist novel. It speaks in many languages: 'listen: here you can hear the politico, the ideologue, the comic, the powerful, the weak ... but also history, society, language itself' (Fuentes 1990: 256). His cannibalistic use of language seeks to subvert cultural hegemony in the Spanish/English borderland he inhabits. Compared with his earlier work, *Christopher Unborn* is more self-con-sciously against the fundamentalism of nationalism: 'Mexicans we are because we are progressive because we are revolutionary because we are liberal because we are reformists ... because we are Spaniards because we are Indians because we are *mestizos*' (Fuentes 1990: 153–4). Emblematic of a peripheral postmodernism, this novel is a bridge between the modernism of the boom proper and the new postmodern novel of the neo-liberal era.

Mario Vargas Llosa (born in Peru in 1936) was not only a major figure of the boom, but has remained an internationally renowned writer to the present day as well as a somewhat more controversial politician. Following the success of his *La ciudad y los perros* (The City and the Dogs) of 1963, he wrote *La Casa Verde* (The Green House) in 1966 that is still a marvellously evocative rendering of the everyday lives and hopes of ordinary people in Latin America. In this novel he breaks with chronological time, which, instead, is shown as constantly shifting. For Jean Franco, through this device 'Vargas Llosa suggests the intricate weave and warp of existence with criss-crossing threads of relationships, with the conditioning of past actions on the present and the effect of time itself' (Franco 1970: 255). In terms of the broader cultural politics of Latin America, this weaves in with the analysis of mixed temporalities by which we refer to the uneven development of the continent which is, at one and the same time, premodern, modernizing and, in many ways, postmodern.

In political terms Vargas Llosa is a pessimist, which has led him perhaps, contrary to the strong left-wing flavour of the boom writers generally, to espouse right-wing politics. In his early *La ciudad y los perros*, the 'dogs' were the sordid and cruel inmates of a military academy where the middle class sent their sons to have 'discipline' installed in them. The city was a freer, more civilized space but, ultimately, the dogs would invade it. Equally bleak was his 1969 hit, *La conversación en la catedral* (Conversation in the Cathedral), which painted a picture of a squalid and unjust Latin American city (Lima). For 'Lima the horrible' there is no solution, or as Vargas Llosa puts it: 'Peru fucked up, Carlitos fucked up, everyone fucked up.' Other more popular, less political novels by Vargas Llosa (such as *La tía Julia*, or Aunt Julia) have been much lighter and have, for good reason, been popular among a wide range of readers.

With Gabriel García Marquez (born in Colombia in 1927) the Latin American boom novel undoubtedly reached a peak and became a global presence. And, if there is one text which signals the high point of his work it is the itself mythical novel *Cien años de soledad* (One Hundred Years of Solitude; 1967) which tells the story of the Buendía family in the mythical land of Macondo. Historical events, like the famous banana plantation workers strike of 1928, merge seamlessly with the most fantastic people and their doings. Cut off from the outside world, the Buendías exist in a condition of original innocence. Biblical-style natural disasters are then joined by evil brought from the outside which leads to death and destruction. Towards the end, the protagonist Aureliano Babilonia is able to decipher the reality he lived in; he 'breaks out of false circularities, meaningless repetitions, the prehistory before the dawn of true historical consciousness' (Martin 1998: 191).

Cien años appeared in the same year that Ché Guevara was killed in the jungles of Bolivia, which are not unlike the mythical Macondo for that matter. Politically progressive and stylistically advanced, this novel also marked a certain 'end of innocence' or the waning of optimism. The postwar period of economic development was coming to an end and the cycle of political authoritarianism was also opening up. The Cuban Revolution was no longer looking as fresh and attractive as it once had, with economic stagnation and political bureaucratization setting in. In seeking to unravel the magical reality of *Cien años* in Latin America, García Marquez seemed to have found a way out of the labyrinth of history. Unfortunately the euphoria of *Cien años* was to be short-lived, the definitive liberation of Latin America did not occur and the new dependency of neo-liberal globalization was already on the horizon.

The phrase used most widely to describe the style of the new Latin American novel of the 1960s is that of 'magical realism'. Although that term is by now a bit of a cliché in that it is oversimplified and overused, it is still useful shorthand. Originally 'magical realism' was applied to writers such as Alejo Carpentier (*Los pasos perdidos* – The Lost Steps), but it was subsequently generalized. Although he considers that the term may be 'ideologically dangerous', Gerald Martin defines it as something which is 'exotic and tropical, overblown and unrestrained, phantasmagorical and hallucinatory' (1998: 164). Related to surrealism, the term represents a break with the earlier modernist mood of social realism. The novels of the land of an earlier era were giving way to the theme of the labyrinth. The 'magical' note was, in part, a refusal of Western rationality and part a redefinition of Latin American identity in order to reclaim the indigenous and African elements of myth and belief.

After the 1960s, there was a move in cultural politics towards the postmodern and postcolonial as part of the post-boom mood. But the literary boom remained a significant landmark and its reverberations are still felt today. Postmodernism speaks about a decentred world and of a periphery which becomes more central. Yet this state of affairs does not seem so novel in Latin America. As Octavio Paz observed in his 1960s classic *El laberinto de la soledad* (The Labyrinth of Solitude):

> We had lived in the periphery of history. Today, the centre, the nucleus of world society has come apart and we have all become peripheral beings. We are all at the margins because there is no longer any centre. (Paz 1967: 152)

It is as though Latin America even while it struggled to modernize was already postmodern in some ways. The intricacies of magical realism and the transformation of cultural politics in Latin America through the literary boom of the 1960s made the continent a key element of global culture in the decades which followed.

Popular Culture

The notion of a popular culture is a contested one but it nevertheless points to a cluster of issues crucial to our understanding of cultural politics in Latin America. The main division is between those who regard popular culture as a part of resistance to the dominant cultural order, and those for whom it refers essentially to commercial or 'mass' culture. We can, of course, conceive of it in both senses. For Stuart Hall:

> [I]n one sense, popular culture has its base in the experiences, the pleasures, the memories, the traditions of the people but it also at the same time the scene, *par excellence*, of commodification of the industries where culture enters directly into the circuits of a dominant technology – the circuits of power and capital. (1996: 469)

In Latin America there is a general tendency to take culture in the first Gramscian sense in which it contests capitalist hegemony. In the shifting sands of cultural politics in Latin America today we inevitably also have to touch on the second sense of popular culture as a capitalist commodity.

As European settlers began to make a new 'Latin America', so they created a new popular culture. Many immigrants simply reproduced the culture and tradition of their home countries, but many became criollos (creoles) with a particular blend of Hispanic and indigenous customs. The image of the gaucho, at least in the Southern Cone, was often the archetypal presentation of this synthesis. The nascent mass media would take up the melancholy frustrations and resentments of the gaucho as representing the popular culture of the new urban masses. The musical element was provided by the tango, of uncertain, possibly African origins, which began to flourish in the 1920s and 1930s, an early example of Latin America's transnational cultural impact. The tango was, as Ferrer puts it: 'a constant and important cultural phenomenon, an indispensable element in the life of our people' (Ferrer 1960: 56). The tango at this time reflected the tensions, frustrations and aspirations of urban working-class life. It spoke to the social and economic uncertainties of the period and looked back to a simpler and more secure past.

From the 1930s through to the early 1960s it was the radio and the cinema which built a popular culture which was distinctively nationalist. The radio reached even the illiterate at first with the tango and the bolero that became 'massified'. It seemed that the traditional and modern merged in this new medium which went a long way to forging a national identity in the populist or statist era (see Chapter 2). As Martín-Barbero explains, in this period of populist modernization: 'the communications industries contributed to the gestation of a powerful Latin American imaginary made up of cinematographic (Maria Félix, Cantinflas) and musical (*tango, bolero, ranchera*) symbol' (Martín-Barbero 2000: 37). Latin American cinema achieved considerable presence during this period, with Argentina, Brazil and Mexico even exporting films. That this film era was dynamic and even progressive in a general sense is especially clear in retrospect; it is not surprising that Diego Rivera included Cantinflas in one of his magnificent Mexican Revolution murals.

The 1960s were a mixed decade as they marked a period of great innovation and a flourishing radical popular culture, but also the beginning of a genuinely transnational mass commercial culture. This was the era of the so-called 'new' cinema in Latin America, self-consciously 'vanguardist' in political and cultural terms. The Cuban Revolution cast a spell over the cultural politics of the whole region and nationalist development strategies also provided an optimistic impetus to a broadly progressive mood. The intensity of this period has few parallels and the whole meaning of cultural politics was brought into question. Yet this radical era was also the period when the commercialization of popular culture also took a great leap forward. As Martín-Barbero notes, while cinema (and, of course, television) expanded, 'the entry of their cultural production into the global market has been accompanied by a clear weakening of its capacity for cultural *differentiation*' (Martín-Barbero 2000: 37). In the era of globalization the listening and viewing public were to become more undifferentiated (to not say bland) so that a progressive cultural politics became more difficult to sustain.

Box 8.4   Tropicália: music and politics

In 2003 singer-songwriter Gilberto Gil became minister of culture in Lula's first Workers' Party administration in Brazil. Gil was co-founder in the 1960s of the Tropicália movement and when he took office he declared himself a *Tropicalista*. While opposed by some on the left, such as the legendary Augusto Boal, founder of the theatre of the oppressed movement, as a backward, elitist and romanticist appointment, it was undoubtedly significant and, by and large, very popular. Many could cast their minds back to 1968 when Brazil's post-1964 military rulers greatly tightened up repression in response to an incipient armed struggle movement. In a country of huge social discrepancies but also enormous cultural vitality Gil and his group took inspiration from the *favelas* (shanty towns) and the famous samba schools to create their own version of the 1960s counter-culture.

While the name Tropicália was borrowed from the visual arts this was a largely musical movement. This was a period in which Brazil's bossa nova had arrived on the international cultural scene with the 1964 hit *The Girl From Ipanema* by Antonio Carlos Jobim. Gil and his colleagues were not from Río, however, but, rather, from the impoverished and more Afro-Caribbean north-eastern city of Bahía. In terms of musical style the bossa nova mixed with urban samba, along with rhythm and blues, soul and funk. This was the period when Bob Dylan was called 'Judas' for introducing the electric guitar into traditional music. The Tropicalistas refused the left war on pop and scorned folklorist notions of musical authenticity. Tropicália was a very particular response from Latin America to the rise of mass consumerism and popular culture. It was part of the global 1960s but inextricably Brazilian. Its motto was probably Gil's co-founder Caetano Veloso's oft-used phrase '*E prohibido prohibir*' (It is forbidden to forbid). Gilberto Gil, as minister of culture, is bound to disappoint many of his one-time followers but he will certainly not be constrained by dogma or be predictable.

Source: Jaggi (2006).

Commercialization (and the transformation) of popular culture continued apace in the 1970s and 1980s. The cinema, which had been central to a national popular culture, declined dramatically. Cinema audiences declined by half or more and national film production declined from 100 per year to less than 10 in Argentina, Brazil and Mexico, the countries where it had been strongest. The importance of video increased dramatically, with 80 per cent at least of all cassettes coming from the United States. Popular culture was becoming more privatized, not coincidentally with the rise of the neo-liberal economies (see Chapter 3) and its emphasis on individualism. As popular culture becomes commercialized it also becomes 'commodified' (everything can be bought and sold) and there was a general homogenization of the cultural domain. However, it is important to note that this is not simply imposed from the 'outside', as it were, as the theory of 'cultural imperialism' in the 1960s and 1970s argued. Rather, the globalization of popular culture occurred as part of transformation within the various countries of Latin America reflecting socio-economic changes but also impacting on these in significant ways.

One of the best-known forms of popular culture in Latin America today is the *telenovela* (TV novel or, rather, soap), which Brazil famously exports even to the USA. Its origins lay in the much earlier *folletín* (magazine serials) and *radioteatro* (radio theatre), the medium where Eva Perón made her name, for example. Drawing on these earlier genres the rise of the *telenovela* coincided with the consolidation of the large national media conglomerates like Globo in Brazil and Televisa in Mexico. Often very realistic, they use cinematic techniques in a novel way, sometimes portraying social issues of the day in a sympathetic manner. They were the main product which took Latin American audio-visual culture into the global markets. As Ana López writes: 'Thoroughly grounded in perhaps the most conservative Western dramatic form, the melodrama, the *telenovela* is also paradoxically the principal emblem of Latin American television's modernity' (2000: 169). In some ways the *telenovela* is also a good example of how Latin American culture tends to absorb and transform in an original way the currents of so-called global culture.

Another icon of popular culture is the carnival in which, for a few days, the world is supposedly 'turned upside down', where roles are transgressed and play rules over work. Even in the 1930s the carnival (especially in its internationally most famous Brazilian variant) was losing its violent, transgressive character and becoming part of the nationalizing, civilizing ethos. The samba schools were to become a major element through which popular culture still impacted on the carnival spectacle, but even they were often co-opted by the state. The carnival, like many other popular cultural festivals, has of course become part of the global tourist consumption circuits. This does not necessarily mean that these events have become 'globalized' and devoid of popular meaning. In fact they are good examples of how the local/global construction of popular culture occurs today in a complex interaction of public/private, traditional/ modern relations that cannot be reduced to simplistic notions of culture becoming universalized or simply commercialized.

If the profane carnival is part of popular culture, so too is religion in many forms. Popular religiosity is an integral element of popular culture in Latin America, and is deeply festive in character, reflecting the popular culture of particular regions and ethnic groups. For Cristián Parker (1996), popular Christianity, as he calls it, is central to Latin American cultural identity and it articulates a distinct cultural logic as an alternative to Western rationalism. In spite of secularization and globalization, religion continues to be (and increasingly so we could argue) a reference point for popular culture. With the collapse of socialism and communism as alternative ideologies for social change it is hardly surprising that religion should play this role. For Parker, 'Christianity, thus understood as a cultural factor, may well be the novel horizon for the construction of a new Latin American civilisation for the twenty first century' (1996: 263). Be that as it may, we cannot divorce popular culture from religion in contemporary Latin America.

Going back from the sacred to the profane, we need to say a few words about football, which today is much more what Marx would have called the 'opium of the masses' than religion ever was. An English cultural tradition imported into Argentina and Uruguay in the first instance, football or soccer is today a major element in Latin American and global popular culture. Pre-1970s there were national styles of football and, for example, Brazilian 'football became a vehicle through which class, ethnic and neighbourhood allegiances were articulated, while also integrating them within a broader emergent national identity' (Rowe and Schelling 1991: 139). The symbiosis of football and radio in this period took on a different form in the era of television and, later, of globalization. Football has been mobilized by dictatorships, as in Brazil and Argentina (World Cup 1982, most notoriously), but it has also served a strong populist, if not always democratic, cultural function. As with the samba schools, the football clubs play an important role in shaping an egalitarian, optimistic and joyous popular culture which cultural politics ignores at its peril.

We can now reconsider 'popular culture' in a way that is relevant for cultural politics as the theme of this chapter. At one time popular culture referred to tradition and folklore. The national popular culture pointed towards the 'authentic' indigenous traditions and to the gaucho as bearer of nationhood in a sense. Yet it also smacked of underdevelopment and backwardness, of tradition as a roadblock for the juggernaut of progress.

We can no longer sustain this view either in its negative variant of its positive proclamation of an unpolluted popular culture opposed to 'bourgeois hegemony'. There is no clear distinction either between 'Latin American culture' and the new global culture: where, for example, would we place the tango, Celia Cruz, Havana Rum, salsa, Buena Vista Social Club, or Ronaldo for that matter?

9

International Context

Latin America, like other regions of what used to be called the Third World, is impacted on in a whole series of ways by the international context within which it exists. This chapter begins with a broad review of the international context of economic and political development in Latin America from the age of colonialism to the present era of globalization. Particular emphasis is placed on the massive changes which took place in the decade after the end of the cold war. We then turn to security issues, understood in the broadest sense to include wars and border conflicts but also the debt issue and the increasingly important drugs question. Next there is a shift to the regional dimension with an evaluation of the impact of NAFTA and MERCOSUR (Common Market of the South), which are transforming the north and south of the subcontinent respectively. Finally, we examine the role of Latin America in the world today in terms of international organizations such as the UN (United Nations), the OAS (Organization of American States) and the global social movements concerned with the environment.

Colonialism to Globalism

What we know today as Latin America was created by the era of colonialism when the European powers set across the globe seeking territories and peoples to dominate and profit from. Soon after Columbus announced his 'discovery' of America in 1492, the rivalry between the European powers for domination of the region began. While Spain began as the lead power in the Conquest period, by the early 1600s Britain had moved into that role mainly as a reflection of the changing balance of power in Europe. Meanwhile, Portugal remained ensconced in Brazil, and Holland and France moved into some areas. By the early 1800s, the newly emergent United States in North America was becoming a powerful player. For the USA the main issue was to reduce European power in South America and to that end support was given to various independence movements. The US aspirations to regional hegemony were proclaimed in the Monroe Doctrine of 1823 which declared that the American continents 'are henceforth not to be considered as subject for future colonization by any European power'.

In the nineteenth century, the US intelligentsia constructed a strongly racist discourse to legitimize and justify their growing role and weight across the Americas. Thus Professor John W. Burgess from Columbia University could state in 1923:

> there are vast differences in political capacity between the races ... it is the white man's mission, his duty, and his right to hold the reins of political power in his own hands for the civilization of the world and the welfare of mankind. (Cited in Smith 2000: 47)

This racist hierarchy had the Anglo-Saxons at the top and indigenous peoples and Afro-Americans at the bottom. In between were the Japanese and Chinese, the Spanish and Italians, occupying a place akin to that of the 'coloureds' in apartheid-era South Africa. From the standpoint of assumed racial superiority it was easy for the USA to at best assume a role of 'trusteeship' over the lesser races to the south, and at worst intervene openly when their interests were considered to be at stake.

The most blatant episode in early US imperial expansion occurred in relation to Mexico. In the 1820s the USA had sought a unilateral 'rectification' of the border with Mexico as regards Texas. By 1845 the US Congress felt sufficiently bold to simply declare the 'annexation' of Texas into the United States. The inevitable war with Mexico lasted 2 years and at the end of it the USA had increased its territory by a fifth through the forceful acquisition of 850 000 square miles of Mexican territory. More poignantly, Mexico lost half of its national territory, a wound that is felt clearly to this day. Some 100 years later, the USA was still intervening unilaterally through force of arms in Latin America. A moderate reformist government in Guatemala was overthrown in a CIA-backed military coup in 1954, motivated by the unacceptable nationalization of United Fruit, a US company. By now the USA did not see European power in 'its' continent as the main problem but, rather, the threat of communism loomed large in the minds of that country's leaders.

Following the Second World War, the USA found itself locked into the cold war with the Soviet Union, which it accused of seeking to export communism to the 'Free World' – as it chose to dub its sphere of influence in the world. In 1947, US President Harry S. Truman codified the new US strategy in the Truman Doctrine. It declared openly that the

USA would actively support 'free peoples' (however defined) from external and also internal foes. The door was opened for intervention in the affairs of other countries in the Americas under the pretext of 'hemispheric security'. The USA was proclaiming itself a global policeman, not least in the region it now openly considered to be its own backyard. The inter-American system was placed on a more established footing with the formation of the OAS during a pan-American conference held in Bogotá in 1948, although it only commenced to operate officially in 1951 after being duly ratified. The OAS served effectively as the US colonial department for a long time, although later it did achieve some independence.

The cold war era was marked by a series of US interventions in Latin America to stem the 'communist threat', as it saw it. Guatemala in 1954 was the first instance of a Latin American democratically elected government falling to US-sponsored cold war warriors. The communist-threat argument was soon seen clearly to be a foil for a move designed to protect US economic interests in Guatemala closely tied to leading politicians. Cuba was next with an immediate economic embargo declared by the USA after the overthrow of the dictator Batista in 1959. In 1961 the USA openly supported by military and political means an invasion of the island by anti-Castro forces which failed ignominiously at the Bay of Pigs. Then, in 1970, when President Allende was elected in Chile, the USA directed its full venom at independent democratic nationalist government in Latin America. Henry Kissinger criticized the 'irresponsibility' of the Chilean people in voting for Allende, and a CIA memo of October that year declared ominously that: 'It is firm and continuing policy that Allende be overthrown by a coup. We do continue to generate maximum pressure towards this end utilizing every appropriate resource' (cited in Smith 2000: 174). Kissinger and the CIA were to get their way in 1973 when Allende was overthrown and the brutal Pinochet dictatorship installed.

The 1980s saw the cold war turning 'hot' and the locus of conflict shifting to Central America. While Allende represented the threat of electoral or democratic socialism, in Central America the threat was posed by nationalist and socialist guerrillas. The first 'domino' to fall, as the USA saw it, was Nicaragua where the Sandinistas took power in 1979 with widespread support to overthrow the long reign of the dictator Somoza. The loss of US influence in Nicaragua was followed by the very serious threat to the established order in El Salvador by the FMLN (Farabundo Martí National Liberation Front), and the rather more inchoate guerrilla movements in Guatemala. US President Ronald

Box 9.1   US President Reagan on the Latin American threat, 1984

As long as we maintain the strategic balance and make it more stable by reducing the level of weapons on both sides, then we can count on the basic prudence of the Soviet leaders to avoid that kind of challenge to us. They are presently challenging us with a different kind of weapon: subversion and the use of surrogate forces – Cubans, for example. We've seen it intensifying during the last 10 years as the Soviet Union and its surrogates moved to establish control over Vietnam, Laos, Kampuchea, Angola, Ethiopia, South Yemen, Afghanistan, and recently, closer to home in Nicaragua and now El Salvador. It's the fate of this region, Central America, that I want to talk to you about tonight ... The defense policy of the United States is based on a simple premise: we do not start wars. We will never be the aggressor. We maintain our strength in order to deter and defend against aggression – to preserve freedom and peace. We help our friends defend themselves ...

Central America is a region of great importance to the United States. And it is so close – San Salvador is closer to Houston, Texas, than Houston is to Washington, DC. Central America is America; it's at our doorstep. And it has become the stage for a bold attempt by the Soviet Union, Cuba and Nicaragua to install communism by force throughout the hemisphere ...

When half of our shipping tonnage and imported oil passes through Caribbean shipping lanes, and nearly half of all our foreign trade passes through the Panama Canal and Caribbean waters, America's economy and well-being are at stake ...

What we see in El Salvador is an attempt to destablize the entire region and eventually move chaos and anarchy toward the American border ...

As the National Bipartisan Commission on Central America, chaired by Henry Kissinger, agreed, if we do nothing or if we continue to provide too little help, our choice will be a communist Central America with additional communist military bases on the mainland of this hemisphere and communist subversion spreading southward and northward.

Source: Quoted in Holden and Zolov (2001: 295–6).

Reagan probably believed that the domino effect would hit Mexico and even the USA. Whatever his beliefs he authorized a systematic under-mining of the Nicaraguan revolution and support for the 'Contras' (counter-revolutionaries) of Somoza's National Guard in a war against the new regime, likening the Contras to the democratic founding fathers of the USA (see Box 9.1).

The end of the cold war, pursuant on the collapse of communism in the East, had a dramatic impact on international relations in the Americas. The presidencies of George Bush Senior (1989–93) and Bill Clinton (1993–2001) inaugurated a new era which, for optimistic observers, signalled the irrelevance of the Monroe Doctrine. The new spirit of multilateralism was most evident in Central America where the USA withdrew support from the Contras and began to support the regional plans endorsed by the rest of Latin America. The US military occupation of Haiti in 1994 was justified in terms of its support for democracy and was carried out under the auspices of the UN. The republics of Latin America, especially the larger, more powerful ones, were also beginning to recover their voice. Following on from its successful intervention in Central America, a group of countries (Argentina, Brazil, Colombia, Mexico, Panama, Peru and Venezuela) went on to form the so-called Rio Group in 1986 to address issues of democratization and regional integration from a broad Latin American perspective.

Towards the end of 1989, the USA launched a short, sharp military intervention in Panama to kidnap President Manuel Noriega under the pretext of drug trafficking. Indeed, under close supervision by the CIA, Noriega had been involved in drug trafficking, but not since 1986 when he had been indicted in Miami. Operation Just Cause, as it was called, had other strategic objectives to do with the Panama Canal. The war on drugs waged self-righteously by the USA in Latin America was stepped up in the 1990s, and the notorious US policy of 'certification' – that a country was doing sufficient to combat drugs to continue receiving aid – attracted widespread opposition at all levels. Clearly the US drugs policy cannot be seen in isolation from its concern with transnational crime and its broader security interests in Latin America. The concern from a Latin American perspective is that the 'war on drugs' is simply a cover for an increased involvement by the USA in the internal politics of the region.

For the optimistic observer there is a

> conviction that the profound asymmetry of power and resources between the United States of America and the rest of the continent does not have to take its current form of a thoroughly inequitable relationship. (Bulmer-Thomas and Dunkerley 1999: 311)

Certainly the USA has reacted recently in a measured way, for example in relation to trade disputes with Brazil. And the US State Department backed down very rapidly from the support it seemed to give to those seeking to overthrow President Chávez in Venezuela in 2002. Mexico has, to a considerable degree, been brought into a more mutually beneficial relationship with the USA, and certainly the relationships opened up between Latin America and Europe and Japan have introduced a certain multipolarity into the situation. Whether the much-vaunted 'new agenda' represents any more than a benign neglect rather than active intervention, remains on the whole to be seen. Certainly the horizon of possibilities in the USA, in economic and political terms, remains bounded by the parameters of US power.

In the new era of globalization we now live in, US hegemony is as open as it was when Mexico was dismembered in the mid nineteenth century. Now it is Colombia which is treated practically as a province as the war on drugs and the war on terror are stepped up in that country. National sovereignty counts for little and the only consolation is that, on the whole, the USA is not terribly interested in Latin America as a strategic zone. In the mid 1960s under President Lyndon B. Johnson the secretary of state for Latin America was one Thomas C. Mann who declared memorably that: 'I know my Latinos. They understand only two things – a buck in the pocket and a kick in the ass' (cited in Smith 2000: 157). The very least that can be said is that this type of attitude does not augur well for friendly and equal relations between Anglo-America and Latin America.

Regional Integration

The question of regional integration has recently come to the fore in Latin America, especially after the high visibility of NAFTA in 1994. However, the history of the idea or aspiration in Latin America is a long one. If the republics of Latin America could at the very least cooperate economically it was thought that they might be better placed to compete with the 'colossus in the north', that is the USA. The Economic Commission for Latin America (ECLA), formed in 1948, was a crucial force in motivating and organizing the drive towards regional integration in the 1950s and, in particular, in the 1960s. Thus the Latin American Free trade Association (LAFTA) and the Central American Common Market took shape in 1961. Later, in 1969, the Andean Pact brought together Bolivia, Colombia, Ecuador, Peru and Venezuela in a regional integration process, and in 1973 CARICOM (the Caribbean Community) was launched. None of these organizations, however, would stand the test of time.

LAFTA began with an ambitious project to create a large free-trade area but also to engage in regional industrial planning. This was the era of import-substitution industrialization (see Chapter 3) and this joint approach made sense. For a number of reasons, which included the lack of a collective political will, LAFTA ended as simply a series of bilateral trade agreements which did, however, at their peak cover around 40 per cent of trade within Latin America. The Andean Pact also committed to import-substitution industrialization was effective for Colombia, Ecuador and Peru, but the other countries began to break away in practice. Colombia sought to reconstruct the pact in the 1990s along the lines of 'open' regionalism (see below). As to the Caribbean and Central American trading blocs, they have been dealt a severe blow by NAFTA, which we discuss next, as it effectively took Mexico directly and preferentially into the US economic orbit. These groupings of smaller countries could never have the potential that MERCOSUR (see below) has to establish a regional pole of attraction within Latin America.

With the end of the cold war, the USA launched its project for a new world order in the 1990s. However, it must be noted that the initiative to establish a North American free-trade area came from Mexico, and not the USA, following its failure to establish better trading relations with Western Europe. From the US perspective a free-trade agreement with Mexico might lead to a degree of economic regeneration in its southern neighbour which, in turn, might lessen the flow of Mexican migrants coming across the border in search of work. Given the somewhat unexpected enthusiasm of President Bush Senior for this project, Canada felt compelled to join the talks which from early 1991 onwards became trilateral in nature. By mid 1992 the NAFTA (North American Free Trade Association) had been signed up to by the three parties and only awaited approval by the respective national legislatures. This free-trade area would embrace over 360 million people with a combined GDP of some US$6239 billion. It was also to be the first North/South free-trade association bringing a Latin American country into a close embrace with the richest nation in the world.

Approval for NAFTA was by no means a foregone conclusion. Opposition in the USA was intense, and not only from populist-nationalist politicians such as Ross Perot. Some economic groups stood to lose from the deal and the trade union movement (AFL-CIO) was at first vehemently opposed to what it saw as the inevitable 'export of jobs' to the lower-wage Mexican economy. Gradually the unions came round to the idea, in part owing to the intervention of the Canadian unions which had better relations with their Mexican counterparts. Eventually NAFTA went into effect on 1 January 1995 with two so-called 'side agreements' to deal with the two contentious social issues of labour and the environment. President Clinton had eventually thrown his weight behind the agreement and he was soon calling for an American Free Trade Area by 2005, stretching from Alaska to Tierra del Fuego.

NAFTA represented the high tide of faith in the free market and the neo-liberal economic recipes for development. As Anthony Payne puts it: 'The emerging political order in the Americas left no place for political leaders who found it difficult to endorse these nostrums' (1996: 106). Chile was soon clamouring at the door of NAFTA to sign up but the US politicians seemed to lose interest and they were reluctant to grant 'fast-track' status to subsequent negotiations for entry into NAFTA. After the 'lost decade' of the 1980s, in economic terms NAFTA at least seemed to offer some prospects for Mexico in terms of economic regeneration. Free trade now ruled supreme and there was to be absolutely no space for nationally oriented economic development or concerns for issues such as social equity or even a minimal safety net for those who could not compete in the new order.

Meanwhile, to the south of the continent, MERCOSUR (Common Market of the South), which had been created in 1991, was setting up its own common external tariff in 1995. Its core members were Argentina and Brazil, which had in the past sought to develop bilateral trade relations, but it also included the smaller economies of Paraguay and Uruguay. Later Chile and the Bolivia bloc would become associate members of MERCOSUR and Chile was to be torn between the aspiration to join NAFTA and the Southern Cone pull of MERCOSUR. Brazil, given the substantial size of its industrial sector and its reluctance to embrace neo-liberalism wholeheartedly, was the clear driver of this project. While Argentina under the neo-liberal regime of President Menem (1989–99) was a somewhat reluctant partner, it was later to become more enthusiastic in support of MERCOSUR. In theory MERCOSUR could allow for the development of increased regional trade and thus could offer some protection from the full rigour of international competition.

In economic terms MERCOSUR has been, on the whole, successful in spite of periodic problems, particularly between Argentina and Brazil in relation to the auto industry. Brazilian exports to Argentina increased dramatically and its neighbour became its second most important trading partner, behind only the USA. The abolition of internal tariffs within the bloc was not always welcomed by its smaller partners, but overall they too have also benefited. MERCOSUR is not just an economic project,

Box 9.2 Brazil's regional role

During Brazil's long dictatorship (1964–85) there was considerable concern that its military rulers aspired to a sub-imperialist role in South America, possibly in alliance with South Africa, then firmly in apartheid mode. However, during the period when Fernando Henrique Cardoso (1992–2002) was first foreign minister then president, Brazil acquired a strong but progressive and consensual regional role. At pains to disown neo-imperialist domination plans, Brazil's foreign policy concentrated rather on finding common ground with its Spanish-American neighbours and demonstrating the benefits of solidarity in the region when responding to US free-trade ambitions. Brazil's geopolitical importance, market size and security capacity give it an almost natural leadership capacity. While eschewing possibly divisive notions of Brazilian 'leadership' – especially given memories of sub-imperialist ambitions in the 1970s – its foreign policy-makers were quite conscious of the critical mass it represented and how the rest of Latin America (as well as Brazil of course) could benefit from consensual alliance building.

Clearly the unifying factor was the US project to create a Free-Trade Area of the Americas (FTAA) following its successful negotiations in 1994 to set up the North American Free Trade Association (NAFTA) that had already incorporated Mexico. The USA was quite conscious that a resurgent democratic Brazil could act as an alternative pole of attraction and called the 1994 Miami Summit of the Americas to defuse this challenge. In the event Brazilian diplomacy triumphed and the rest of the Latin American countries by and large drew strength from this autonomous and independent stance. Brazil then moved to seek an alliance between MERCOSUR (Mercado Común del Sur or Mercado Comun do Sul) and the rest of Latin America. And with the growing role of Asia (China in particular) in Latin America, more interdependent relationships are being forged between Latin American countries *and reducing the hegemony of the US in the region.*

Source: Burges (2006).

and its flourishing after the mid 1990s coincided with a deepening of democracy in the region. A whole range of social movements, including particularly the trade unions but also the women's and environmental movements, began to organize on a transnational regional basis. In cultural terms Brazilian 'difference' became more relative as a whole series of cultural exchanges, particularly in border regions, began to create a new regional identity.

In terms of the regional balance of force in the Americas, MERCOSUR plays a significant role. While in Argentina, Chile and Mexico regionalism is seen as part of the drive towards an open economy, in Brazil there is a still lingering nationally oriented development aspiration. Under President Cardoso (1995–2002) in particular, Brazil was to show a very clear disposition towards playing a regional leadership role. As Jean Grugel and Almeida Medeiros put it: 'The Brazilian government under Cardoso has been explicit in its championing of MERCOSUR as an alternative model to integration within the Americas' (1999: 59). Implicitly, MERCOSUR can thus be seen as a challenge to NAFTA and the USA project to create a single economic zone across the Americas under its control. When Argentina's economy went into a profound crisis at the end of 2001 the Brazilian government responded with a very clear support for its neighbour and a condemnation of US indifference.

The case of Chile is most interesting because it was torn between NAFTA and MERCOSUR in a way which showed most clearly the distinct character of the two regional blocs. As Chile emerged into the democratic era after 1989 there was an inevitable re-engagement with the rest of Latin America. The strongly outward-oriented development strategy continued under the new democratic governments and this impelled them to support the demand of the dominant economic groups to seek entry into NAFTA. While at one stage in 1994 Chile was invited to join NAFTA, political infighting within the US political system prevented fast-track approval by the US Congress. Partly as a reaction to this rebuff but also out of a desire to join the now strongly democratic Southern Cone bloc of countries Chile sought associate membership of MERCOSUR, and President Cardoso in Brazil smoothed away the remaining economic differences to make this possible. Significantly, when Chilean President Lagos (2000–6) visited Argentina in 2000 he declared that in a world of 'globalizers' and 'globalized' it was the only way the latter could confront the challenges of globalization.

By 2006, the issue of regional integration in Latin America had become clearer. The US-driven Free Trade Area of the Americas (FTAA) initiative had failed. This became clear at the 2005 Summit of the Americas held in Mar del Plata, Argentina, where President Chávez was lauded in the streets, and President Bush did not even find a warm welcome in the conference hall. The notion of a single market across the Americas and embracing 34 countries was a bold project that depended on consolidating neo-liberalism, just at the time when it was beginning to falter in global terms and particularly in Latin America. The inflexibility of the US administration on issues such as agricultural subsidies and anti-dumping practices made even a compromise unlikely. There was also a growing tide of counter-globalization movements in some countries that had some impact. Overall, Washington was unable to impose its regional free-market project, because of the serious erosion since the year 2000 of the neo-liberal economic model across Latin America.

Latin American governments did not, however, move decisively towards regional integration on their own terms during this period. While MERCOSUR (under Brazilian leadership) was able to circumvent the US attempt to isolate it, was not able to break out of the impasse it found itself in, owing to national rivalries. It is often argued that the failures of Latin American integration are due to the 'divide and rule' policies of first British and then US imperialism. In truth, as Carlos Malamud put it: 'The lack of tangible results in the regional and sub-regional integration process in Latin America is due more to internal issues than to external considerations' (Malamud 2005: 4). The rhetoric of integration – such as the so-called Bolivarian project – is not matched by clear political goals and viable transnational cooperation arrangements. Looking inwards to the pressing social and economic problems seems – in the cold light of day – a priority over any 'Latin American project'.

The very term 'open regionalism' used to describe regional integration in Latin America today is, on the face of it, contradictory. The 'new regionalism' as distinct from the ECLA-inspired movement of the 1960s is an integral part of, and complementary to, the process of globalization. It rejects any notion of regional integration behind a protectionist barrier or, even, focused on building up the internal market of the countries concerned. The new regionalism is not a state or interstate project, but responds rather to the needs of international capitalism. In that sense regionalization (as distinct from regionalism) can be seen as part and parcel of globalization. It is designed to deepen the integration of the Latin American economies with the global market, not to strengthen regional integration in the 1960s sense of the term. So today we find NAFTA as a crucial regional expression of globalization, while MERCOSUR has some element of old regionalism about it, in spite of being predominantly an expression of the new regionalism as well.

Security Issues

According to the United Nations Development Project Report: 'The concept of security must change – from an exclusive stress on national security to a much greater stress on people's security' (1997: 2). National security through force of arms is a very restricted view of what human security means. This section will, though, deal with those traditional themes such as wars and conflicts, the geostrategic dimension and the 'drugs war'. However, it will be set in the framework of social and economic development rather than seen as a separate issue. We will also look at foreign debt as an issue which crucially affects human security in Latin America. A human security focus takes us away from the nation-state as the key actor, if not the only one. It also allows us to integrate the issues of peace and security with the broader agenda of sustainable development. Finally it sets the context within which international organizations, including especially the NGOs, might make progressive interventions within Latin America.

The end of the cold war did not lead in Latin America to the unleashing of ethnic, national or border conflicts which had been held in check by the East–West conflict. On the contrary, most civil wars and conflicts in Latin America had been overdetermined by the cold war and its end led to a discernible diminishing of tension. The last inter-state war in Latin America was the so-called 'soccer war' of 1969 between El Salvador and Honduras. Then in the early 1980s there were border skirmishes between Peru and Ecuador and also between Argentina and Chile over the disputed Beagle Channel Islands at the southernmost point of the continent. On the external front the landmark recent conflicts are the 1982 war between Argentina and Britain over the disputed Falklands/Malvinas Islands in the South Atlantic, and then the unilateral US military intervention in Panama in 1989. On both the internal and external fronts then there has been a decidedly less conflictual period since at least the mid 1990s.

The conflicts in Central America were resolved through separate but related peace processes in the mid 1990s, which owed a lot to the end of the cold war. However, in Latin America as a whole we need to find other explanations for the diminishing inter-state tensions in recent years which are creating a genuine 'zone of peace' in the area. As Augusto Varas notes, 'the end of the Cold War has not fundamentally affected defence policies and interests with respect to neighbouring countries and at the regional level' (1998: 16). The main factor influencing internal and regional security policies in Latin America has, in fact, been the consolidation of democracy in the 1990s. Democratic governments, albeit with authoritarian inflections in some cases, have created a favourable atmosphere for non-military resolution of border conflicts, for example. The Argentina–Chile dispute over the Beagle Islands was resolved extremely easily and quickly once democracy was restored in both countries. While democracies have faced up to each other militarily (for example, Peru and Bolivia), on the whole democracy has provided a much better climate for regional tolerance and understanding.

The inter-state system in Latin America has tended to stabilize with the consolidation of democracy and with the advances in regional integration (see next section). However, it is well to recall the close relationship between the politics of geography (or geopolitics) and militarism in Latin America. As Jonathan Barton writes: 'it is this close association of the military with geo-politics that leads to the constant struggle for territorial gain and geo-political advantage' (1997: 63). It is an association that goes back to the young republics which emerged from the Spanish colonial territories with their emphasis on the need to preserve territorial integrity. In a later period under the Brazilian post-1964 rulers we saw an extension of this internal or sub-imperialist will to dominate. In the Brazilian case there was even a strong axis being forged with the apartheid regime in South Africa in a bid to form a SATO (South Atlantic Treaty Organization) to rival NATO (North Atlantic Treaty Organization). This type of geopolitics is now, thankfully, a thing of the past and it is unlikely to revive.

The two most salient geopolitical issues in Latin America today, especially from a global perspective, are the Amazon and Antarctic questions. The Amazon basin is an internal frontier in Latin America with huge territorial and resource implications. Natural resource exploitation – be it of timber or in terms of agricultural potential – is hotly contested, not least in the area of indigenous peoples' rights. It is also a prime site in terms of the international environmental movement's campaign to save the rainforest. The Antarctic, although quite different, is also seen as a frontier but for the whole of humanity. As Barton (1999: 142) says, 'the Antarctic provides a particularly complex problem of multiple state interests suggesting that the frozen continent with be central to Latin America geo-political debates into the next century'. With national sovereign claims temporarily suspended, the issue of the Antarctic (claimed in large measure by the various republics of Latin America) remains a geopolitical timebomb which may make the Amazon pale into insignificance by comparison.

From a US perspective it would probably be the 'drugs question' which would be seen as the most salient security issue in Latin America today. This has become a lucrative transnational industry with a major impact on development in the region. The drugs industry has virtually transformed the economics and politics of the Andean countries – Bolivia and Peru even more than Colombia, although it is usually the latter that is the news. The drugs industry is a dynamic economic sector by any standards and it is totally integrated with the US criminal economy. It reflects the weakness of the state and the ravages of neo-liberalism which have devastated many legal agricultural activities. It is in Colombia where it has had most political impact on democratic politics, feeding on a long-running civil war which the ruling elites had seen no reason to decisively confront and resolve by democratic means. Given the deep roots of the drugs industry and its social embeddedness, it clearly cannot be reduced to a simple security issue to be dealt with by force alone.

As Colin Sage wrote some time ago, 'drug diplomacy now forms a cornerstone of US foreign policy throughout Latin America' (1991: 327). This is largely seen as a region-specific approach as the USA never seriously contemplated cutting off economic and military aid to Pakistan when it was the world's largest heroin producer in the 1990s. The inconsistencies of the US drug certification process can be explained easily by the wider US foreign policy agenda. Thus Syria and Lebanon were dropped from the list of 30 or so countries deemed major drug producers in the late 1990s to 'facilitate' the war against Iraq. Today the epicentre of the US 'war on drugs' is clearly Colombia, but Mexico is also an important target. However, Mexico, being within NAFTA, is treated quite differently from Colombia with a strong guerrilla movement of communist origins, inaccurately dubbed 'narco-terrorists' in the popular press. Illegal drug production and commercialization is a major social and political issue in Latin America, but not one that can be dealt with by fluctuating and self-interested US 'security' measures.

From the point of view of ordinary people in Latin America it would probably be the foreign-debt question and the whole dominant economic strategy which would be seen as the major issue affecting their security. The international financial institutions such as the World Bank, the IMF and the WTO are seeking to create a new world order based on financial integration and political stabilization. They seek to promote 'good governance' and stability within the expansion of globalization. But they do this of course by imposing their own agendas which may contain incentives though they are based strictly on conditions being met. The issue of conditionality has had a massive impact on Latin America from the mid 1980s high-point of the foreign debt crisis through the structural-adjustment period (see Chapter 3) to the present condition of dependence on the multilateral financial agencies. Latin America's financial dependence is now more or less total, with the partial exceptions of Brazil and Mexico which are powerful enough to retain some degree of negotiating power if not independence.

Box 9.3 Drugs: economics, politics and security

There is always considerable media interest in Latin America's *narcotráfico* drugs trade and its relationship to the economics and politics of the area, not to mention its impact on global security. The criminal networks built around the drugs trade inevitably spread widely, becoming involved with money-laundering, arms trafficking and the trade in human beings. In Colombia and Mexico in particular the criminal financial networks are extremely important and merge seamlessly with the legal world of money in the era of globalization. To the finances of drugs and associated markets one needs to add the element of organized violence. The Colombian *sicarios* (killers) are extremely professional and pervasive not only as enforcers but as market-makers and political players. But this is not a purely Latin American phenomenon – because, as Castells explains:

> Latin American-based drugs traffic is an essential component of American crime, to the point that US policy toward Latin America is dominated by the obsession to fight drugs traffic at the point of supply. This is an impossible task, but one that has entirely transformed US–Latin American relations from old-fashioned imperialism to hysterical pursuit of a vanishing enemy which, in its repeated escapes, blows up entire political systems. (Castells 1998: 195)

Colombia is, without doubt, the Latin American country where the drugs trade most seriously impacts on the economy and the political system. It has generally been assumed that the drugs industry harms the legal economy. The illegal drugs trade clearly impacts on employment, money-laundering, land ownership and income inequality. However, a recent study suggests that: 'Colombia's economic problems are more related to political violence than coca production' (Holmes and Gutiérrez de Piñeras 2006: 115). When controlling for violence, the impact of coca production on its Colombian economy is not significant in terms of either exports or gross domestic product. Furthermore when the sources of violence are disaggregated this study found that while right-wing paramilitary violence is related positively to exports and negatively to gross domestic product, FARC (Colombian Revolutionary Armed Forces) revolutionary activities do harm exports but not gross domestic product. So, we need to unpack economics, politics and security when dealing with the drugs issue in Latin America.

The case of Argentina shows most clearly the impact which the international financial agencies can have on human security. From 1990 to 2000 Argentina followed almost to the letter the conditions set by the international financial institutions. However, by the end of 2001 the economy was collapsing as the international banks quickly moved their funds offshore owing to imminent devaluation of the peso which had been artificially pegged to the US dollar. In the economic disintegration which followed, the proportion of the population which lived under officially defined levels of poverty increased to over 50 per cent. Wages were frozen, jobs were lost and prices went up as companies sought to offload any losses on to the public. The IMF economic experts duly arrived on the scene to reinstate the loans the withholding of which in late 2001 had precipitated the crisis; however the conditions of reinstatement were extremely onerous, including widespread sackings in the public administration of the poorer provinces in particular.

What are the prospects, then, for human security in Latin America today? Olga Pellicer echoes a belief widespread in Latin America that, 'It can in no way be claimed that there is any "shared agenda" of security issues between [the USA] ... and the rest of the hemisphere' (1998: 9). There is every reason, in fact, to fear that post-September 11 the USA will simply impose whatever agenda it sees fit on the region. On the other hand, we see distinct signs of the emergence of a new more cooperative hemispheric security agenda and strategy in Latin America itself. From being inward-looking, most nations have perforce become outward-looking in the era of globalization, and a more cooperative regional security regime is flowing from this. Following Augusto Varas we can conclude that:

> Hemispheric co-operative security could be defined as a system of inter-state interactions which, by co-ordinating government policies, anticipates and contains threats to national interests and prevents the perception of such threats by the different governments from turning into tensions, crises or open confrontations. (1998: 11)

In the World Today

Latin America has always been difficult to place in the world. Clearly Western, it also seemed to contain various exotic or primitive elements for some observers. In the radical 1960s Latin America was seen by many to be a leading part of the so-called Third World (except perhaps Cuba), which was in neither the West nor the communist East. In a sense Latin America has always been a hybrid – part Western, part underdeveloped world. In economic terms the weight of Latin America has been steadily declining since the Second World War. In political terms, which we focus on here, the region's influence has waxed and waned but on the whole it has had a fairly peripheral importance. It is in cultural terms that Latin America has really played a significant global role (see Chapter 8), through its literature and dances in particular.

Latin America joined the international community of nations 'officially' after the First World War when the League of Nations was established by the victorious powers. There were 15 of the region's republics at the meeting in 1920, and all 20 were eventually to join. At the League, the Latin American representatives formed a discernible bloc and were seen as such by the other countries present. However, the possibility that the League could act as a counterweight to the United States, emerging as the new hegemonic power after the war, came to nothing in so far as the USA did not even join the League, which became increasingly irrelevant. The League did seek to mediate in the 'Chaco War' between Bolivia and Paraguay, but the US role was soon allowed to dominate. When the United Nations was formed in 1945, following the Second World War, the 20 Latin American republics were there from the start. The UN allowed Latin America to join the growing anti-colonial movement at the international level and to take up issues of economic development in the context of the presence of an overwhelming dominant power such as the USA.

The UN Charter contains a specific compromise between its avowed globalism and Latin American regionalism in the shape of art. 51, which recognizes Latin America's individual and collective right to defence against armed attacks. Another article places great importance on regional bodies in handling peace and security matters before they can be brought to the UN Security Council. In terms of regional economic development issues the UN was a far more progressive vehicle than the League of Nations had been. This can be seen in the foundation of the influential Economic Commission of Latin America (ECLA) in 1948 as an agency of the UN's Economic and Social Council. Significantly based in Santiago de Chile, ECLA was to play an extremely important role in developing a non-orthodox social and economic development strategy. It is no coincidence that Fernando H. Cardoso wrote his influential *Dependency and Development in Latin America* (Cardoso and Faletto 1979) in Santiago at ECLA while a political exile in the mid 1960s from the Brazilian military coup of 1964. Today ECLA continues to develop an unorthodox interpretation of Latin America's role in the world economy and advocates an independent development strategy, as we see in Box 9.4.

The regional counterpart to the UN in Latin America was the OAS (Organization of American States) set up in 1948. To its critics it worked simply as an extension of US foreign policy in Latin America, but it was still an important regional forum. In 1960 another important regional organization was established, the IDB (Inter-American Development Bank), in which the USA played the pre-eminent role as

Box 9.4   The Economic Commission for Latin America and the Caribbean (ECLAC) charts a future agenda for the global arena, 2000

For the influential UN commission for Latin America the future is not constrained by what the neo-liberal world order has to offer. Latin America is called upon to make its own future even in the midst of a difficult international context. It would seem that the dependency tradition of the 1970s is not totally absent from these strategic thoughts on the future of Latin America in the era of globalization:

> There are a number of major obstacles that will have to be surmounted in order to build a new global order. The first is the absence of a set of shared principles that are embraced by all the major players. The second is that, given the asymmetrical power relations found in global society, the various actors differ in their ability to influence this process. The third is the difficulty of forming international coalitions capable of offsetting those inequalities, whether through developing-country partnerships, or international alliances of social sectors which feel that their interests are being harmed by the globalization process ...
>
> In order to surmount asymmetries at the global level, it is important to realize that, in the presence of widely differing positions such as those found in a hierarchical international system, attempts to apply equal terms in order to set up a level playing field will only serve to heighten existing inequalities. In the light of the considerations discussed in the preceding chapter, it becomes clear that the global agenda must include action on three different fronts. The first is to enhance the transmission of growth impulses from developed to developing countries via international trade and technology transfer. The second is to work through international lending agencies to give developing countries more

→

might be expected. The OAS applied sanctions on Cuba after 1962 at the instigation of the USA and supported retrospectively most US military interventions in the region. However, since the end of the cold war in particular the OAS has begun to develop a more clearly independent Latin American position. With the real or imagined threat of communism no longer an issue, the Latin American nations in the OAS began to openly discuss a more independent foreign policy position for this regional body. Thus, for example, in 1991 the General Assembly of the OAS approved the Santiago Commitment to Democracy and Renewal of the Inter-American System that was considerably independent from the Washington Consensus then prevailing.

→

breathing space for the adoption of countercyclical macroeconomic policies, help reverse the international concentration of credit and expedite the financial development of these countries. The third is to make sure that the global agenda places just as much emphasis on the international mobility of labour as it does on the international mobility of capital.

If an international social agenda is to be established, every member of the global society must be acknowledged as a citizen of the world and, hence, as possessing certain *rights*. The most cogent expressions of these rights are found in international declarations on civil, political, economic, social, cultural and labour rights, on the rights of women, children and different ethnic groups, and on the right to development ...

The construction of a truly new international architecture is founded upon the overall effect of global and regional institutional reforms. Unfortunately, many of the proposals put forward in recent years regarding the financial and, above all, social aspects of the international architecture focus almost entirely on adapting national structures to the global era. In other words, these proposals are looking at the *national* rather than the international architecture, and this is precisely their main weakness ...

Globalization has increased the demands of international competitiveness and strengthened the interrelationship between competitiveness and employment. It has also given rise to new social risks. On the social front, national globalization strategies should therefore focus on three areas: education, employment and social protection. Progress in these three areas is a prerequisite for equitable participation in the global era. Moreover, such progress is essential for the implementation of a rights-based international agenda at the national level.

Source: ECLAC (2000: 96–108).

The post-cold-war loosening of US control over the OAS is relative of course, but the topics being opened up for discussion are nevertheless significant. According to a senior Mexican Foreign Affairs official (Dieguez 1998: 105) the issues on the table include:

- Are regional or global solutions more appropriate to deal with Latin American problems?
- What does a threat to collective security mean in the post-cold-war period?
- Is the shared security issue one between Latin American nations and the USA or one common to themselves?

These are issues or debates which simply could not have surfaced at the height of the cold war. They signal a certain porousness in US–Latin American relations as against the fairly hermetic relationships of the past. We can also add that the OAS, or Organización de Estados Americanos (OEA), as it is known in Latin America, is now taking up a much broader 'security' agenda to include environmental degradation and human-rights violations, for instance.

Having examined Latin America's participation in the official global (UN) and regional (OAS) institutions, we turn now to the 'Third-Worldist' alternative. The principle of non-alignment between West and East goes back at least to the Perón government in Argentina (1946–55) which clearly articulated this philosophy in a similar way to Nasser in Egypt or Nehru in India. However, as Pope Atkins notes: 'Latin American nonalignment has been a multifaceted objective variously interpreted by Latin American governments' (1999: 105). Different motives and very different politics could sit behind the non-aligned banner. Perón's non-alignment, for example, was not Third-Worldist in seeking alliances with liberation movements in Africa or Asia; indeed, he would have been horrified by any suggestion that Argentina was a Third-World country. It meant simply that in a conflict between European countries (Axis versus Allied) or between the USA and Russia, Latin America should, in its own interests, maintain a prudent neutrality.

At its height in the 1970s, Latin American and Caribbean countries were members of the Non-Aligned Movement, the only exceptions being Paraguay and a few countries in Central America. At this stage the meaning of non-alignment had changed somewhat to focus predominantly on the economic dimension of international relations. There was a call for a new international economic order based on more equitable trading relations, and there was also an implicit attempt to lose this assumed neutrality between East and West to obtain concessions from both sides. For some countries such as Cuba and for a while Nicaragua, alignment with the Soviet bloc was preferred but this was clearly a minority position. Under the military dictatorships of the 1980s and in the 'new democracies' following the neo-liberal economics of globalization, even non-alignment was too radical. There was in many countries an unashamed endorsement of 'Western-Christian' civilization against any other culture or ideology.

The era of globalization since 1990 has brought Latin America more squarely into the world on a uniform platform of acceptance of free-market economics and Western models of democracy. Thus Latin America is more clearly 'in the world' as never before and not a place apart. What this has led to, apart from an increasingly uniform set of economic strategies, is greater global communication. Indeed, many analysts now refer to a 'global civil society' where citizens from all over the world can communicate, share aspirations and develop common projects. It is now more likely that a young educated person in Mexico City, São Paulo or Buenos Aires will have contact with their counterparts overseas through the internet than with those in the remoter parts of their own countries. This greater transnational fluidity and contact may have led to a greater distance within the various countries of Latin America between their globalized cities and more traditional hinterlands.

Where Latin America has most clearly become part of a global civil society has been in relation to the new or alternative transnational social movements. The UN Rio Conference of 1992 focused on the environment and brought the issue to the fore in Latin America. Henceforth there would be an active Latin American presence in the international environmental movement. The 1995 UN Beijing Conference on Women attracted an even stronger Latin American women's movement participation. The work preparatory to and after Beijing has helped consolidate a transnational Latin American women's movement which has played an energetic role in the global forums. Finally, the World Social Forum which began meeting in 2000 in the Brazilian city of Port Alegre has played a very important role as a pole of attraction for the anti-globalization movement worldwide. While economic participation by Latin America in the world may be more passive than it was, the voices of Latin American civil society in the global arena have become much more proactive.

In conclusion, then, while the cold war era from the Second World War to 1990 was characterized by geopolitical issues and ideological conflict as the main parameters of Latin America's insertion in the world, the period since then is nowhere near as structured, nor are the geo-strategic rules of the game at all clear. Peter Smith rightly calls the period since 1990 'the age of uncertainty' (2000: 357); ideology now plays a clearly subordinate role to economic issues. Globalization seems in principle to provide a multipolar world for Latin America to relate to, with Europe and Japan providing important economic and political linkages. However, it must be said that after September 11 the world looks distinctly unipolar, with US hegemony hardly contested anywhere, least of all in Latin America. In its way this new order is perhaps recreating the colonial era of Latin America, suitably modernized for our new times.

There is, however, nothing inevitable about this scenario and for every hegemonic project 'from above' there is a counter-hegemonic project 'from below' as it were. At the start of his administration US President George W. Bush had declared that Latin America would be a priority for US foreign policy but all this changed in September 2001 when Washington effectively lost interest in Latin America. US disillusionment went further in 2003 when most of Latin America refused to endorse the war in Iraq. As Peter Hakim, president of Inter-American Dialogue, recalls:

> [O]f the 34 Latin American and Caribbean countries, only seven supported the war. Six of them (Costa Rica, the Dominican Republic, El Salvador, Honduras, Nicaragua and Panama) were engaged in trade negotiations with the United States at the time. And the seventh, Colombia, receives more than US$600 million a year in US military aid. (2006: 3).

Venezuela has proven particularly troublesome to the USA, and its political system easily shook off the attempted US-backed coup in 2002. Venezuela has now joined MERCOSUR (an increasingly powerful counter-weight to US-led free-trade projects), is seeking to create a confederation of the region's state-owned petroleum companies and is even suggesting a nuclear energy consortium with Argentina and Brazil. Hakim concludes that: 'There is little reason to expect that US relations with Latin America will improve soon. More likely they will get worse' (2006: 7). While the USA is facing increasing challenges to its global hegemonic role in Iraq and Afghanistan it is clearly losing the battle 'for hearts and minds' in Latin America. In the meantime the European influence in Latin America is growing and a new economic, political and military power – China – is beginning to spread its wings in the region.

10
Conclusion: Futures Imperfect

There is a saying that the only thing that is certain about Latin America's future is uncertainty. Almost certainly it will also be imperfect, as we can discount steady, sustained and irreversible progress towards something dubbed modernity. This chapter begins by examining the global context within which Latin America's futures will be constructed, essentially the process of globalization in all its complexity. On that basis we examine in turn the economic prospects and the political challenges which lie ahead. In international terms these debates are critical because they raise such fundamental questions as 'What is development?' and 'What do we mean by citizenship in the era of globalization?' Finally, we can return to an underlying theme of this whole text, namely the nature of modernity in Latin America. Is Latin America heading towards the recognized Western notion of modernity or something else entirely? How can the same continent seem to be premodern and postmodern at the same time?

The Global Context

The last decade of the twentieth century was undoubtedly the decade of globalization; the world became more integrated economically, politically and culturally. It seemed that the world had shrunk as a result of the information revolution and vastly cheaper international transport costs. The free-market economic reforms were presented as part of a broader reform process and democratization, and it seemed that the modernization theory of the 1950s had been reinvented and reinvigorated. Economic reform, political democratization and social modernization went hand in hand. It was not hard to see how in this context Francis Fukuyama (1992) could proclaim the 'end of history' in the sense that the model of Western (more specifically US) capitalism was universalized as the only true path to modernization. By the end of the century it was hard to discern any alternatives other than wholehearted immersion in the new sea of globalization. But as we moved into the mid 2000s there was a growing feeling that the high tide of globalization was over and that the days of the unchallenged rule of the USA as global superpower were numbered.

The free-market reforms were effectively locked into the political systems of Latin America because no significant political force could discern an alternative. Even the once fiercely socialist or at least nationalist parties were now constructing their visions of the future within the tight parameters of what became known as the Washington Consensus. Economic internationalization, as the core of the globalization process, was taken for granted and each individual country (as well as the region as a whole) could simply seek the most advantageous integration within it. Southeast Asia with its dynamic NICs (newly industrializing countries) was seen as the positive role model. On the other hand, the whole sections of sub-Saharan Africa which virtually ceased to exist as viable entities because they were excluded from the globalization process served as very powerful negative role models in Latin America at the start of the twenty-first century. This meant the various countries inevitably had to engage with the new global order, but how they did so was obviously not predetermined.

Clearly there are always alternative options and it is only ideological certitude (or blindness) that prevents us recognizing these. On the other hand the Washington Consensus on which globalization was based seemed distinctly less consensual in the early twenty-first century. Essentially there was a growing recognition that the free operation of market forces could not resolve everything. In reality it was states that had created this 'free-market' ideology and they had to intervene constantly to sustain it. Nation-states are run by governments and these are in turn elected. In the 1990s after military regimes and bouts of hyperinflation it was easy enough to persuade a Latin American electorate that the Washington way was the only way. Gradually, however, the spell wore off or, rather, the acute social contradictions of the model became apparent and the democratic paradise it promised seemed always to be over the next horizon.

Latin America's politically uneven integration into the dominant world system is best exemplified by Brazil. Already in the 1980s reference was being made to Brazil being, in international comparative terms, a 'Belindia' – an amalgam of 'a Belgium and an India'. That is to say the south-east of the country is comparable to a small to medium-sized industrial European country, while the impoverished north-east is

---

Box 10.1   Nations challenging globalization

The G20 is a group of developing countries in the global South that came together in August 2003 in the lead-up to the World Trade Organization (WTO) ministerial conference in Cancún, Mexico. Its most powerful members are Brazil, China and India, but in Latin America it also brings together Argentina, Bolivia, Chile, Cuba, Guatemala, Mexico, Paraguay, Uruguay and Venezuela. The Brazilian role in creating this counter-hegemonic alliance was crucial. Its original aim was to create a developing-country counterweight in the agricultural negotiations that the WTO was to hold in Cancún. The group adopted a common position on US and EU agricultural subsidies that was circulated as an official document of the WTO both before and after Cancún. The leverage of the G20 was first seen when the WTO at Cancún failed to reach agreement on the basis suggested by the richer countries of the North that in the past might have prevailed. The importance of the G20 in agricultural matters in particular is due to the fact that it represents almost 60 per cent of the world's population and accounts for 25 per cent of global agricultural exports.

The G20 is essentially an intergovernmental organization of the South committed to pressuring the industrialized nations to end subsidies to their farmers so as to allow for the free trade they preach through the WTO. Thus the founding Brasilia Declaration signed by Brazil, China, India and South Africa regretted that major trading partners are still moved by protectionist concerns in their countries' less competitive sectors ... and emphasized how important it is that the results of the current round of trade negotiations provide especially for the reversal of protectionist politics and trade-distorting practices.

While the emphasis on trade issues and agriculture in particular is clear, a group such as G20 cannot but revive memories of the 1960s when the non-aligned movement was at its peak. If it continues to coordinate its members and the G4 core group (Brazil, China, India and South Africa) are able to work together this would represent a major step in the loosening of the ties that bind the South to the dominant neo-liberal globalization project. And Latin America as a whole – led by Brazil – will undoubtedly play a positive role in this process.

---

comparable to a country such as India. The point, though, is that these two countries are in fact one in Brazil due to an uneven and combined development processes. This process has since been termed 'Brazilianization' by some European sociologists such as Ulrich Beck (2000). What is meant by Brazilianization is the spread of this profoundly uneven development model to Europe and elsewhere with a small proportion of the population becoming an integral part of the dynamic globalization process and the vast majority left by the wayside.

It will become increasingly clear that Brazilianization is an integral element of the globalization process. The social and political implications of the economic internationalization processes are already being widely felt. The virtual economic meltdown of Argentina in 2001 is having an impact across Latin America in political terms as much as in the direct economic impact. Basically, governments are questioning the wisdom of slavishly following a modernization model that is 'made in the USA'. Whatever free markets can achieve in terms of economic rationalization they cannot build better health or education systems. Nor can the much-vaunted economic competitiveness be built on the basis of an impoverished population. Even from the perspective of those who benefit from globalization there is a danger that without some degree of social regulation the system will simply race out of control as financial fluidity corrodes all forms of social and political stability.

If at the level of political economy we can detect a degree of flexibility or openness at the global level, the same cannot be said about the geostrategic dimension of the 'new imperialism'. Even before September 11 the United States was reasserting its full hegemony over Latin America. Foreign ministers reported a revitalized imperialist arrogance and there was a fear that the bad old days of the 1950s were coming back. In geostrategic terms access to and stability of oil production in Latin America was a key issue. This influenced US policy in relation to Venezuela of course, but also Colombia, Ecuador and Mexico. The 40-year US embargo of Cuba was visibly crumbling but its abandonment would have been seen as a relaxation of imperial control in Latin America. The long-term goal of a Free Trade Area of the Americas remained a US priority whatever compromising might be necessary in relation to the MERCOSUR trading bloc and the powerful regional economic aspirations of Brazil.

The fates of Mexico and Central America are intimately linked to developing US strategy for the region. The bid to create an integrated sphere of influence (or more precisely neo-colonialism) in that region could yet be challenged by a shift to China as the next large low-wage area to exploit. The more directly interventionist tendency has been evident in Colombia and in Venezuela. In Colombia the USA has thrown its full weight behind one side in a long-running civil war, but the so-called 'war on terror' has simply made that political choice easier to justify, at least at home. In Venezuela the USA has already intervened in 2002 to seek the overthrow of the nationalist Chávez regime, and although this may have been more subtle than in Chile in 1973, the imperial designs are there for all to see. In Argentina, finally, as the economic crisis unfolds, the USA finds itself in a position where its influence on the multilateral economic institutions can quite literally determine which way the political process will develop and which party will make up the next government.

Globalization has not superseded dependency for Latin America; it has simply rendered it more complex. Rather than a North/South or a rich/poor divide we now have a more multipolar world but also one where these divides are present within countries as much as between them. As Cardoso explains: 'In the dependency theory vision we learnt that the international situation modelled Latin American societies "from within". Today this process continues, although with globalization its effects are much sharper' (1995: 24). In the world of flows and networks, continually developing and spreading, globalization is not just 'outside' but well and truly within all societies including those of Latin America. This is a more complex and rapidly evolving world than that described by dependency theory in the 1970s. It is no more benign for Latin America and few believe it will deliver democratic development for Latin America any more than the modernization approach did.

The vast majority of the citizens of Latin America wish to be 'citizens of the world'; there is very little atavistic desire to pursue lost roots or a 'true' Latin American identity. There is a cultural confidence in Latin America that renders the risks of globalization more than acceptable. The problem is that most governments in Latin America do not see their citizens' global or cosmopolitan aspirations as a priority. For them, globalization spells economic problems and an internationalization of politics that makes their jobs far more difficult. These governments necessarily work inwards to secure a level of stability and legitimacy to confront an outside world seen, more or less uniformly, as hostile. There will inevitably in the future be a resurgence of nationalism of a populist and also rightist flavour if Latin America's insertion into the globalization process is not achieved on a more equitable and sustainable basis.

In conclusion, we should probably question the novelty of the globalization paradigm for an understanding of Latin America. Latin America was always part of a global system and that element of the dependency theory has never really been contested. Centuries of colonialism were not just wiped away when independent nation-states were formed in the nineteenth century. To refer to Latin America as postcolonial is seen as inaccurate and misleading by many intellectuals in Latin America, but surely it has some relevance. Latin America today is at the opposite end of the spectrum from autarchy in relation to the global system. A powerful economic and military machine to the North, the USA, sets the terms

204 Contemporary Latin America

of reference for any development option. There are options, as we shall see in the section below, but on the whole the global context is not favourable for democratic development in Latin America.

Economic Prospects

If European thinkers now ponder the dangers of 'Brazilianization', Latin American intellectuals have turned recently to consider the 'Puertoricoization' of their countries. Puerto Rico is a 'Latin' country, Spanish is spoken there, there is a thriving independence movement, but it is an integral part of the United States. The prospect of Latin America's Puertoricoization acts as a 'scarecrow' for Arnold Antonin, but it 'may now become a voluntary and attractive process for the impoverished masses of Latin America given the failure of economic and political elites' (1995: 69). According to this scenario, articulated by a Haitian intellectual, if Latin Americans cannot all get to the USA to share in the 'American Way of Life' they will end up inviting the USA to their countries to recreate them in their own image. In this nightmare scenario nation-states will be replaced by drug cartels, and national governments will be replaced by colonial administrations.

As with most images, that of Puertoricanization captures some of the trends at play but also exaggerates them. A realistic prospect for Haiti is not necessarily so realistic for Brazil. While the dynamic of recolonization is countered by strong nationalistic and regionalist tendencies, globalization is having a powerful economic effect. However, it is not leading to a homogenization of Latin America's economies (whether in an upward or a downward direction), but rather to their increased differentiation. The logic of globalization is not one of even development but, in fact, one of growing fragmentation. As dependency theory showed in its day, increased international integration leads to increased national disintegration in Latin America. While globalization plays the dominant role in structuring the region's economic relations with the world around it, within the region social fragmentation rules as there is no unifying logic comparable to that played in the past by national economic development strategies.

In the immediate future the economic prospects of Latin America must be declared uncertain at best. For Rosemary Thorp, taking a long-term view of the twentieth century we can conclude that: 'Despite the setbacks of recent years, the trade structures of the larger and even some of the smaller countries have been transformed over the century, away from dependence on a few primary exports' (1998: 281). Certainly, as we saw in Chapter 1, the social indicators that measure development improved dramatically in the second half of the twentieth century. Economic policy-making is more sophisticated even though the range of choices may be more limited; governments have become more pragmatic and knowledgeable in dealing with the economic crises that have come their way. But can we really argue, as Thorp does, that governments in Latin America 'are beginning to recognize the potential for complementarity between growth and equity' (1998: 281)?

The neo-liberal agenda stressed above all the efficiency of the market in allocating economic resources. Questions of equity were either postponed or relegated to the political realm. That is, unless one chose to believe that in the 'long term', rational allocation of resources by 'the market' would be to everyone's advantage. Bulmer-Thomas, in concluding a major research project on the new economic model (NEM) in Latin America, argued that: 'The scale of poverty and the degree of income inequality continue to be the scourge of Latin America. The NEM does not provide a simple answer to either problem' (Bulmer-Thomas 1996: 312). Yet all the evidence points to the neo-liberal agenda having no answer at all to the problem of poverty beyond demanding faith in the market or providing better education for young aspiring labour market entrants in the hope that they might be able to compete in the labour market. This political dead-end for neo-liberalism is now widely recognized as a problem.

In the years to come we can imagine that there will be a keen bid to find alternative economic policies. As Korzeniewicz and Smith argue, 'embryonic and fragmentary efforts are already underway in Latin America that make it possible to visualize a "high road" to economic growth, hemispheric integration and globalization' (2000: 29). The economic strategies pursued by Chile or Brazil today cannot be reduced to seeking a low-wage niche in the global market. Their formulators recognize the crucial role of the state in regulating the market, a function it cannot perform itself. The strategies focus crucially on the social and institutional agenda which was so clearly neglected by the first wave of economic reforms in the 1980s. The economic crisis in Mexico in 1994 and the virtual meltdown of Argentina's economy in 2001 provided clear indications that integration with the world economy carried risks. If only out of self-interest, economic policy-makers in Latin America do now look beyond the Washington Consensus.

If globalization creates a new dualism between those included and those excluded from its dynamic, then the tasks of any economic strategy

Box 10.2   People challenging globalization

People are increasingly challenging neo-liberal globalization in diverse ways – economic, political, social and cultural – and at different levels or scales of social activity from the global to the local, passing through the regional, national and maybe city levels. In Latin America there is a particularly vigorous resistance to globalization at a popular level, from street demonstrations against neo-liberal economic policies through struggles over water privatization to the reassertion of traditional indigenous values and ways of social interaction.

In Central America there was a general move in the 1990s away from a period of civil war and economic stagnation towards more active integration with the US economy. There was now an emphasis on negotiated settlements and renewed efforts at regional integration, taking up initiatives of the 1960s. This was, of course, the post-cold-war period when globalization was at its most virulent phase. Rural producers in particular had to face intense international competition and consumers struggled to get by.

It was in this context that the search for economic alternatives began, to counter social exclusion and to create new spaces (*crear espacio*). In Honduras one such entity arose in response to this situation, and in 1995 a clear-cut project emerged. Small-scale agricultural producers in Honduras, organized in cooperatives, church-based organizations, women's organizations and farmworkers' associations, proposed to transform their local economies via active and sustainable commercial relations. In the absence of a market system that could provide a decent

→

must necessarily include seeking to overcome this divide. The 'digital divide' between those linked electronically to the new economy and those not is one important element. There is also a gender divide with women still, and increasingly more likely to be, on the low road to globalization rather than the high road. There are also regional divides between those parts of a country linked into the global economy and those which are increasingly becoming an economic backwater. To overcome these complex and interrelated dualisms, and the inequalities they cause or exacerbate, is a massive task. It is clearly not just an economic issue and involves all levels of social interaction, especially the political dimension (see next section) but also the cultural one. A cultural revolution to get beyond the restrictive choices present in economic policy-making today is also necessary for development to be prioritized.

Absolutely crucial to any new economic policy seeking to bridge the gap between equity and efficiency will be the role of the states. The

→

livelihood to the producer and render a fair price to consumers, a network of social organizations from the productive sector would market basic grains and staple items of daily consumption to rural and marginalized urban communities.

The idea took on a name, the Alternative Community Trade Network (COMAL). A *comal* is a traditional cooking instrument found throughout Central America, round in shape and usually handmade from natural clay. The *comal* is placed, like a skillet, over an open fire or stove to cook maize tortillas, a staple in most Central American cultures. The choice of the *comal* as a symbol became a reaffirmation of food security at the most basic level, of both men's and women's contributions to economic livelihood, and of the endurance of cultures and traditions at risk.

COMAL had an ambitious agenda: to ensure that local organizations could effectively coordinate actions, to achieve the volume needed to become economic and political players. Community stores, already established by many organizations on a small scale and in sometimes isolated locations, would benefit from quality products at better prices and access to greater technical skills, and as such could better serve low-income populations. The initiative was highly grassroots-oriented, with a strong commitment from the American Friends Service Committee (AFSC) to support organization, assist in building an administrative and legal base, form a technical team and accompany a complex process of building bridges across sectors and borders. Four initial programmes developed in planned phases: Education and Training, Price Information System, Marketing and Institution Building.

Source: McCann Sánchez (2002: 103–7).

neo-liberal economic reforms of the 1980s ended the cycle of state-led development. At its bluntest it meant the dismantling of the state's economic functions, to be replaced by the 'invisible hand' of the market. National development was to be replaced by a global development model. Now, some 20 years after this dramatic economic transformation process was launched its success is far from clear. Even among supporters of the NEM, the talk now is of reforming the state rather than simply downsizing it. The Latin American Centre for Development Administration argues that total market predominance does not make economic or political sense today and that 'rather than dismantling the state structure, the solution would lie in its reconstruction' (CLAD 2002: 1). Even if the state is no longer seen as having a necessary role in production, its regulatory capacity is seen as more important than ever before.

State reform is an integral element of redemocratization in Latin America and, conversely, the new state needs to be more democratic (see Chapter 4). To tackle the social inequalities of the region the new democratic state will necessarily be more efficient than its counterpart in the 1950s. While economic stabilization has been achieved through the economic reforms of the 1980s, social legitimacy has yet to be achieved. For that to happen, the Latin American state will not only need to be more efficient than in the past: it will need to address social development issues which, even in the medium term, can hold back economic development. As CLAD puts it: 'In the process of rebuilding the Latin American State, the greatest challenge lies in rendering changing world trends compatible with the region's specificities' (2002: 3). The danger is that in moving from a protectionist, inward-looking state into the era of global competitiveness (the 'competitive state') national development priorities will be ignored altogether. Following that path would make the Latin American state a simple transmission belt for IMF policies.

Over and beyond the questions of political economy and economic policy-making lies the underlying question of what development actually means in the era of globalization. Following the Second World War, development was taken to mean nationally managed economic growth. Towards the end of the twentieth century as the era of globalization began, development became redefined as the extent of participation in and integration with the world market; the role of the state was now simply to enforce the *global* rules of economic management. Yet this model or understanding of development has been contested. The classic problems of underdevelopment persist and cannot be wished away. Development needs to be sustainable in the long term, so ecological issues simply demand attention. Also, gender is also now a decisive element in any development policy debate, while social justice and the rights of minorities are now crucial to a broadly defined concept of development.

If development is redefined so would be our understanding of Latin America's economic prospects. The companies that regularly produce risk-index studies of Latin America are usually linked to the large transnational banks. They decide that a country is a greater or a lesser risk to international investors purely on the criteria of profitability (and stability, up to a point). On the other hand, as a study of black community organizations in Colombia found:

> For the ethno-cultural organizations, development must be guided by principles derived from the rights and aspirations of the local communities and must propend for the affirmation of cultures and the protection of natural environments. (Grueso *et al.* 1992: 212)

In this people-centred meaning of development we find equity and sustainability at the top of the agenda rather than profitability and openness to the world market. It is a conception gaining ground in Latin America as the 'downside' of the neo-liberal strategy for development becomes more apparent.

Political Challenges

Undoubtedly the main political challenge facing Latin America today is the question of governability in the era of globalization (see Chapter 5). How can a modicum of political stability and consensus be maintained by governments of countries that are being buffeted by the increasing pressures of economic internationalization? Democratic governability and what is known as 'good' government are essential ingredients for any stable political system, but they are in particular demand in Latin America at the present time. We would appear to be witnessing a transitional political period both globally and in Latin America. How can the undoubted dynamism of economic globalization be matched through a process of global governance? How can Latin American governments construct the institutions of democratic governance when social and economic inequality are increasing? These are the main political challenges in Latin America today.

The crisis of governability in Latin America today is most acute in the Central American countries, where the failure of the movements striving for social transformation in the 1980s had a long-term effect. The integration of Mexico with the USA and Canada pushes Central America further into peripherality. Peru also suffers from ungovernability as do Bolivia and Ecuador, if to a lesser extent. For O'Donnell the main means to achieving governability are 'a relatively high homogeneity (especially territorial) and a solid historical democratic tradition' (1993: 69). Scoring high in these terms are Chile, Uruguay and Costa Rica (the Central American exception to the rule). Countries such as Argentina, Colombia and Venezuela fall somewhere in between in so far as they have overcome heterogeneity to some extent and have strong democratic traditions, but these are jeopardized by the pressures created by globalization over the last decade or so.

One of the main reasons for increasing ungovernability, apart from the pressure of globalization, is the growing disenchantment with the democratic process. When elected governments returned to the region from the mid-1980s onwards, hopes were high that democracy would deliver economic, political and social benefits to all. However, as this process of democratization coincided with the neo-liberal economic 'revolution', this was not to be the case. What had emerged by the 1990s was a widespread disenchantment (*desencanto*) with democracy generally. Neo-liberalism tended to decentre politics and to destructure pre-existing social and political identities. The market, as it were, 'dissolved' these identities and devalued politics. The rule of the market and the prioritizing of individualism in economic theory had the political effect of demobilizing civil society. As people emerged from the dictatorships to become citizens in the new democracies, so the new economics led them to withdraw from the public area to the private.

The expectations that democracy would deliver were undoubtedly inflated, but the global context and the local neo-liberal agenda made it almost impossible. The result was a certain disengagement from democracy and the election in the 1990s of authoritarian figures such as Menem in Argentina and Fujimori in Peru. In so far as the state had turned into a dictatorship in the previous period, the electorate were also receptive to the anti-state message of the neo-liberals. The new democracies were also inevitably going to suffer from wear and tear (*desgaste*) owing to the pressure of seeking to govern under conditions of increased international competition and the burden of the foreign debt. Democracy, or the actual form it took in Latin America at the turn of the century, has not been able to satisfy people's expectations. The ensuing disenchantment could lead to the emergence of authoritarian regimes promising a way out of the apparent impasse in democratic governability, but that is by no means an inevitable outcome.

To overcome disenchantment and create the conditions for democratic governability, a new conception of citizenship seems necessary. Citizenship needs to be more active and more participatory to counteract the inevitable tendencies towards what we have called the disenchantment with democracy. At present we see in Latin America a tendency towards a critique of all politics and representative politics in particular, and anti-politics can easily take an authoritarian direction as we have mentioned. Politics seems to become irrelevant as the market spreads its influence from the economic to the electoral sphere, yet the power to transform society and influence the global context lies mainly in the political arena. Participation in politics inevitably has high points and low points, but there are signs of popular reinvolvement. Reactions in Venezuela after the attempt to overthrow Chávez in 2002, and those by the people in Argentina faced with economic catastrophe, point to a new era of popular involvement in politics.

Democracy is clearly a process and not a one-off event, and democratic citizenship needs to be constructed rather than assumed. The key countries which will determine whether Latin America moves in that direction are, undoubtedly, Brazil and Mexico. In terms of our typology above, with Uruguay and Chile at the stable end and Central America and Peru at the unstable end, these two countries stand somewhere in between. They are highly heterogeneous and even face territorial fragility in the Amazon and Chiapas regions respectively. However, the long decades of authoritarian and centralized government in both Mexico and Brazil have generated a certain political stability. In Mexico, the unthinkable happened in 1999 and the PRI (Revolutionary Institutional Party) suffered electoral defeat. In Brazil a highly mobilized electorate and competitive party system has led to left-led governorships in hugely important provinces, and it is now possible even to think of a national left-wing government that is overthrown by a military coup.

Whether a new form of citizenship is constructed in Latin America or not depends on how the current period of political transition is resolved. The era now coming to a close is the era of the Mexican Revolution which began in 1910. That revolution symbolizes the national democratic transformation of Latin America. It meant modernization, universal education, land redistribution and the building of a national identity. When Mexico chose to join NAFTA in 1994 that whole era had clearly come to an end. National sovereignty seemed a quaint archaism and the US model of democracy seemed the only one worth pursuing. The old regime was dead but it still was not clear what was to replace it, in so far as Mexico could never become a Puerto Rico. What the future might hold was signalled by another event early in 1994, namely the start of the Zapatista revolt that was to have a significant effect on the growing anti-globalization movement.

The Zapatista revolt seemed to open up a new period in Mexico's history. While its roots lie deep in the colonial past it is also a clear reflection of resistance to globalization's effects. Relatively unaffected by the transformations unleashed in 1910, this region has been hit particularly hard by neo-liberalism. The revolt is seeking reforms not unlike those demanded by the revolutionaries of 1910: land, work, education, home. However, these demands are not easily met in the present situation and would entail essentially a 'revolution in the revolution'. Given the information revolution and the contiguity between struggles which globalization allows, Chiapas is not an island. Indeed, perhaps more important than its global effects (often rather romantic and simplified) is its impact on the rest of Mexico. Today the need for another democratic

Box 10.3   Zapatistas speak out

For Subcomandante Marcos, spokesperson of the Zapatistas speaking in early 1994:

> it is perhaps for this reason – the lack of interest in power – that the word of the Zapatistas has been well received in other countries across the globe, above all in Europe. It has not just been because it is new or novel, but rather because it is proposing this, which is to say: to separate the political problem from the problem of taking power, and take it to another terrain.

> Our work is going to end, if it ends, in the construction of this space for new political relationships. What follows is going to be a product of the efforts of other people, with another way of thinking and acting.

He went on to say that:

> What upsets the Pentagon is when you punch Zapatista into the computer, nothing comes out that says, Moscow, or Havana, or Libya, Tripoli, Bosnia or any other group. And the left, accustomed to the same way of thinking, says, well, they don't fit in anywhere. It doesn't occur to them there might be something new, that you have to retheorize. And they say, well then, these poor people don't know what they want, we need to help them ... I have seen various magazines ... of Trotskyites and Maoists, of all the orthodox leftists and of the old dinosaurs that say, well, the ELZN [Ejército Zapatista de Liberación Nacional/Zapatista National Liberation Army] is very good and what they've done is very good and all, but they lack a program, so here's a program. They lack a party so here's a party. They lack a leader so here's a leader.

→

revolution in Mexico – and the rest of Latin America – is back on the agenda, owing at least in part to the example of Chiapas. For some insight into Zapatista thinking see Box 10.3.

Mexico's modernist revolution of 1910 and its arguably postmodern revolution (however localized) of 1994 are crucial events in Latin America. Cultural critic Néstor García Canclini writes that 'For many decades Latin American societies placed their faith in this modernity project' (García Canclini 2000: 44). The modernist revolution went far beyond politics as conventionally understood; industrialization, migration to the cities and universal education are all part of a modernizing dream.

→

As to Zapatista politics:

> We do not want others, more or less of the right, centre or left, to decide for us. We want to participate directly in the decisions which concern us, to control those who govern us, without regard to their political affiliation, and oblige them to 'rule by obeying'. We do not struggle to take power, we struggle for democracy, liberty and justice. Our political proposal is the most radical in Mexico (perhaps in the world but it is still too soon to say) ...

> We hope that the people understand that the causes that have moved us to do this are just, and that the path that we have chosen is just one, not the only one. Nor do we think that it is the best of all paths ... We do not want a dictatorship of another kind, nor anything out of this world, not international Communism and all that. We want just where there is now not even minimum subsistence ... We do not want to monopolize the vanguard or say that we are the light, the only alternative, or stingily claim the qualification of the revolutionary for one or another current. We say, look at what happened. This is what we had to do.

For the Zapatistas, politics is global:

> We will make a collective network of all our particular struggles and resistances. An intercontinental network of resistance against neoliberalism, an intercontinental network of resistance for humanity. This intercontinental network of resistance, recognising differences and acknowledging similarities, will search to find itself with other resistances around the world. This intercontinental network of resistance will be the medium in which distinct resistances may support one another. This intercontinental network of resistance is not an organising structure; it doesn' t have a central head or decision maker; it has no central command or hierarchies. We are the network, all of us who resist.

Source: http://flag.blackened.net/revolt/zapatista.html.

As García Canclini writes, 'parents sent their children to school en masse believing that it was a means of social mobility' (2000: 44). Today education is being privatized and the dream of a national health service has evaporated. Industries close down and the great cities sink under the weight of pollution and overcrowding. It is clearly too early to say whether Chiapas 1994 will inaugurate a continent-wide process of transformation as the earlier Zapatistas of 1910 did. According to John Peeler:

> Latin America ... has an opportunity to make a major contribution to the political theory and practice of democracy by pushing forward with a vision of radical democratic reform at a time when the stable democracies of the north seem unable to move. (1998: 201)

While on the face of it this view is unduly optimistic, it does reflect a distinct possibility. Latin America, whatever its problems, is not a jaded society unable to reinvent itself. In fact, as we shall see in the next section, Latin America has shown huge political and cultural creativity in forging a distinct identity. Radical democracy may never be achieved in Latin America but it is being built in many corners of civil society. A new mood of democratic experimentalism is evident in the new social movements, in local democratic experiences and in the refusal of the Puerto Rico model of subordination to the imperial power to the north. After neo-liberalism, democracy is being reconstructed.

After Modernity

The modernizing project which began in the 1950s across most of Latin America is now in crisis. Modernizing technologies still make their impact felt, but modernity is still as far away as ever. So what happens after modernity? Is Latin America still really 'pre'modern vainly seeking to catch up with the West? Or is Latin America simply following a different path to modernity? These are not abstract philosophical debates because they speak to 'what' Latin America is. Identity is a crucial issue today, no less so for nations and regions than for individuals. As globalization seemingly dissolves difference then questions of identity will come more to the fore. I will examine two positions, the first that Latin America is still essentially premodern, and the second that stresses Latin America's difference. My own position, which is distinct from both these main positions, follows.

There is still a strand of analysis that follows on from the racist stereotypes of the nineteenth century. The 'Iberian-Catholic' heritage is seen to account for the particularities of Latin America's modernity, or failure to achieve it, and features such as the authoritarianism of military rule and the role of women in society are explained in terms of the colonization by Spain and Portugal. In the 1990s, Latin America was also viewed in a similar way by writers such as Samuel Huntington (1996), who viewed the world in terms of a global culture clash. Modernization and development were seen by him as specifically Western attributes. Democracy, stability, wealth and equity are aspirations for Westerners, while other cultures may prefer authoritarianism, hierarchy, religion, austerity and discipline as values to rule their lives by. Islamic societies are obviously the main 'other' Huntington has in mind, but the Latinos to the south of his homeland would also be considered rather different in some essentialist way.

In Latin America a parallel position has been developed recently by Claudio Veliz (1994), in an influential overview of modernity and tradition. While Latin America was inclined to centralism, tradition and order, the Anglo-Saxon countries prioritized mobility, modernity and change. The aversion to change of the Spanish *conquistadores*, with their spirit of the Counter-Reformation, has persisted until the present day for Veliz. Only now with globalization are the Anglo-Saxon values penetrating Latin America and allowing space for modernization. For Veliz, 'in spite of its reputation for frequent and violent upheaval, the principal feature of modern Latin America is its overwhelming stability' (1994: 86). It is the cultural identity of Latin America which has prevented modernization according to this perspective; Latin Americans are sent to live imprisoned in their own past, unable to accept change and unreasonably distrustful of anything new.

The problem with the positions of Samuel Huntington and Claudio Veliz is that they simply assume the superiority of the North American development model, which is no different in essence from the position taken by Domingo Faustino Sarmiento in the nineteenth century when he contrasted Latin America's 'barbarism' with the 'civilization' of the Europeans (see Chapter 8). Modernization can only come from without, brought to the barbaric and backward regions by the enlightened Europeans or, now, North Americans. Not only does it rely on racist assumptions, but this is also a theory which has been applied from the colonial era until today without success. The diffusion of Western values and Western consumer goods has been going on for a long time, and unless we believe that Latin American cultural identity is incredibly hardy as well as backward, it is difficult to understand why cultural assimilation has not occurred and led to modernization. In fact, as we shall see later, modernization has occurred; it has simply been of a particularly peripheral nature given Latin America's position in the global economy.

At the other extreme are those views that stress the specificity of Latin America in a positive sense. In the literary boom of the 1960s there emerged a new term, 'magical realism', which could be said to encapsulate Latin America's uniqueness. It is a cultural model often called *macondismo*, named after the mythical village Macondo in Gabriel García Márquez's *Cien años de soledad*. Macondo serves as a metaphor for the recalcitrant, indigenous and magical reality of Latin America. As Larrain puts it: 'Latin America is supposed to be the world of the unexpected and of uncontrollable telluric forces' (2000: 137). This world will resist the Western notion of modernization to seek its own magical mode. It rejects the model of Western rational–formal man based on individual economic calculations. Instead, there is an emphasis on indigenous knowledge, a different way of seeing the world and acting within it. There is an emphasis on reciprocity and solidarity against Western possessive individualism.

There are two main variants of the belief that Latin America is different from the West or the north. One of these stresses the recovery of the indigenous values destroyed by the Iberian conquest. Eduardo Galeano, the extremely influential Uruguayan author, writes in this vein that

> It is out of hope, not nostalgia, that we must recover a community-based mode of production and way of life, founded not on greed, but on solidarity, age-old freedoms and identity between human beings and nature. (1991: 14)

This utopia is to be sought, according to Galeano, from among the Indo-American communities. The religious variant of this vision stresses the meeting between indigenous cultural values and Catholicism. This Latin American religiosity is seen as beyond Western instrumental rationality. It stresses intuition over scientific knowledge and morality over the world of business. Modernization seen as rationalization is alien to this ethos that would stress, conversely, the benefits of a communal or people-led development effort.

The main problem with this cluster of views on Latin America's identity is its essentialism. That is to say they rely on a concept of identity as something innate and immutable over time. As Larrain puts it, however, 'it is difficult to accept that Latin American cultural identity was fixed once and for all in the sixteenth century, in a symbolic dramatic matrix standing fundamentally in opposition to the Enlightenment' (2000: 158). In many ways this procedure is simply the mirror opposite of negative stereotyping of those who argue for an innate Iberian-Catholic identity that held back modernization. In its recovery and revaluing of indigenous traditions this perspective is, in essence, a form of anti-modernism. While these traditions can be incorporated into a new identity and a movement for social transformation they cannot simply be 'revived'. Otherwise we end up in a similar position to the romantic anti-Enlightenment movement in Europe that was not able to significantly impact on the rise of capitalism.

Rather than argue whether Latin America was premodern (as per Claudio Veliz) or anti-modern (as per *macondismo*), we could consider the analogy with postmodernism. We can take postmodernism, not as something 'after' modernity but as a particular version of it. In Latin America there is a particular symbiosis between archaic social and

economic relations and ultra-modern ones, reflected in popular culture
for example (see Chapter 7). These are hybrid societies with an uneven
development in which premodern, modern and 'postmodern' features
combine in a form of syncretism. They are labile societies and political
systems, constantly pulled between the traditional and the modern, the
local and the global. Even time does not seem to follow the logic of
Western sequential temporality. Rather, in Latin America we see mixed
temporalities where the old mixes with the new quite effortlessly. We
can see this in the realm of music or in the indigenous-based Zapatistas'
use of the internet to pursue 'traditional' demands. We see it also in the
use of language such as that of the novel by Carlos Fuentes, *Christopter
Unborn*:

> We are all Columbuses, those of us who bet on the truth of our
> imagination and win; we are all Quijotes who believe in what we
> imagine; but ultimately, we are all Don Juans who desire as soon as
> we imagine and who quickly find out that there is no innocent desire,
> the desire to complete oneself takes over the other, changes him,
> makes him one's own: not only do I desire you, I desire besides that
> you desire as I do, that you be like me, that you be I: Christopher,
> Quijote, Juan, our fathers who art on earth, our everyday Utopia, give
> it to us tomorrow and forgive us our debts ($1,992 billion, according
> to this morning's *Gall Street Journal*!), although we (Aztecs! Incas!
> Sioux! Caribs! Araucanians! Patagonians!) will never forgive our
> debtors: yessir, make us fall into temptation, because pleasure without
> sin is not pleasure ... I don't want a pacific world which we will not
> deserve as long as we don't resolve what's going on inside here, my
> father says to us, with all that which we are, good and bad, bad and
> good, but still unresolved; wife, son, we shall arrive at Pacifica one
> day if we first stop being North or East in order to be ourselves, West
> and all. (1990: 522–3)

From a postmodern perspective all traditions are culturally constructed,
as is modernity of course, so that we cannot take them as pure essences.
The notion of 'hybridity' associated with the postcolonial form of literary analysis can also be useful in terms of our social and political focus.
If Latin America is a hybrid social formation, that means its modernity
is particular: clearly it has been constructed on the periphery of the
world system, from the era of colonialism to the new imperialism of
today. The notion of hybridity allows us to reject the notion that globalization is creating a homogenous world when Latin America is so clearly
heterogeneous. Likewise, however, it is a concept which allows us to

---

Box 10.4   García Canclini's vision

Néstor García Canclini is an anthropologist and cultural theorist born in
Argentina but who has been working in Mexico for many years. His best-
known work is *Cultura Híbridas/Hybrid Cultures* (1995). In 2002 he won
the Fundación Cardoza y Aragón Hispanic American literary essay prize
for his anonymously presented *Latinoamericanos buscando lugar en este
siglo* (Latin Americans Searching for a Place in this Century) which
asks the deceptively simple question: 'What does it mean to be a Latin
American (today)?' He sees neo-liberalism as corroding our societies but
cultural diversity as everywhere flourishing. We are caught between the
loss of viable national development projects and the promises of the new
global cosmopolitanism. For García Canclini the meaning of 'Latin
American' might emerge from new open and solidarity based exchanges in
the era of globalization. We need to respond creatively to globalization and
not just accept is as a given.

In García Canclini's own words:

> What does it mean to be Latin American? I have tried to essay the way
> in which this question has been changing and new answers are being
> constructed. There are still historical voices in this debate but other
> different ones are added, sometimes with new arguments. Also, the
> scale has expanded: the current condition of Latin America overflows
> its territory. Those who have left their countries and now extend our
> cultures beyond the region, show the painful dislocation of the Latin
> Americans and also the opportunities offered by global exchanges. I
> wanted to capture the indecision that our ambivalent insertion into the
> current conflicts of capitalism leads us to: we are globalized as cultural
> producers, as migrants and as debtors ... We will thus arrive with more
> subjections than assets to the functions that various nations of the
> continent will mount to celebrate in 2010 the second centenary of their
> independence.

Source: García Canclini (2002: 12–13; my translation).

---

question the notion of some essential 'Latin Americanness' be it indigenous or religious in character. Against any totalizing logic we should,
perhaps, follow García Canclini in recognizing that Latin America's
'multicultural and multitemporal heterogeneity does not constitute an
obstacle to be eliminated but a basic fact for any programme of development and [regional] integration' (1997: 31).

This book began by asking 'where' Latin America is in the world in
terms of its nation-states, its physical landscapes and its peoples. We can

probably now close appropriately by asking 'what' is Latin America? It is part of the West but not quite. It is modern but not quite. Some authors go on to say that 'Latin America belongs not quite anywhere' (Schelling 2000: 9). I prefer to pursue the analogies with hybridity, mixed temporalities, and a condition of liminality (betwixt and between). These are concepts and frameworks which do allow us to make sense of the uneven but combined development processes described in the chapters above. Finally, we can say that Latin America is in a sense a process and not a predefined entity. It is as Aricó from Argentina once put it: 'an unfinished construction, a project to be realized, an unfulfilled project always set on our horizons' (cited in Calderón and Dos Santos 1995: 19).

Latin America is today one site of the battle of ideas between neo-liberal globalization/the US model/the market model and all the alternative sources of power and different social and political logics. Taking a global view, Perry Anderson concludes that in Latin America we find a much stronger and more promising combination of factors pointing towards an alternative model. That is because

> here, and only here, the resistance to neo-liberalism and to neo-imperialism melds the cultural with the social and national. That is to say, it implies the emerging vision of another type of organization of society and another model of relations among states. (Anderson 2004: 42)

Thus it is not only an alternative social model that is emerging from below, there is also a new level of inter-state cooperation that refuses to go along with a simple US-led world order. While in Europe popular opinion may have opposed the US war in Iraq, most European governments acquiesced. It was only in Latin America that resistance to the new worldwide hegemonic ambitions of the USA stretched from the streets to the presidential palaces.

Latin America is also particular because as Anderson reminds his Northern audience, it is 'the only region of the world with a continuous history of revolutionary upsets and radical political struggles that extend for somewhat more than the last century' (Anderson: 2004: 42). From the Mexican Revolution at the start of the century to the Bolivarian Revolution at its close there has been a cycle of major revolutionary upheavals including Bolivia in 1952, Cuba in 1959, Nicaragua in 1979 and so forth. The revolutionary tradition – in its nationalist but also socialist variants – has strong roots and was never really overcome by the collapse of communism in the 1990s. This is not to say it is a uniquely revolutionary region waiting to explode in flames. What it means is that history counts in Latin America – a region where Fukuyama's optimistic prediction of the 'end of history' in 1990 cut little ice. There is a quite uniquely fluid relationship between the past, the present and the future in Latin America where they all interact and form part of one another. The story we have recounted in this little book is far from over.

Recommended Reading

Rather than seeking to be comprehensive in any way, this list is quite selective, focusing on key issues and drawing attention to central texts. It is also limited in that it keeps to the English-language material when, in reality, a closer knowledge of the situation demands access to the literature in Spanish and Portuguese. Rather than provide a list of further reading for each chapter, I prefer to categorize broadly through four main headings, General, Economic, Political and Social, taken purely as labels of convenience. Last, but definitely not least, there is a guide to contemporary and internet sources.

General

Encyclopedias do not immediately come to mind as a good read but the *Cambridge Encyclopaedia of Latin America and the Caribbean* edited by Simon Collier and Thomas Skidmore (1992) is well informed and extremely readable. For more detail and a far more academic treatment you may dip into the 10-volume *Cambridge History of Latin America* series edited by Leslie Bethel (1984–96).

For a broad single-authored history of Latin America few can compare with Tulio Halperín Doughi's (1993) much reprinted work, while Schneider (2006) offers a chronologically ordered study of Latin America's political history from colonial times to the twenty-first century. A traditional, country-by-country approach is the student-friendly text by Thomas Skidmore and Peter Smith (2001), and a broad analytical overview of democracy in Latin America can be found in Smith (2005). Of the many 'readers', which often suffer from lack of focus or detailed treatment of issues, that of Jan Knippers Black (2005) stands out as useful. For a critical Latin American view of the twenty-first-century options see Manuel Antonio Garretón and co-authors (2002) and Gwynne and Kay (2004) which provides much material to follow through on the introductions to the various themes provided in this text.

From more disciplinary perspectives one could start with Tessa Cubitt's (1995) broad sociology of Latin America, Jonathan Barton's (1997) political geography, Geraldine Lievesley's (1999) political science approach and Jorge Larrain's (2000) cultural sociology perspective. Swanson (2003)provides a lively and up-to-date companion to literary and cultural studies; for a transdisciplinary perspective which takes up broad theoretical concerns in relation to Latin America see Centeno and López-Alves (2001).

It is quite impossible to provide a guide to reading for all of the republics of Latin America. However, on Argentina you could consider the broad overview by David Rock (1987), on Brazil that by Thomas Skidmore (1999), and for Chile a useful introduction by Antonio Garretón (1989). On Mexico the literature is nearly as vast as that for the rest of Latin America put together, but a good start is Knight (2002) and not to be missed is Gilly (2006) on the history of the Mexican Revolution from a sympathetically critical perspective. For Central America a good overview in English is that by James Dunkerley (1988) and also the more recent collection by Booth *et al.* (2005) that stresses the relationship between global forces and social rebellions. On Colombia, with a focus on the recent violence period, see Charles Bergquist and co-authors' study (Bergquist *et al.* 2001) and for a broad historical sweep Palacios (2006) that is both readable and reliable. On Peru see Carrion (2006) on the legacy of the Fujimori era and on Venezuela Daniel Levine (1992) provides a good overview. On Cuba you may usefully consult Janette Habel's (1991) introduction and Gott (2005), a broad sweeping history with many insights. On the Zapatistas a useful introduction is that by Neil Harvey (1998) and on Chávez or Chavismo in Venezuela see Richard Gott (2001) for a sympathetic but independent view.

For a general undergraduate bibliography see Ana Maria Cobos and Ana Lya Sater (2002) which will also have a dedicated website constantly updated.

Economic

To understand the contemporary political economy of Latin America one perforce needs to take a historical perspective. Victor Bulmer-Thomas (1994) covers the economic history of Latin America, while Rosemary Thorp (1998) focuses on the twentieth century. The impact of neoliberalism is considered in considerable detail in a thematic collection edited by Bulmer-Thomas (1996) and in that edited by Smith *et al.* (1994), with Haggard and Kaufman (1996) providing a broad overview of the political economy of democratic transition.

The political economy of Latin America has also given rise to a whole series of polemics and critiques of the mainstream. Critical overviews include those by Henry Veltmeyer *et al.* (1997) and essays collected by Philip Oxhorn and Graciela Ducatenzeiler (1998), while Frederick Weaver (2000) provides a succinct but informative radical overview of Latin America in the world economy.

On the question of regional integration there are a number of solid studies one can consult. These include the collection edited by Victor Bulmer-Thomas (2001) and the broader Third-World perspective on regionalization and globalization edited by Felix Fernández-Jilberto and André Mommen (1998).

Political

The domestic, regional and international political dimensions of Latin America have a vast literature dedicated to them. Some of this is conjunctural, commenting on events which may not seem so relevant in a few years' time, but there is now a solid tradition of comparative politics to draw on. For an introduction to this field see Wiarda and Kline (2006), which provides an overview of the political factors that condition socio-economic development.

One of Latin America's main contributions to comparative politics has been in the area of democratization. The literature is vast and has become somewhat overspecialized, but see the classic *Transitions from Authoritarian Rule* (O' Donnell *et al.* 1986). Worthwhile studies include the collections edited by Linz and Valenzuela (1994), by Mainwaring *et al.* (1992) and (with a Central American focus) by Seligson and Booth (1995). For brief critical introductions to the issue of democracy in Latin America see the accessible books of John Peeler (1998) and by Geraldine Lievesley (1999). For a more advanced recent focus on democratization see the Garretón and Newman (2002) collection.

The collection edited by Elizabeth Dore (1997) engages with some of the key issues in the gender debates; the accessible Latin American Bureau publication by Sylvia Chant and Nikki Craske (2003) examines the changing patters of gender relations; and finally, Maxine Molyneux (2000) engages with Latin America from a broad gender politics perspective.

On the law in Latin America, or more precisely the lack of it, see the collection edited by Méndez *et al.* (1999), which provides an illuminating if disturbing overview. On legislative politics in Latin America a useful overview is that provided by the collection edited by Morgenstern and Nacif (2006). Another key political issue of the day is the current reform of the state, on which see the collection of Vellinga (edited by Menno Vellinga 1999) and that by Carlos Luiz Bresser-Pereira (1999) with a strong Brazilian focus. On the politics of the environment and of non-governmental organizations in Latin America, see Bebbington and Thiele (1993). On the troubled relationship between drugs and democracy see Arias (2006).

The external dimension in Latin America is inevitably dominated by relations with the United States, on which one may consult the Bulmer-Thomas and Dunkerley (1999) collection on 'the new agenda', the thematic overview by G. Pope Atkins (1999) and the brilliant critical history of Peter H. Smith (2000). On Latin American-European relations see Lawrence Whitehead (1996) on the European dimension of democratization in Latin America.

Social

The social arena is more diverse than the economic and the political in so far as it is not unified to the same extent by the dominant discipline, in this case sociology. Much of the research in this area (which I take to include the cultural) is thus interdisciplinary.

We have already mentioned in the general section above Tessa Cubitt's (1995) overview of Latin American society. One could move from there to Alan Gilbert's (1998) overview of the Latin American city, Bryan Roberts (1995) on migration to the city and Jim Thomas (1995) on the urban informal sector.

The study of social movements in Latin America has received considerable interest. Joe Foweraker (1995) provides a general introduction and one can then consult Eckstein (1989), Escobar and Alvarez (1992) and Alvarez *et al.* (1998) for a whole range of studies, mainly from a radical perspective, with the recent addition of Eckstein and Wickham-Crowley (2003) to consider. On religion in Latin America see, among others, the studies by David Lehman (1996), David Martin's (1990) popular study of Pentecostalism, and the critical insider account of liberation theology by Cristián Parker (1996) with background information provided by Penyak and Petry (2006).

For a more strictly sociological review of contemporary social structure, Tardanico *et al.* (1997) examine the impact of structural adjustment on urban employment, Smith and Korzeniewicz (1997) examine the growing differentiation of households among other topics, while O' Donnell and Tokman (1997) bring to our attention some of the most solid research on contemporary social and economic inequality we have available.

For the cultural politics of contemporary Latin America there are now several recent studies including those by Jorge Larrain (2000) and the collections edited by Vivian Schelling (2000) and Anny Brooksbank-Jones and Ronaldo Munck (2000) respectively. Important texts on specific topics would include Néstor García Canclini (1995) on 'hybrid cultures', Beatriz Sarlo (1993) on the great writer from Argentina, Jorge Luis Borges, and Liam Kane's (2001) review of popular education which focuses on Paulo Freire in particular. On Latin American film see John King's (1990) fascinating history, and on literature Gerry Martin's (1999) 'journey through the labyrinth'. For a broad survey of art and revolution in Latin America, Craven (2006) is a brilliant read and the state/culture relationships are explored in terms of the iconography of power in Andermann and Rowe (2006).

Contemporary

Inevitably, what is contemporary today is old news tomorrow, which means anyone wishing to keep up with current affairs needs to avail themselves of the specialist journals and the myriad sources now accessible through the internet. Journals focusing on Latin America include:

Australian Journal of Latin American Studies (Australia)
Bulletin of Latin American Research (UK)
Canadian Journal of Latin American and Caribbean Studies (Canada)
Hispanic American Historical Review (USA)
Journal of Latin American Cultural Studies (UK)
Journal of Latin American Studies (UK)
Latin American Perspectives (USA)
Latin American Politics and Society (USA)
Latin American Research Review (USA)

While articles in specialist journals such as those listed above help bridge the gap between the contemporary event and the definitive books on the topic, for real-time coverage one needs access to the news. In the UK the main source of news and analysis is the *Latin American Weekly Report* published by Latin American Newsletters in London. The US-based *NACLA's Report on the Americas* is a bimonthly news/analysis magazine with a radical take on events.

The most direct way to access news for a particular country is through its own news outlets. To obtain access to these the simplest way is to use the internet in so far as few libraries stock newspapers from Latin America.

Internet

It is now virtually impossible to do research on or learn about Latin America without access to the internet. There is so much information and analysis that simply is not stored in traditional libraries any more that it has become indispensable.

The researcher in Latin America is fortunate to have a most impressive 'gateway' provided by the University of Texas LANIC page http:// lanic.utexas.edu/las.html, now recognized as the World Wide Web (WWW) Virtual Library for Latin American Studies. Here you may start your research according to topics – for example, Economy, Government, or Society or Culture, which correspond roughly with the categories of this guide to further reading. But you will also find topics such as Education and Sustainable Development, not to mention Recreation. You will find links to a whole range of material, much of it in Latin America itself, which is often not the case for search engines generally. If your interest is in a specific country you can enter the site through its name, under which you will find well-ordered and regularly updated information on just about any issue. If you only use the internet once, make sure it is the LANIC site!

Economic data on Latin America can also be found at the sites of the World Bank http://www.worldbank.org, the Inter-American Development Bank http://www.iadb.org and the Economic Commission for Latin America and the Caribbean (ECLAC) http://www.eclac.cl/.

Political data on Latin America can be sourced at the surprising reliable US State Department Notes http://www.state.gov/r/pa/ei/bgn/. For up-to-date analysis and a useful archive try the *Washington Post* http://www.washingtonpost.com/ or the less comprehensive but more progressive *Guardian* site http://www.guardian.co.uk/. For newspapers and magazines from Latin America you may either try the Yahoo country pages or the section Media and Communication on the LANIC site http://www.lanic.utexas.edu/subject/media.

For social/cultural issues you wish to research, a good place to start would be one of the major search engines such as Yahoo http://www. yahoo.com/ and even better access is gained through the Yahoo country pages http://www.yahoo.com/Regional/Countries/[NAME OF COUNTRY]/. You can find there the URL ('address') for the Zapatistas http://www. ezln.org/ or the Colombian FARC http://www.contrast.org/mirros/farc/, or on how to organize travel to Latin America (for example http://www.

journeylatinamerica.co.uk/) or cook a typical dish of the region www.cs.
yale.edu/homes/hupfer/global/regions/sam.html (for Central America
and the Caribbean replace 'sam' with 'cam'). You will also obtain access
to many specialized and most informative discussion groups on almost
any issue of the day you might be interested in.

For more analytical social science research you should try the Latin
American Council for the Social Sciences http://www.clacso.edu.ar
based in Buenos Aires, and the US-based Latin American Studies
Association http://lasa.international.pitt.edu/.

Bibliography

Almond, G. and Verba, S. (1963), *The Civic Culture: Political Attitudes and Democracy in Five Countries*, Princeton, NJ: Princeton University Press.

√ Alvarez, S. (1998), 'Latin American Feminisms "Go Global": Trends in the 1990's and Challenges for the New Millenium', in S. Alvarez, E. Dagnino and A. Escobar (eds), *Culture of Politics, Politics of Culture: Re-Visioning Latin American Social Movements*, Boulder, CO: Westview Press.

Alvarez, S., Dagnino, E. and Escobar, A. (1998), 'Introduction: The Cultural and the Political in Latin American Social Movements', in S. Alvarez, E. Dagnino and A. Escobar (eds), *Cultures of Politics. Politics of Cultures*, Boulder, CO: Westview Press.

Andermann, J. and Rowe, W. (eds) (2006), *Images of Power: Iconography, Culture and the State in Latin America,* Oxford: Berghan Books.

Anderson, P. (2004), 'The Role of Ideas in the Construction of Alternatives', in A. Borón (ed.), *New Worldwide Hegemony. Alternatives for change and social movements*, Buenos Aires: CLACSO.

√ Angell, A. and Reig, C. (2006), 'Change or Continuity? The Chilean Election of 2005/2006', *Bulletin of Latin American Research*, Vol. 25, No. 4, pp. 481–502.

Antonin, A. (1995), 'La visión de los cientistas sociales', *Nueva Sociedad*, No. 139 (Sept.–Oct.), pp. 19–25.

√ Arias, E. D. (2006), *Drugs and Democracy in Rio de Janeiro: Trafficking, Social Networks, and Public Security* : Chapel Hill, North Carolina: University of North Carolina Press.

Atkins, G. Pope (1999), *Latin America and the Caribbean in the International System*, Boulder, CO: Westview Press.

Auyero, J. (2000) *Poor People's Politics*: *Peronist Survival Networks and the Legacy of Evita*, Durham, NC: Duke University Press.

Bartolomé de las Casas (1971), *History of the Indies* (translated by André Collard), New York: Harper & Row.

√ Barton, J. (1997), *A Political Geography of Latin America*, London: Routledge.

Barton, J. (1999), 'The Environmental Agenda: Accountability for Sustainability', in J. Buxton and N. Phillips (eds), *Developments in Latin American Political Economy*, Manchester: Manchester University Press.

√ Bebbington, A. and Thiele, G. (1993), *Non-Governmental Organizations and the State in Latin America*, New York: Routledge.

Beck, U. (2000), *The Brave New World of Work*, Cambridge: Polity Press.

Benoit, H. (2006), 'Brazil: The social contradictions underlying the violent eruption in São Paulo', *World Socialist Website*, http://www.wsws.org/

√ Bergquist, C., Peñaranda, R. and Sanchez, G. (2001), *Violence in Colombia 1990–2000: Waging War and Negotiating Peace*, Delaware: Scholarly Resources Inc.

√ Bethel, E. (ed.) (1984–96), *The Cambridge History of Latin America, Vols 1–10*, Cambridge: Cambridge University Press.

√ Black, G. (1984), *Triumph of the People: Sandinista Revolution in Nicaragua*, London: Zed Books.

√ Booth, J. A., Wade, C. J. and Walker, T. W. (2005), *Understanding Central America: Global Forces, Rebellion and Change*, Boulder, CO: Westview Press.

Bresser-Pereíra, L. C. (1999), 'From Bureaucratic to Managerial Public Administration in Brazil', in L. C. Bresser Pereíra and P. Spink (eds), *Reforming the State. Managerial Public Administration in Latin America*, London: Lynne Rienner.

Brodeur, J. P. (1999), 'Comments on Chevigny', in J. Mendez, G. O'Donnell and D. Pinheiro (eds), *The (Un)Rule of Law and the Underprivileged in Latin America*, Notre Dame, IN: University of Notre Dame Press.

Brooksbank-Jones, A. and Munck, R. (eds) (2000), *Cultural Politics in Latin America*, London: Palgrave Macmillan.

Bruce, I. (2004), *The Porto Alegre Alternative. Direct Democracy in Action*, London: Zed Books.

√ Bruhn, K. (2006), 'Is Latin America Turning Socialist? The Region's Electoral Trend', *ReVista*, Spring–Summer, pp. 42–43.

√ Bulmer-Thomas, V. (1994), *The Economic History of Latin America Since Independence*, Cambridge: Cambridge University Press.

Bulmer-Thomas, V. (1996), *The New Economic Model in Latin America and its Impact on Income Distribution and Poverty*, London: Palgrave Macmillan.

√ Bulmer-Thomas, V. (ed.) (2001), *Regional Integration in Latin America and the Caribbean*, London: Institute of Latin American Studies.

√ Bulmer-Thomas, V. and Dunkerley, J. (1999), 'Conclusions', in V. Bulmer-Thomas and J. Dunkerley (eds), *The United States and Latin America: The New Agenda*, London: Institute of Latin American Studies, and Cambridge, Mass: David Rockefeller Centre for Latin American Studies.

√ Burbach, R. (2005), *The Pinochet Affair. State Terrorism and Global Justice*, London: Pluto Press.

√ Burges, S. (2006), 'Without Sticks or Carrots: Brazilian Leadership in South America During the Cardoso Era, 1992–2003', *Bulletin of Latin American Research*, Vol. 25, No. 1, pp. 23–42.

Burns, B. (1977), *Latin America. A Concise Interpretative History*, New Jersey: Prentice Hall.

√ Buxton, J. (2005), 'Venezuela's Contemporary Political Crisis in Historical Perspective', *Bulletin of Latin American Research*, Vol. 24, No. 3, pp. 328–47.

Calderón, F. and Dos Santos, M. (1995), *Sociedades sin Atajos*, Buenos Aires: Paidos.

√ Cardoso, F. H. (1995), 'El pensamiento socioeconómico latinoamericano', *Neuva Sociedad*, No. 139 (Sept.–Oct.), pp. 68–70.

Cardoso, F. H. (1999), 'Foreword', in L. C. Bresser Pereíra and P. Spink (eds), *Reforming the State. Managerial Public Administration in Latin America*, London: Lynne Rienner.

Cardoso, F. H. (2001), *Charting a New Course. The Politics of Globalization and Social Transformation*, New York, Oxford: Rowan & Littlefield Publishers.

Cardoso, F. H. and Faletto, E. (1979), *Dependency and Development in Latin America*, Berkeley, CA: University of California Press.

√ Carmen Feijoo, M. and Gogna, M. (1990), 'Women in the Transition to Democracy', in E. Jelin (ed.), *Women and Social Change in Latin America*, London: Zed Books.

Carrión, J. (ed.) (2006), *The Fujimori Legacy: The Rise of Electoral Authoritarianism in Peru*, Pennsylvania: Pennsylvania State University Press.

Carvalho, J. J. de (2000), 'An Enchanted Public Space: Religious Plurality and Modernity in Brazil', in V. Schelling (ed.), *Through the Kaleidoscope*, London: Verso.

Cassen, B. (1998), 'Democratie Participative a Porto Alegre', *Le Monde Diplomatique* (Août).

√Castañeda, J. (1993), *Utopia Disarmed. The Latin American Left after the Cold War*, New York: Knopf.

Castañeda, J. (2006), 'A Tale of Two Lefts', *Foreign Affairs*, 85, 3, pp. 28–43.

Castells, M. (1998), *The Information Age. Economy, Society and Culture, Vol. III End of Millennium*, Oxford: Blackwell.

Castells, M. (2001), *The Internet Galaxy*, Oxford: Oxford University Press.

√ Centeno, M. A. (2004), 'The Return of Cuba to Latin America: The End of Cuban Exceptionalism?', *Bulletin of Latin American Research*, Vol. 23, No. 4, pp. 403–413.

Centeno, M. A. (2006), '¿Votos para qué? The Fragile Democratic Consolidation in Latin America', *ReVista*, Spring–Summer, pp. 48–50.

Centeno, M. A. and López Alves, F. (eds) (2001), *The Other Mirror. Grand Theory Through the Lens of Latin America*, Princeton: Princeton University Press.

√ Chant, S. (1999), 'Population, Migration, Employment and Gender', in R. Gwynne and C. Kay (eds), *Latin America Transformed, Globalisation and Modernity*, London: Arnold.

√ Chant, S. with Craske, N. (2003), *Gender in Latin America*, London: Latin American Bureau/Rutgers University Press.

Chestnut, R. A. (1997), *Born Again in Brazil: The Pentecostal Boom and the Pathogens of Poverty*, New Brunswick, NJ: Rutgers University Press.

Chevigny, P. (1999), 'Defining the Role of the Police in Latin America', in J. Mendez, G. O'Donnell and D. Pinheiro (eds), *The (Un)Rule of Law and the Underprivileged in Latin America*, Notre Dame, IN: University of Notre Dame Press.

CLAD (Latin American Centre for Development Administration) (2002), *A New Public Management for Latin America*, http://www.clad.org.ve/gespin.html.

Cobos, A. M. and Sater, A. L. (2002), *Latin American Studies. An Annotated Bibliography of Core Works*, North Carolina: McFarland & Co.

√ Collier, S., Skidmore, T. and Blakemore, H. (eds) (1992), *The Cambridge Encyclopaedia of Latin America and the Caribbean*, Cambridge: Cambridge University Press.

√ Cott, D. L. van (2005), 'Building Inclusive Democracies: Indigenous Peoples and Ethnic Minorities in Latin America', *Democratization*, Vol. 12, No. 5 (December), pp. 825–42.

√ Craven, D. (2006), *Art and Revolution in Latin America, 1910–1990*, New Haven: Yale University Press.

Crisp, B. and Botero, F. (2006), 'High Emotions, Little Content. Colombia's Presidential Election', *ReVista*, Spring/Summer, pp. 24–25.

Cubitt, T. (1995), *Latin American Society*, Harlow: Longman.

Dieguez, M. (1998), 'Regional Mechanisms for the Maintenance of Peace and Security in the Western Hemisphere', in O. Pellicer (ed.), *Regional Mechanisms and International Security in Latin America*, New York: United Nations University Press.

Dore, E. (ed.) (1997), *Gender Politics in Latin America*, New York: Monthly Review Press.

Dos Santos, S. A. (2006), 'Who is Black in Brazil? A Timely or a False Question in Brazilian Race Relations in the Era of Affirmative Action?', *Latin American Perspectives*, Vol. 33, No. 4, pp. 30–48.

Dos Santos, T. (1970), 'The Crisis of Development Theory and the Problem of Dependence in Latin America', in H. Bernstein (ed.), *Underdevelopment and Development*, London: Penguin.

√ Dunkerley, J. (1988), *Power in the Isthmus: A Political History of Modern Central America*, London: Verso.

Eckstein, S. (ed.) (1989), *Power and Popular Protest: Latin American Social Movements*, Berkeley, CA: University of California Press.

Eckstein, S. E. and Wickham-Crowley, T. P. (eds) (2003), *Struggles for Social Rights in Latin America,* New York: Routledge

⋉ ECLAC (Economic Commission for Latin America and the Caribbean) (2000), *Globalisation and Development*, Santiago, Chile: ECLAC.

⋎ ECLAC (2001), *Social Panorama of Latin America, 2000–2001*, Santiago, Chile: ECLAC.

√ ECLAC (2006), *Social Panorama of Latin America, 2005*, Santiago, Chile: ECLAC.

Escobar, A. and Alvarez, S. (eds) (1992), *The Making of Social Movements in Latin America*, Boulder, CO: Westview Press.

√ Fernández-Jilberto, A. and Mommen, A. (eds) (1998), *Regionalization and Globalization in the Modern World Economy*, London: Routledge.

√ Ferrer, H. (1960), *El Tango: Su Historia y Evolución*, Buenos Aires: Losada.

Fine, B. (2001), *Social Capital Versus Social Theory*, London: Routledge.

Fisher, J. (1992), 'Iberian Colonial Settlement', in S. Collier, T. Skidmore and H. Blakemore (eds), *The Cambridge Encyclopaedia of Latin America and the Caribbean*, Cambridge: Cambridge University Press.

Fitzgerald, E. V. K. (1996), 'The New Trade Regime, Macroeconomic Behaviour and Income Distribution in Latin America', in V. Bulmer-Thomas (ed.), *The New Economic Model and its Impact on Income Distribution and Poverty*, London: Palgrave Macmillan.

Foweraker, J. (1995), *Theorising Social Movements*, London: Pluto Press.

√ Foxley, A. (1983), *Latin American Experiments in Neo-Conservative Economics*, Berkeley: University of California Press.

Franco, J. (1970), *The Modern Culture of Latin America. Society and the Artist*, London: Penguin.

Freitlowitz, M. (1998), *A Lexicon of Terror. Argentina and The Legacies of Torture*, New York and Oxford: Oxford University Press.

Freyre, G. (1951), *Brazil: An Interpretation*, New York: Alfred Knopf.

Frieden, J., Pastor, M. and Tomz, M. (eds) (2000), *Modern Political Economy and Latin America. Theory and Policy*, Boulder, CO: Westview Press.

Fuentes, C. (1990), *Christopher Unborn*, London: Picador.

Fukuyama, F. (1992), *The End of History and the Last Man*, London: Hamish Hamilton.

⌡ Galeano, E. (1987), *The Open Veins of Latin America*, New York: Monthly Review Press.

Galeano, E. (1991), 'The Blue Tiger and the Promised Land', *Report on the Americas* (New York: North American Congress on Latin America), Vol. 24, No. 5.

García Canclini, N. (1995), *Hybrid Cultures: Strategies for Entering and Leaving Modernity*, Minneapolis: Minnesota University Press.

García Canclini, N. (1997), *Imaginarios Urbanos*, Buenos Aires: Editorial Sudamericana.

García Canclini, N. (2000), 'Contradictory Modernities and Globalisation in Latin America', in V. Schelling (ed.), *Through the Kaleidoscope*, London: Verso.

⧸ García Canclini, N. (2002), *Latinoamericanos buscando lugar en este siglo*, Buenos Aires: Pardós.

García Márquez, G. (1971), *One Hundred Years of Solitude*, New York: Avon Books.

√ Garretón, M. A. (1989), *The Chilean Political Process*, Boston: Unwin Hyman.

Garretón, M. A. (2004), 'La indispensable y problemática relación entre partidos y democracia en América Latina', in UNDP (ed.), *Contribuciones para el Debate (Libro y Resumen)*, New York: UNDP.

√ Garretón, M., Cleaves, P., Cavarozzi, M., Hartlyn, J. and Gereffi, G. (2002), *Latin America in the Twenty-First Century*, California: Lynne Rienner.

Garretón, M. and Newman, E. (eds) (2002), *Democracy in Latin America*, Washington, DC: The Brookings Institute.

Gilbert, A. (1998), *The Latin American City*, London: Latin American Bureau.

Gilly, A. (2006), *The Mexican Revolution: A People's History,* New York: New Press.

Gonzalez, A. (1998), 'Physical Landscapes and Settlement Patterns', in J. Knipper Black (ed.), *Latin America: Its Problems and its Promises*, Boulder, CO: Westview Press.

√ Gott, R. (2001), *In the Shadow of the Liberator: The Impact of Hugo Chavez on Venezuela and Latin America*, London: Verso.

√ Gott, R. (2005), *Cuba. A New History*, New Haven and London: Yale University Press.

Grueso, L., Rosero, C. and Escobar, A. (1992), 'The Process of Black Community Organising in the Southern Pacific Coast Region of Colombia', in A. Escobar and S. Alvarez (eds), *The Making of Social Movements in Latin America*, Boulder, CO: Westview Press.

√ Grugel, J. and Almeida Medeiros, M. (1999), 'Brazil and MERCOSUR', in J. Grugel and W. Hout (eds), *Regionalism Across the North–South Divide*, London: Routledge.

Gwynne, R. and Kay, C. (eds) (1999), *Latin America Transformed. Globalisation and Modernity,* London: Hodder Arnold.

√ Gwynne, R. and Kay, C. (eds) (2004), *Latin America Transformed. Globalisation and Modernity – Second Edition,* London: Hodder Arnold.

√ Habel, J. (1991), *Cuba: The Revolution in Peril*, London: Verso.

Haggard, S. and Kaufman, R. (1996), *The Political Economy of Democratic Transition*, Princeton, NJ: Princeton University Press.

√ Hakim, P. (2006), 'Is Washington Losing Latin America?', *Foreign Affairs*, Vol. 85, No. 1, pp. 39–53.

√ Hall, S. (1996), 'What is this "Black" in Black Popular Culture', in D. Morley and K.-H. Chen (eds), *Stuart Hall. Critical Dialogues in Cultural Studies*, London: Routledge.

Halperín Doughi, T. (1993), *The Contemporary History of Latin America*, Durham, NC: Duke University Press.

Hartlyn, J. and Valenzuela, A. (1998), 'Democracy in Latin America since 1930', in L. Bethel (ed.), *Latin America: Politics and Society since 1930*, Cambridge: Cambridge University Press.

√ Harvey, N. (1998), *The Chiapas Rebellion. The Struggle for Land and Democracy*, Durham: Durham University Press.

Higgott, R. (2000), 'Contested Globalisation: The Changing Context and Normative Challenges', *Review of International Studies*, No. 26, pp. 131–53.

√ Holden, R. and Zolov, E. (eds) (2001), *Latin America and the United States. A Documentary History*, New York and Oxford: Oxford University Press.

√ Hollander, N. C. (1974), 'Si Evita Viviera', *Latin American Perspectives*, Vol. 1, No. 3, pp. 42–57.

√ Holmes, J. and Gutiérrez de Piñeres, S. A. (2006), 'The Illegal Drugs Industry, Violence and the Colombian Economy: A Department Level Analysis', *Bulletin of Latin American Research*, Vol. 25, No. 1, pp. 104–18.

√ Huber, E. (1996), 'Options for Social Policy in Latin America: Neoliberal Versus Social Democratic Models', in G. Esping-Anderson (ed.), *Welfare States in Transition. National Adaptations in Global Economies*, London: Sage.

Human Development Report (2006), *Beyond Society: Power, Poverty and the Global Water Crisis*, New York: UNDP.

Humphrey, J. (1982), *Capitalist Control and Workers' Struggles in the Brazilian Auto Industry*, Princeton: Princeton University Press.

Huntington, S. (1996), *The Clash of Civilisations and the Remaking of World Order*, New York: Simon & Schuster.

IDB (1997), *Latin America after a Decade of Reforms. Economic and Social Progress: 1997 Report*, Washington, DC: IDB.

IDB (2000), *Development Beyond Economics*, Washington, DC: IDB.

Jaggi, M. (2006), 'Blood on the Ground', *Review, Saturday Guardian*, (13 May), p. 14.

Kane, L. (2001), *Popular Education and Social Change in Latin America*, London: Latin American Bureau.

Kay, C (1999), 'Rural development: from agrarian reform to neoliberalism and beyond', in R. Gwynne and C. Kay (eds), *Latin America Transformed: Globalization and Beyond*, London: Arnold.

King, D. (2006), 'Constitutional Reform in Bolivia. The 2005 Presidential Election', *ReVista*, Spring/Summer, pp. 12 and 15.

King, J. (1990), *Magical Reels. A History of Cinema in Latin America*, London: Verso.

Knight, A. (2002), *Mexico*, Cambridge: Cambridge University Press.

Knippers-Black, J. (ed) (2005) *Latin America: Its Problems and its Promise – A Multidisciplinary Introduction*, Boulder, CO: Westview Press.

Korzeniewicz, R. and Smith, W. (2000), 'Poverty, Inequality and Growth in Latin America: Searching for the High Road to Globalisation', *Latin American Research Review*, Vol. 35 No. 3, pp. 7–54.

Laite, J. (1981), *Industrial Development and Migrant Labour*, Manchester: Manchester University Press.

Landim, L. (1996), 'Non-governmental Organizations in Latin America', in R. I. Camp (ed.), *Democracy in Latin America: Patterns and Cycles*, Delaware: S. R. Books.

Larrain, J. (2000), *Identity and Modernity in Latin America*, Cambridge: Polity Press.

Lechner, N. (1986), 'De la revolución a la democracia', *La Ciudad Futura* (Buenos Aires), No. 2 (October).

Lechner, N. (1999), 'La reforma del estado y el problema de la conducción política', in B. Revez (ed.), *Descentralización y Governabilidad en Tiempo de Globalización*, Lima: Instituto de Estudios Peruanos.

Lehman, D. (1990), *Democracy and Development in Latin America*, Cambridge: Polity Press.

Lehman, D. (1996), *Struggle for the Spirit: Religious Transformation and Popular Culture in Latin America*, Oxford: Blackwell.

Lehman, D. and Bebbington, A. (1998), 'NGOs, the State and the Development Process: The Dilemmas of Institutionalisation', in M. Vellinga (ed.), *The Changing Role of the State in Latin America*, Boulder, CO: Westview Press.

Levine, D. (1992), *Conflict and Political Change in Venezuela*, Princeton, NJ: Princeton University Press.

Lievesley, G. (1999), *Democracy in Latin America, Mobilisation, Power and the Search for a New Politics*, Manchester: Manchester University Press.

Linz, J. and Bresser-Pereíra, J. C. (eds) (1999), *Reforming the State*, California: Lynne Rienner.

√ Linz, J. and Valenzuela, A. (eds) (1994), *The Failure of Presidential Democracy: The Case of Latin America*, Baltimore: Johns Hopkins University Press.

√ López, A. (2000), 'A Train of Shadows: Early Cinema and Modernity in Latin America', in V. Schelling (ed.), *Through the Kaleidoscope*, London: Verso.

McCann Sánchez, M. (2002), 'Constructing Economic Solidarity', in J. Feffer (ed.), *Living in Hope. People Challenging Globalization*, London: Zed Books.

√ McFarlane, A. (1992), 'African Slave Migration', in S. Collier, T. Skidmore and H. Blakemore (eds), *The Cambridge Encyclopaedia of Latin America and the Caribbean*, Cambridge: Cambridge University Press.

MacDonald, G. J., Nielsen, D. L. and Stern, M. A. (eds) (1997), *Latin American Environmental Policy in International Perspective*, Boulder, CO: Westview Press.

Mainwaring, S., O'Donnell, G. and Valenzuela, A. (1992), *Issues in Democratic Consolidation: The New South American Democracies in Comparative Perspective*, Notre Dame: University of Notre Dame Press.

Mainwaring, S. and Scully, T. (1995), 'Introduction: Party Systems in Latin America', in S. Mainwaring and T. Scully (eds), *Building Democratic Institutions. Party Systems in Latin America*, Stanford, CA: Stanford University Press.

Mainwaring, S. and Shugart, M. (1997), *Presidentialism and Democracy in Latin America*, New York: Cambridge University Press.

√ Malamud, C. (2005), 'The Obstacles to Regional Integration in Latin America', Madrid: AREA. Latin America, ARI No. 134/2005.

Marshall, T. H. (1963), *Sociology at the Crossroads and Other Essays*, London: Heineman.

Martin, D. (1990), *Tongues of Fire*, Oxford: Blackwell.

Martin, G. (1998), 'Narrative since c. 1920', in L. Bethel (ed.), *A Cultural History of Latin America*, Cambridge: Cambridge University Press.

√ Martin, G. (1999), *Journeys Through the Labyrinth: Latin American Fiction in the Twentieth Century*, London: Verso.

Martín-Barbero, J. (2000), 'Transformations in the Map: Identities and Culture Industries', *Latin American Perspectives*, Vol. 27, No. 4, pp. 27–48.

√ Menchu, R. (1984), *I, Rigoberta Menchu*, London: Verso.

Mendez, J., O'Donnell, G. and Pinheiro, D. (eds) (1999), *The (Un)Rule of Law and the Underprivileged in Latin America*, Notre Dame, IN: University of Notre Dame Press.

Merick, T. (1998), 'The Population of Latin America, 1930–1980', in L. Bethel (ed.), *Latin America: Economy and Society Since 1930*, Cambridge: Cambridge University Press.

√ Molyneux, M. (2000), *Women's Movements in International Perspective*, London: Palgrave Macmillan.

√ Montecinos, V. (1998), 'Economists in Party Politics: Chilean Democracy in the Era of the Markets', in M. Centeno and P. Silva (eds), *The Politics of Expertise in Latin America*, London: Palgrave Macmillan.

Moore, B. (1969), *Social Origins of Dictatorship and Democracy*, London: Penguin.

Morgenstern, S. and Nacif, B. (eds) (2002), *Legislative Politics in Latin America*, Cambridge: Cambridge University Press.

Moreno-Bird, J. C. and Paunovic, I. (2006), 'Old Wine in New Bottles? Economic Policymaking by Left-of-Center Governments in Latin America', *ReVista*, Spring–Summer, pp. 44–47.

Munck, G. (2006), 'Latin America: Old Problems, New Agenda', *Democracy at Large*, Vol. 2, No. 3, pp. 11–13.

Munck, R. (1988), *The New International Labour Studies*, London: Zed Books.

Munck, R. (with R. Falcón and B. Galitelli) (1987), *Argentina: From Anarchism to Peronism*, London: Zed Books.

√ Navía, P. (2006), 'Bachelet's Election in Chile. The 2006 Presidential Elections', *ReVista*, Spring/Summer, pp. 9–11.

Newson, L. (1992), 'Pre-Columbian Settlement', in S. Collier, T. Skidmore and H. Blakemore (eds), *The Cambridge Encyclopaedia of Latin America and the Caribbean*, Cambridge: Cambridge University Press.

Nun, J. (1967), 'The Middle-Class Military Coup', in C. Veliz (ed.), *The Politics of Conformity in Latin America*, New York: Praeger.

√ O'Brien, P. (1985), 'Authoritarianism and the new economic orthodoxy: the political economy of the Chilean regime', in P. O'Brien and G. Cammack (eds), *Generals in Retreat. The Crisis of Military Rule in Latin America*, Manchester: Manchester University Press.

O'Donnell, G. (1993), 'Estado, democratización y ciudadanía', *Nuevo Sociedad*, No. 128 (Nov.–Dec.), pp. 62–87.

O'Donnell, G. (1997), 'Poverty and Inequality in Latin America: Some Political Reflections', in G. O'Donnell and V. Tokman (eds), *Poverty and Inequality in Latin America*, Notre Dame, IN: University of Notre Dame Press.

O'Donnell, G. (1999a), 'Polyarchies and the (Un)Rule of Law in Latin America: A Partial Conclusion', in J. Mendez, G. O'Donnell and D. Pinheiro (eds), *The (Un)Rule of Law and the Underprivileged in Latin America*, Notre Dame, IN: University of Notre Dame Press.

O'Donnell, G. (1999b), *Counterpoints: Selected Essays on Authoritarianism and Democratisation*, Notre Dame: University of Notre Dame Press.

O'Donnell, L., Schmitter, P. and Whitehead, L. (eds) (1986), *Transitions from Authoritarian Rule: Latin America*, Baltimore, MD: John Hopkins University Press.

O'Donnell, G. and Tokman, V. (eds) (1997), *Poverty and Inequality in Latin America*, Notre Dame, IN: University of Notre Dame Press.

√ Oliveira, O. D. and Roberts, B. (1994), 'Urban growth and urban social structure in Latin America, 1930–1990,' in L. Bethell (ed.), *The Cambridge History of Latin America*, Vol. VI, Cambridge: Cambridge University Press, pp. 253–324.

√ Oxhorn, P. and Ducatenzeiler, G. (eds) (1998), *What Kind of Democracy? What Kind of Market? Latin America in the Age of Neoliberalism*, Pennsylvania: Pennsylvania University Press.

√ Palacios, M. (2006), *Between Legitimacy and Violence: A History of Colombia, 1875–2002*, Durham, North Carolina: Duke University Press

Panizza, F. (2004), 'Brazil Needs to Change: Change as Iteration and the Iteration of Change in Brazil's 2002 Presidential Election', *Bulletin of Latin American Research*, Vol. 23, No. 4, pp. 465–82.

√ Parker, C. (1996), *Popular Religion and Modernization in Latin America. A Different Logic*, New York: Orbas Books.

Payne, A. (1996), 'The United States and its Enterprise for the Americas', in A. Gamble and A. Payne (eds), *Regionalism and World Order*, London: Palgrave Macmillan.

Paz, O. (1967), *The Labyrinth of Solitude*, London: Lane.

Peeler, J. (1998), *Building Democracy in Latin America*, Boulder, CO: Lynne Rienner.

Pellicer, O. (1998), 'Introduction', in O. Pellicer (ed.), *Regional Mechanisms and International Security in Latin America*, New York: United Nations University Press.

√ Penyak, L. and Petry, W. (eds) (2006), *Religion in Latin America: A Documentary History*, New York: Orbis Books

Petras, J. and Veltmeyer, H. (1998), 'Social Structure and Change in Latin America', in J. K. Black (ed.), *Latin America: Its Problems and its Promise*, Boulder, CO: Westview Press.

Petras, J. and Veltmeyer, H. (2001), *Globalisation Unmasked*, London: Zed Books.

√ Petras, J. and Veltmeyer, H. (2005), *Social Movements and State Power. Argentina, Brazil, Bolivia, Ecuador*, London: Pluto Press.

Pinheiro, D. (1999), 'The Rule of Law and the Underprivileged in Latin America. Introduction', in J. Mendez, G. O'Donnell and D. Pinheiro (eds), *The (Un)Rule of Law and the Underprivileged in Latin America*, Notre Dame, IN: University of Notre Dame Press.

Plant, R. (1999), 'The Rule of Law and the Underprivileged in Latin America. A Third Perspective', in J. Mendez, G. O'Donnell and D. Pinheiro (eds), *The (Un)Rule of Law and the Underprivileged in Latin America*, Notre Dame, IN: University of Notre Dame Press.

Portes, A. (1985), 'Latin American Class Structures: Their Composition and Change During the Last Decade', *Latin American Research Review*, Vol. xx (3), pp. 7–39.

Pratt, M. L. and Newman, K. (eds) (2000), *Critical Passions. Selected Essays of Jean Franco*, Durham: Duke University Press.

Przeworski, A. (1986), 'Some Problems in the Study of the Transition to Democracy', in G. O'Donnell, P. Schmitter and L. Whitehead (eds), *Transitions from Authoritarian Rule, Prospects for Democracy*, London: John Hopkins University Press.

Radcliffe, S. (1999), 'Civil society, social difference and politics: issues of identity and representation' in R. Gwynne and C. Kay (eds), *Latin America Transformed: Globalization and Modernity*, London: Arnold.

Remmer, K. (1991), 'The Political Impact of Economic Crises in Latin America in the 1980s', *American Political Science Review*, No. 85, pp. 777–800.

Roberts, B. R. (1995), *The making of citizens: cities of peasants revisited*, London: Edward Arnold.

Rock, D. (1987), *Argentina, 1516–1987: From Spanish Colonization to Alfonsín*, California: University of California Press.

Rowe, W. and Schelling, V. (1991), *Memory and Modernity. Popular Culture in Latin America*, London: Verso.

Sader, E. (2005), 'Taking Lula's Measure', *New Left Review*, May/June, No. 33, pp. 59–79.

Sage, C. (1991), 'The Discourse on Drugs in Latin America', *Bulletin of Latin American Research*, Vol. 10, No. 3, pp. 325–32.

Sáinz, P. (2006), 'Equity in Latin American in the 1990's, *DESA Working Paper No. 22*.

Salman, T. (2006), 'The Jammed Democracy: Bolivia's Troubled Political Learning Process', *Bulletin of Latin American Research*, Vol. 25, No. 2, pp. 163–82.

Sanchez, O. (2005), 'Argentina's Landmark 2003 Presidential Election: Renewal and Continuity', *Bulletin of Latin American Research*, Vol. 24, No. 4, pp. 454–75.

Sarlo, B. (1993), *Borges: A Writer on the Edge*, London: Verso.

Sarlo, B. (2000), 'The Modern City: Buenos Aires, The Peripheral Metropolis', in V. Schelling (ed.), *Through the Kaleidoscope: The Experience of Modernity in Latin America*, London: Verso.

Sarmiento, D. F. (1960), *Facundo* (selected and edited by X. A. Fernandez and R. F. Brown), Boston, MA: Ginn.

Sarmiento, D. F. (1961), *Facundo: Civilización y Barbarie*, Buenos Aires: EUDEBA.

Schelling, V. (2000), 'Introduction: Reflections on the Experience of Modernity in Latin America', in V. Schelling (ed.), *Through the Kaleidoscope: The Experience of Modernity in Latin America*, London: Verso.

Schneider, R. (2006), *Latin American Political History: Patterns and Personalities,* Boulder, CO: Westview Press

Seligson, M. and Booth, J. (eds) (1995), *Elections and Democracy in Central America Revisited*, Chapel Hill: University of North Carolina Press.

Selverston, M. (1999), 'The Politics of Identity Reconstruction: Indians and Democracy in Ecuador', in D. Chalmers *et al.* (eds), *The New Politics of Inequality in Latin America*, Oxford: Oxford University Press.

Shefner, J. (1998), 'The Redefinition of State Policies in the Social Arena: The Case of Mexico', in M. Vellinga (ed.), *The Changing Role of the State in Latin America*, Boulder, CO: Westview Press.

√ Shifter, M. (2006), 'In Search of Hugo Chávez', *Foreign Affairs*, Vol. 85, No. 3, pp. 45–59.

Skidmore, T. (1999), *Brazil: Five Centuries of Change*, New York: Oxford University Press.

Skidmore, T. and Smith, P. (2001), *Modern Latin America* (5th edn), Oxford: Oxford University Press.

Smith, C. (1992), 'Geography', in S. Collier, T. Skidmore and H. Blakemore (eds), *The Cambridge Encyclopaedia of Latin America and the Caribbean*, Cambridge: Cambridge University Press.

Smith, P. (2000), *Talons of the Eagle. Dynamics of US-Latin American Relations*, Oxford: Oxford University Press.

Smith, P. (2005), *Democracy in Latin America: Political Change in Comparative, Perspective,* New York: Oxford University Press.

√ Smith, W. and Korzeniewicz, R. (eds) (1997), *Politics, Social Change and Economic Restructing in Latin America*, Miami: North-South Centre Press.

Smith, W. C., Acuña, A. U. and Gamarra, E. A. (eds) (1994), *Latin American Political Economy in the Age of Neoliberal Reform*, New Brunswick, NJ: Transaction Publishers.

Sondereguer, M. (1985), Aparición con vida (El movimiento de derechos humanos en Argentina)', in E. Jelin (ed.), *Los nuevos movimientos sociales*, Buenos Aires: Centro Editor de América Latina.

√ Stallings, B. (1992), 'International Influence on Economic Policy: Debt, Stabilization and Structural Reform', in S. Haggard and R. Kaufman (eds), *The Politics of Economic Adjustment*, Princeton NJ: Princeton University Press.

√ Sternbach, N., Navarro-Aranguren, M., Chuchryk, D. and Alvarez, S. (1992), 'Feminisms in Latin America: From Bogotá to San Bernando', in A. Escobar and S. Alvarez (eds), *The Making of Social Movements in Latin America*, Bolder, CO: Westview Press.

Sunkel, O. (1993), 'Towards a neostructuralist synthesis', in O. Sunkel (ed.), *Development from Within: Towards a Neostructuralist Approach for Latin America*, Boulder: Lynne Reinner.

Swanson, P. (ed.) (2003), *The Companion to Latin American Studies,* London: Arnold.

Tardanico, R. and Menjívar Larín, R. (eds) (1997), *Global Restructuring, Employment and Social Inequality in Urban Latin America*, Miami, FL: North-South Centre.

√ Tedesco, L. (1999), 'NGOs and the Retreat of the State: The Hidden Dangers', in J. Buxton and N. Phillips (eds), *Developments in Latin American Political Economy*, Manchester: Manchester University Press.

Thomas, J. J. (1995), *Surviving in the city: the urban informal sector in Latin America*, London: Pluto Press.

Thorp, R. (1998), *Progress, Poverty and Exclusion. An Economic History of Latin America in the 20th Century*. Washington, DC: IDB.

Torres-Rivas, E. (1999), 'Epilogue: Notes on Terror, Violence, Fear and Democracy', in K. Koomings and D. Kruigt (eds), *Societies of Fear: The Legacy of Civil War, Violence and Terror in Latin America*, London: Zed Books.

Tulchin, J. and Bland, G. (eds) (1994), *Peru in Crisis. Dictatorship or Democracy*, Boulder, CO: Lynne Rienner.

Turner, M. and Hulme, D. (1997), *Governance, Administration and Development*, London: Palgrave Macmillan.

√ Ugalde, L. C. (2006), 'The Challenges of Democratic Consolidation in Mexico', *ReVista*, Spring/Summer, pp. 19–20.

UNDP (1997), *Human Development Report 1997*, New York: Oxford University Press.

UNDP (2004), *Ideas and Contributions. Democracy in Latin America. Towards a Citizen's Democracy*, New York: UNDP.

Valença, M. M. (2002), 'The Politics of Giving in Brazil. The Rise and Demise of Collor (1990–1992)', *Latin American Perspectives*, Vol. 29, No. 1, pp. 115–52.

√ Van Coett, D. (ed.) (1994), *Indigenous Peoples and Democracy in Latin America*, Washington, DC: Inter-American Dialogue.

Varas, A. (1998), 'Cooperative Hemispheric Security After the Cold War', in O. Pellicer (ed.), *Regional Mechanisms and International Security in Latin America*, New York: United Nations University Press.

Veliz, C. (1994), *The New World of the Gothic Fox: Culture and Economy in English and Spanish America*, Berkeley, CA: University of California Press.

Vellinga, M. (1999), *The Changing Role of the State in Latin America*, Boulder, CO: Westview Press.

√ Veltmeyer, H., Petras, J. and Vieux, S. (1997), *Neoliberalism and Class Conflict in Latin America*, London: Palgrave Macmillan.

√ Wade, P. (1997), *Race and Ethnicity in Latin America*, London: Pluto Press.

Weaver, F. (2000), *Latin America in the World Economy*, Boulder, CO: Westview Press.

Whitehead, L. (1996), *The International Dimensions of Democratisation: Europe and the Americas*, Oxford: Oxford University Press.

Whitehead, L. (1998), 'State Organisation in Latin America since 1930', in L. Bethel (ed.), *Latin America. Economy and Society Since 1930*, Cambridge: Cambridge University Press.

Wiarda, K. and Kline, H. (2006), *A Concise Introduction to Latin American Politics and Development,* Boulder, CO: Westview Press.

World Bank (1997), *World Development Report 1997*, New York: Oxford University Press.

√ World Bank (2002), *World Development Report 2002. Building Institutions for Markets*, Oxford: Oxford University Press.

World Bank (2006), *World Development Report 2006*, New York: Oxford University Press.

Index